GRADING
From the
Inside Out

Bringing Accuracy to Student Assessment
Through a Standards-Based Mindset

TOM SCHIMMER

Solution Tree | Press

a division of
Solution Tree

555 North Morton Street
Bloomington, IN 47404
800.733.6786 (toll free) / 812.336.7700
FAX: 812.336.7790

email: info@solution-tree.com
solution-tree.com

Visit **go.solution-tree.com/assessment** to download the free reproducibles in this book.

Printed in the United States of America

20 19 18   13 14 15

FSC
www.fsc.org
MIX
Paper from
responsible sources
FSC® C011935

Library of Congress Cataloging-in-Publication Data

Names: Schimmer, Tom.
Title: Grading from the inside out : bringing accuracy to student assessment
    through a standards-based mindset / Tom Schimmer.
Description: Bloomington, IN : Solution Tree Press, [2016] | Includes
    bibliographical references and index.
Identifiers: LCCN 2015043182 | ISBN 9781936763856 (perfect bound)
Subjects: LCSH: Grading and marking (Students)--Standards. | Students--Rating
    of.
Classification: LCC LB3051 .S3155 2016 | DDC 371.26--dc23 LC record available at http://lccn
.loc.gov/2015043182

Solution Tree
Jeffrey C. Jones, CEO
Edmund M. Ackerman, President

Solution Tree Press
President: Douglas M. Rife
Senior Acquisitions Editor: Amy Rubenstein
Editorial Director: Lesley Bolton
Managing Production Editor: Caroline Weiss
Senior Production Editor: Suzanne Kraszewski
Copy Editor: Miranda Addonizio
Proofreader: Elisabeth Abrams
Cover and Text Designer: Laura Kagemann

This book is dedicated to teachers who, without any fanfare or notoriety, continually put *who* they teach above *what* or *how* they teach. It is also dedicated to those teachers whose unwavering commitment to our most vulnerable learners serves as an inspiration to us all!

ACKNOWLEDGMENTS

While my name is on the front cover of this book, books are never the result of one person's effort. Without the incredible support of those who surround me, this project never would have been possible.

To Rick Stiggins, Jan Chappuis, Ken O'Connor, Rick Wormeli, Thomas Guskey, and Lee Ann Jung: My work is built upon your examples and your incredible contributions to the field of assessment and grading, which serve as the foundation for us all to become better at what we do. I am humbled to call you my colleagues and friends. I can only hope to live up to the lofty example you've set for me and everyone else hoping to make as meaningful a contribution to education as you have.

To Douglas Rife, Claudia Wheatley, and the entire Solution Tree team: Thank you for believing I had something meaningful to contribute to the conversation about sound grading practices. Your unwavering support is very much appreciated, and I look forward to our future work together.

To Amy Rubenstein, Lesley Bolton, Caroline Weiss, Suzanne Kraszewski, Miranda Addonizio, and Elisabeth Abrams: Your vision and editing have turned a manuscript into a cogent presentation of ideas. To Laura Kagemann: Thank you for what is an amazing cover design. All of you are the unsung heroes of this book, and I am truly grateful for your contributions

To Katie While, Mandy Stalets, Garnet Hillman, Stephanie Harmon, Ken Mattingly, Darin Jolly, Charity Stephens, Cindy Warber, Sherri Nelson, April Davenport, Courtney Bebluk, Lara Gilpin, and Erin Wilson: Your personal contributions to each chapter are an essential part of this book. These stories from the field bring the ideas within this book to life and allow readers a clear vision of what putting theory into practice can look like.

To Cassandra Erkens and Nicole Vagle: I am so proud and humbled by my opportunity to work with two of the sharpest assessment minds in the business and two of the most genuine people I know. Personally, our friendship is invaluable to me. Professionally, your attention to detail and your depth of assessment knowledge are inspiring. What we are building together is going to be special, and I am so excited by what the future holds!

To my wife, Monica, and my children, Samantha and Adrian: I am so grateful for your love, support, and encouragement. Your understanding and patience are extraordinary and are ultimately what drives me to succeed and to make you proud. I wouldn't be where I am today without you!

Solution Tree Press would like to thank the following reviewers:

Sofia Georgios
Social Studies Teacher
Oak Lawn-Hometown Middle School
Oak Lawn, Illinois

Jon F. Hasenbank
Assistant Professor of Mathematics Education
Department of Mathematics
Grand Valley State University
Allendale, Michigan

Darin Johnston
Sixth-Grade Teacher
North Fayette Valley Middle School
Elgin, Iowa

Matt Townsley
Director of Instruction and Technology
Solon Community School District
Solon, Iowa

Wes Weaver
Principal
Licking Valley High School
Newark, Ohio

April Zawlocki
Assistant Professor of Education
College of DuPage
Glen Ellyn, Illinois

Visit **go.solution-tree.com/assessment** to download the free reproducibles in this book.

TABLE OF CONTENTS

ABOUT THE AUTHOR

Tom Schimmer is an author and a speaker with expertise in assessment, grading, leadership, and behavioral support. An educator for more than twenty years, Tom is a former district-level leader, school administrator, and teacher. As a district-level leader, he was a member of the senior management team responsible for overseeing the efforts to support and build the instructional capacities of teachers and administrators.

Tom is a sought-after speaker who presents internationally to schools and districts.

He earned a teaching degree from Boise State University and a master's degree in curriculum and instruction from the University of British Columbia.

To learn more about Tom's work, visit www.tomschimmer.com, follow Tom on Twitter @TomSchimmer, and visit http://allthingsassessment.info, the Solution Tree All Things Assessment website.

To book Tom Schimmer for professional development, contact pd@solution-tree.com.

INTRODUCTION

I have a confession to make: I was the no-second-chances guy. When I first started as a high school social studies teacher, I was the guy who gave zeros, the guy who imposed penalties for late work—the guy who offered no second chances. I deducted 10 percent per day for late assignments and gave out zeros like candy. If anyone had looked up *punitive grader* in the dictionary at that time, my picture would have been there, and I would have been smiling, with two thumbs up. I had systems!

If a student turned something in late, I would take a blue marker and put a dot in the upper left corner of the assignment, so when I got around to scoring it I would know that I should reduce the score by 10 percent. I didn't want to embarrass the student by writing "−10%" on the paper, so I developed a coding system. If an assignment were two days late, I used a red marker and a red dot; three days was green; four, not coincidentally, was black—the dot of death—since after the fourth day, it was over and I would no longer accept the assignment. The student should have made the effort to get it in on time, I would self-righteously think.

I also had back-up plans. If, for example, my blue marker were to run dry, not to worry, I would take any

1

colored marker and write a small *B* in the top left corner to remind me that a blue dot was supposed to be there and that I should only deduct 10 percent. Two days and no red pen meant a small *R* in the corner, and so on. After all, ink doesn't last forever and the supply closet wasn't always stocked. I had to develop back-up systems to manage my comprehensive score-reduction plan. Sounds exhausting, right?

Well, at the time I didn't think so. I was supposed to do this; it was what happened when I was in school. While I don't recall ever receiving a late penalty myself, I knew that response was possible if I delayed submission of my work by a day or more. In college, it was more of the same; half the time I didn't even know what my professors' grading procedures were. I would spend hours writing extensive papers, only to have them returned with a letter of the alphabet, often accompanied by a plus or a minus, on the back page.

My teaching career began with no formal assessment training. Punitive responses seemed like the right thing to do, not because I had reflected on what the foundation for my grading systems should be, but because that was the only thing I knew. I don't think like that anymore; in fact, I haven't thought that way for a long time.

Since the early 1990s there have been monumental changes in pedagogy and assessment. While in the midst of those changes, I quickly realized that many of the grading practices I used in the past were no longer relevant within the new collective approach to teaching and assessment. After a series of professional epiphanies, I realized I was talking out of both sides of my mouth. How could I say I was all about learning and then use nonlearning factors (such as punctuality, effort, and attitude) to influence student grades? How could I claim to recognize that some students take longer to learn, but then go about grading every move my students made? As much as we may want to cling to the procedures of the past, now is the time to reform grading practices to align how we teach with how we report.

Times Have Changed

Changing grading practices doesn't mean that the practices of the past were wrong, necessarily; rather, they are wrong in today's context. What we used to do was right for how we used to teach, but we don't teach like that anymore. Things change, and hopefully, we can begin to embrace the change to grading the way we've embraced it in so many other aspects of education and life in general.

Remember when watching a movie at home, unless it was on network or cable television, meant getting in the car and driving to the video store? We had to hope that Blockbuster had a few copies of the new release we wanted to watch.

We don't do video that way anymore, and what's more, no one longs for the days of the video store. With Netflix, iTunes, on-demand offerings from satellite and cable companies, and a whole host of other online options, the thought of not watching a movie when we want to is absurd. That said, Blockbuster was not wrong back then—it's just wrong given the realities of today.

Education, like society as a whole, continues to evolve, and as a result, some aspects that were once habitual are no longer applicable. In the grand scheme, standards-based instruction is relatively new. For example, the curricular standards in place at the time of this writing didn't exist forty years ago. Even twenty years ago, traditional grading practices still aligned somewhat with the instructional paradigm, but today they don't.

When I initially made changes to my grading practices, I was wrought with guilt. I thought I was doing everything I could for my students, but when I looked back, I realized I wasn't. Honorable intentions don't justify the use of misguided practices that no longer fit. These traditional grading practices (like averaging, giving penalties, grading everything, and using weighted task types), in fact, are downright wrong given today's pedagogical landscape and what we now know about instruction and assessment. This book challenges some viewpoints on grading, but my intent is not to question honorable motives.

I almost felt compelled to offer a collective apology to the students whose success I undercut with my ruthless approach to grading. I eventually realized that guilt was not helpful, so I suggest skipping that part. Instead, those reading this can start right away (if they haven't already) changing the grading paradigm they use within their own classrooms or schools.

The Standards-Based Mindset

We must change how we think about grading—our mindset—before we can make any physical changes to our grade reporting structures and routines. We need a completely new paradigm to replace the traditional view of grades as a commodity or reward. The new grading paradigm shifts grades from something the teacher randomly doles out to a reflection of learning the student earns.

A Shift in Our Grading Paradigm

While Thomas Kuhn, in his 1962 work *The Structure of Scientific Revolutions*, is widely credited with introducing the world to the idea of a paradigm shift, it's Stephen Covey who brought the idea to the mainstream. In his groundbreaking book *The Seven Habits of Highly Effective People*, Covey (1989) puts forth two important ideas relevant to our grading discussion. The first is this idea of a paradigm shift. In the general sense, Covey (1989) explains that a *paradigm* is "the way we 'see' the world—not in terms of our visual sense of sight, but in terms of perceiving, understanding, interpreting" (p. 23). In essence, Covey (1989) says, a paradigm is built around an assumption "that the way we see things is the way they really are or the way they should be" (p. 24). In today's education climate, the traditional grading paradigm is incongruous with how we teach. We need to see the act of grading differently.

As Covey (1989) writes, "[Thomas] Kuhn shows how almost every significant breakthrough in the field of scientific endeavor is first a break with tradition, with old ways of thinking, with old paradigms" (p. 29). We need to break with the tradition of grading. It's time we pushed aside our old ways of thinking and took a fresh look at how we report student achievement. Developing a new grading paradigm is the necessary first step toward significant grading reform, but we can't make this breakthrough unless we are prepared to renounce our traditional approach to grading. The new grading paradigm is the standards-based mindset.

Why a Shift in Mindset Is Necessary

I have had the good fortune of working with schools and districts throughout North America as well as internationally. During my work, I have noticed a very predictable pattern emerging: schools repeatedly start and stop their attempts to overhaul their grading and reporting paradigms. By and large, schools would inform me that they had changed their report card template and adopted standards-based proficiency scales, but they still struggled with making their changes take hold. As I inquired further, I could see that, in most cases, schools followed a favorable process on paper but failed to establish a new culture of grading that would lead to a new reality of organizing and reporting the evidence of achievement. Without first establishing a standards-based mindset, many teachers still found themselves entrenched within traditional grading thought processes.

The advantage of working on our mindset first is that success is not contingent on moving to full standards-based grading and reporting. Sure, that might be the desired long-term outcome, but teachers can start it on a much smaller scale. Teachers who begin to shift their grading mindset can make significant changes even if a single grade is required, if the electronic gradebook hasn't changed, or if a new report card is nowhere in sight. Whole-system changes do take time, but that shouldn't stop individual teachers from taking immediate action.

Establishing the standards-based mindset is both easy and challenging. It's easy because there are only a few simple ideas to consider; it's challenging because breaking old habits doesn't happen overnight. Instituting this mindset will put teachers in a different frame of mind to address the complexities of assessing student achievement. Grading is mostly mindset. How we think about grades and grading impacts how we respond to late work, cheating, conflicting evidence, the lack of responsibility, and a whole slew of idiosyncratic grading situations that will undoubtedly arise. Our standards-based mindset is the foundation from which all practices and decisions flow; if we shift how we think, we'll change how we grade.

What Is the Standards-Based Mindset?

The *standards-based mindset* comprises three components that, when put together, reshape the grading paradigm. I explore the details of each component in more depth in chapters 5, 6, and 7 of this book, but as a starting point, figure I.1 highlights the interconnectedness of the three elements.

1. Give students full credit for what they know.

2. Redefine accountability.

3. Repurpose the role of homework.

When we commit to these three elements, we establish a new grading paradigm that will create the foundation for more relevant and meaningful grading practices. The overlapping circles represent the interaction between the three elements. The combination of the three is what fully develops the mindset. Each element can exist on its own, but each one is better when aligned with the other two.

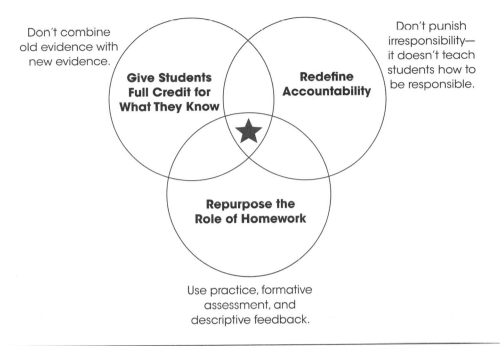

Figure I.1: The standards-based mindset.

About This Book

This book takes the reader through the process of establishing a new mindset, followed by new practices that will alter the grading and reporting realities within any classroom.

The first three chapters of the book focus on establishing the foundation and context for grading reform. Chapter 1 highlights the realities of our modern assessment paradigm and makes the case that the assessment landscape has changed so much that grading reform is no longer optional. Chapter 2 establishes the ideas of accuracy and confidence as the true north, allowing grading practices to follow an unwavering path aligned with the modern assessment paradigm. Chapter 3 examines—and debunks—five myths of standards-based grading that often impede a school's or district's ability to move ahead with necessary changes. While addressing the myths early on may feel premature, it is important to address them before exploring the standards-based mindset more deeply.

The middle chapters focus on what I call *grading from the inside*. Chapter 4 begins with an in-depth overview of the standards-based mindset. From there, it outlines the specifics of standards-based grading. Chapter 5 establishes the fundamental goal of giving students full credit for what they know. Chapter 6 explores the repurposing of homework as more of a formative process focused on feedback and learning, rather than on verification. Chapter 7 redefines accountability, allowing teachers to hold students accountable without compromising the integrity of the proficiency grade.

Finally, the last part of the book is about *grading from the outside*—that is, making the overt changes to practices and processes that lead to standards-based grading and reporting systems. Chapter 8 focuses on levels of proficiency and how teachers may determine them in a manner incongruent with traditional averages and percentage increments. Chapter 9 explores student attributes. The separation of attributes from proficiency grades doesn't mean they're not important. In fact, chapter 9 will make the case that this separation raises the profile of the important attributes to a level unfamiliar to most. Finally, chapter 10 concludes the book by highlighting standards-based reporting and explaining the potential options for schools and districts to organize gradebooks, report proficiency, and tell the story of progress.

This book is full of features that I hope will make the reading experience enjoyable and productive, such as grading dilemmas, vignettes from the field, personal reflections, ideas for dealing with parents, and questions for learning teams.

Two Requests

As you read this book, I have two requests. First, I ask you to continually contextualize the ideas within it. It is not possible to give an example from every level, every subject, every configuration, every province, every state, or every country. As you work your way through the book, keep asking yourself, "How could I make that work in my classroom?" or "How could we adapt that given our circumstances?" or "What would we have to do differently given certain policies are already in place?" You know your context better than anyone, and undoubtedly some of the ideas as presented in this book may not be possible in your context. Rather than dismissing those ideas, contextualize them to see if they could fit for you and how.

Second, I ask that you keep an open mind. The ideas within this book challenge the very core of traditional grading. You might not agree with every premise that I put forth; remember that we grow professionally when we find common ground with those who appear to have the opposite opinion of an idea. Have the courage to question your own beliefs, your own assumptions, and your own practices. We cannot accomplish significant grading reform until we align it with our grading purpose and our practices. Traditional grading has run its course; the time for change is now.

CHAPTER 1

The Modern Assessment Paradigm

The past 20 years have seen an accelerating growth in studies of formative assessment. However, this has not been matched by a corresponding development in summative assessment. The net effect has been that the changes have not improved the state of discord between these two functions.

—Paul Black

Since the mid-1990s, educators have been making a prodigious move toward incorporating more formative assessment into their instructional routines—a collective shift toward using assessment in service of learning rather than exclusively for evaluation. We have learned that, at its best, the formative use of assessment results has allowed teachers to more precisely identify next steps for learning and increased student engagement (Black & Wiliam, 1998; Shepard, 2000; Stiggins, 2005). In other words, we have come to know that maximizing the potential success of each student occurs only when we pair a laser-like focus on the intended learning with formative practices that reveal the gap between where the student is and where he or she is going. Despite this good work in formative assessment, we have not improved our summative assessment practices, or evaluation of learning.

As well, the standards-based instructional paradigm, also known as *outcome-based education*, has brought to light the need for more accuracy with how we assess work, verify learning, and report achievement. The pursuit of explicit curricular standards has transformed the instructional landscape and created a more definitive focus on what it is we expect students to achieve;

school is no longer about the completion of a series of activities, but rather the pursuit of proficiency as a set of outcomes that students achieve through the instructional experience. This shift toward definitive standards, and our accelerated use of formative assessment practices, has disjointed the instructional and reporting processes. Curricular standards, whether Common Core or other standards, are the modern instructional reality; it's time we realigned our summative assessment paradigm with this reality so that it can return to fulfilling its role within a balanced approach to classroom assessment.

The Advent of Curricular Standards

The purposeful shift toward establishing more rigorous curricular standards did more than set a minimal level of expectations for school performance. Countries around the world began to eye curricular standards that rose to the desired level of proficiency required for students to be successful post-graduation.

More Rigorous Standards

In the United States, many point to the report *A Nation at Risk* (National Commission on Excellence in Education, 1983) as the root cause of the standards movement in education (Brown, 2009; Holme, Richards, Jimerson, & Cohen, 2010). Among many of its findings, the report submitted that the nation had "lost sight of the basic purposes of schooling, and of the high expectations and disciplined effort needed to attain them" (National Commission on Excellence in Education, 1983, pp. 5–6) and scathingly criticized the collective expression of "educational standards and expectations largely in terms of '*minimum requirements*'" (National Commission on Excellence in Education, 1983, p. 14). While much of the report refers to *standards* in terms of *expectations*, the collective interpretation of the report by education professionals led to a more precise definition that better reflects our modern view of rigorous curricular standards (Brown, 2009; Hamilton, 2003). While the validity of the statistics used within the report was subsequently questioned and criticized (Berliner & Biddle, 1995), the report's impact on the educational landscape was, nonetheless, significant.

The move to establish more rigorous standards and focus on "exit outcomes" (Spady, 1994) is not exclusive to the United States; in fact, it seems that a desire not to fall behind other countries led to reorganizing and repurposing curricula around what is essential for all students to be able to do successfully at the end of their learning experience. After all, international test scores have increasingly become a prominent measure of a successful education system. While outcome-based elements both within and beyond the education realm had existed previously (for example, swimming programs), the serious push toward establishing these rigorous standards began in earnest in the 1980s.

As curricular standards were established, attention in the 1990s turned toward their assessment. In the United States, exit tests, once dismissed for their low threshold of acceptable performance, reemerged in the form of more rigorous standards-based exams to ensure students' mastery of higher-level skills that would allow them to remain competitive (Holme et al., 2010). The continued emphasis on establishing curricular standards throughout the 1990s led almost every state to adopt academic standards of some kind.

In 2001, the reauthorization of the Elementary and Secondary Education Act (No Child Left Behind [NCLB]) signaled a doubling down of the standards movement through the presupposition that high standards and measureable goals would lead to increased educational outcomes for every child. Nearly a decade later, the adoption of the Common Core State Standards (NGA & CCSSO, 2010a), which sought to align what each state meant by *proficiency*, solidified the prominent (and quite possibly permanent) role of curricular standards within the modern classroom.

The standards or outcome-based movement, and much of the political action on its behalf (such as NCLB and the Common Core), has never been without critics; however, the debate about the merits of standards-based education is best left for another discussion. The current reality is that teachers are expected to teach—and students to reach—established curricular standards through a demonstration of proficiency at the end of the instructional experience.

Outcome in Place of Input

Clarifying the focus of education, expanding opportunities for students, and establishing high expectations are the underlying principles of the standards-based reform movement (Davis, 2003). Ronald Harden and his colleagues suggest:

> Outcome-based education can be summed up as "results-orientated thinking" and is the opposite of "input-based education" where the emphasis is on the educational process and where we are happy to accept whatever is the result. In outcome-based education, the outcomes agreed for the curriculum guide what is taught and what is assessed. (Harden, Crosby, Davis, & Friedman, 1999, p. 8)

The two components of the educational experience—what students learn and how they are assessed—are now as aligned as they have ever been.

Most of us at some point, whether in our K–12 or university experiences, have completed a test that we perceived to have nothing to do with the content that was covered; for some, it was more common than uncommon. While today it would be unacceptable, there was a time when few questioned the practice. The standards movement seeks to eliminate the guesswork through a predetermined sequence of curriculum, instruction, and assessment. The outcome (standard) becomes the end while the input (process of learning) relocates as the means.

Standards, Not Standardization

One of the unfortunate byproducts of the standards movement has been the onslaught of standardized testing. It is worth mentioning here that *standards* and *standardization* are not always the same; the former refers to the quality that the demonstration of learning must exhibit, regardless of format, whereas the latter embeds the quality by making the demonstration of learning universal. The leap from standards to standardization is unnecessary, but it's one that has been made time and time again. Teaching to standards of quality does not mean the assessment of those standards has to be identical from student to student. We can establish clear standards for writing without requiring students to write about the exact same topic; we can have students demonstrate proficiency in science through an enriching project without them being identical.

Having curricular standards is analogous to having building codes. In every jurisdiction, there are well-established codes that builders must adhere to. Despite the existence of these codes, not every building looks the same. In fact, architects enjoy much creative flexibility as long as their designs are up to code. In that same sense, we want our students to be up to code, yet they don't have to demonstrate their learning in exactly the same way. Teaching to standards does not equate to standardized assessment. Yes, if we're assessing writing, then all students will have to write, but beyond that, students should have ample opportunity to exercise individual license with their work.

Teaching and assessing standards are based on an established set of criteria that highlight what quality writing, comprehension, critical thinking, performance, problem solving, products, and so on look like—the characteristics, not necessarily the format. As demonstrations become more complex, teachers must skillfully infer quality, since standards rarely dictate specific aspects of specific assignments. We will further explore this ability to recognize quality when grading in subsequent chapters.

The Resurgence of Formative Assessment

The standards movement (and the aggressive testing protocols that followed) precipitated a renewed interest in what might be the most favorable course of action to prepare students to meet the expected standards. As the standards movement embedded itself as an enduring aspect of the educational landscape, researchers reinvigorated their search for the most promising practices. What emerged was an almost unified belief that formative assessment practices were the most effective and efficient way to increase student achievement.

This section is not intended to provide a comprehensive review of the formative assessment and feedback literature. Rather, I simply want to highlight the reality that during the height of the standards movement, a body of evidence emerged that revolutionized instruction and created the modern assessment paradigm. This assessment revolution altered how teachers approach instruction and how they organize and report the evidence of learning.

Formative Assessment

In 1998, *formative assessment* was not a new concept. After all, Michael Scriven (1967) first coined the term *formative evaluation* thirty-one years earlier. Benjamin Bloom (1969) also made the distinction between formative and summative evaluation by stating that the effective use of formative evaluation was maximized when it was separated from the grading process (as cited in Wiliam, 2011). Though the next few decades produced some important research findings on the significance of classroom assessment in raising achievement levels, it wasn't until the latter half of the 1990s that our collective attention turned back to classroom assessment for learning rather than for evaluation.

There is almost unanimous acknowledgment that researchers Paul Black and Dylan Wiliam are most responsible for the universal pivot toward rethinking our day-to-day classroom assessment practices. In their article "Inside the Black Box: Raising Standards Through Classroom Assessment," Black and Wiliam (1998) argue that "standards can be raised only by changes that are put into direct effect by teachers and pupils" and that "there is a body of firm evidence that formative assessment is an essential component of classroom work." In fact, Black and Wiliam (1998) went so far as to argue that they "know of no other way of raising standards for which such a strong prima facie case can be made." These findings, supported within their research review, left no doubt that effective formative assessment practices could bring about unprecedented achievement gains (Black & Wiliam, 1998). What followed was an extensive examination of classroom assessment practices that continues today.

We now embrace the idea that formative assessment is essential to closing the gap between where the student is and where the student should be (Chappuis, 2015; Heritage, 2010; Sadler, 1989). Never before have we understood what quality assessment looks like and how vital it is that our classroom assessment practices are both accurate and communicated effectively (Chappuis, Stiggins, Chappuis, & Arter, 2012). There is little doubt that teachers can carry out assessment during the instructional process to improve both teaching and learning (Shepard, Hammerness, Darling-Hammond, & Rust, 2005). The strategic use of classroom assessment along an intentional learning progression (a sequenced set of knowledge and skills) creates an efficient, effective path toward proficiency (Heritage, 2010; Popham, 2008).

The Formative-Feedback Loop

Assessment is information gathering; using assessment information for an instructional purpose (rather than to evaluate) makes an assessment formative (Black, 2013). A key component of the resurgence of formative assessment was the increased attention educators gave to descriptive feedback. The purpose of formative assessment is not just to collect information about student learning, but to do something productive in response; assessment is the *gathering* while feedback is the *action*. While we can consider grades a type of feedback, they fall well short of being effective; grades by themselves are not descriptive and provide no direction to the student on what he or she must do to improve. The research on formative assessment and descriptive feedback became almost synonymous; effective assessment practices leaned on effective feedback, and effective feedback depended on accurate assessment. At its best, the relationship between formative assessment and descriptive feedback is a continuous loop that constantly fuels learning.

As the research on feedback deepened, it became more obvious that summative grades were insufficient. John Hattie and Helen Timperley (2007), in their article *The Power of Feedback*, made it clear that "to be effective, feedback needs to be clear, purposeful, meaningful, and compatible with students' prior knowledge and to provide logical connections" and that "it is the feedback information and interpretations from assessments, not the numbers or grades, that matter" (p. 104). With their thorough analysis of the feedback literature, Hattie and Timperley (2007) find that "the highest effect sizes involved students receiving information feedback about a task and how to do it more effectively. Lower effect sizes were related to praise, rewards, and punishments" (p. 84). While feedback powerfully influences student achievement, Hattie and Timperley made clear that feedback can have a positive or negative impact. The quality and type of feedback, as well as its timing, make the difference in whether students productively respond to it.

The research on feedback is rich and enduring. Feedback provided in lieu of grades and scores increases the likelihood of a positive effect (Black & Wiliam, 2010; Butler, 1988) and it is, in essence, the positive response that classifies feedback as effective (Kluger & DeNisi, 1996; Wiliam, 2011). Feedback must encourage student thinking and identify what's next (Hattie, 2012; Wiliam, 2011); grades, scores, and levels don't do that. As well, we know that we can enhance the effectiveness of feedback when we give students a clear vision of the learning, when we align our instruction to the learning, and when we organize our assessments so that students can easily discern what they know and what they still haven't learned (Chappuis, 2012).

Balanced Assessment

The net result of the assessment feedback research was a call for a balanced approach to assessment (Stiggins, 2008), in which educators understand and maximize the role of assessment for feedback (formative) and assessment for verification (summative). At their best, formative and summative assessment can have a mutually supportive relationship that allows formative assessment to fulfill its promise to improve learning (Black, 2013). The balance between formative and summative assessment is analogous to the relationship between practice and games, between rehearsal and performance. We know that there are typically more practices than games, more rehearsals than performances; likewise, balance doesn't mean a 1:1 ratio of formative to summative—it means we effectively use both.

While assessment for learning revolutionized the instructional paradigm for teachers (and the classroom experience for students), the need to verify and report learning to others (parents) is no less important today. There is certainly much to discuss about how we design and use summative assessments and make them relevant, but the summative process itself remains important. Our assessment literacy (Chappuis et al., 2012; Erkens, 2009) has, at least in theory, never been collectively stronger, yet a truly balanced assessment system remains elusive in some places. The knowing-doing gap is still the assessment challenge most teachers must work to overcome.

Katie White (@kw426), North East School Division, Melfort, Saskatchewan

When the Ministry of Education of Saskatchewan began the renewal process and many renewed curricula began to flow out of the agency over the course of a very short period of time, our division (district) was faced with making a decision about how to approach this volume of renewal. We began by trying to figure out how an outcome-based curriculum would change our business of teaching and learning. Before we knew it, we were using outcome-based rubrics and a divisionwide gradebook and report card. On our journey, when one thing changed, everything changed.

As we worked with the renewed curricula, we discovered that the shift to outcome-focused learning meant that the platform of understanding broadened for students: the ways they were invited to demonstrate their learning opened up and the continuum of learning offered more possibility. This was exciting, but it meant that we had to spend time in teacher groups considering how each outcome might look during teaching and learning. We started with a collaborative model of curriculum exploration using Understanding by Design (Wiggins & McTighe, 2005). We unpacked the outcomes and then focused on clarifying the continuum of learning using a four-part rubric for each outcome. We shared our work and provided supports for collaborative opportunities to accomplish the task of designing rubrics for each outcome in each curriculum and at each grade level. As a result, we deepened our collective understanding of what we were trying to accomplish each and every day in our classrooms.

Once we unpacked the outcomes and designed our rubrics, we realized we had to spend time planning how we would assess the learning. It was one thing to clarify the learning continuum, but quite another to plan ways to ensure learning developed and was measured in a timely fashion to offer sufficient feedback to allow learning to continue in ways that maximized student potential. Our assessment journey took on another layer. This is when the learning really opened up. We revisited our assessment philosophies, exploring the ideas of observation, formative assessment, redemonstration, and summative assessment once again in the context of our new outcome-focused world. This was not easy work, and we had to explore and discuss many real-life scenarios that presented complexities that a philosophy could not fully capture. We reworked our learning plans, revised our assessment plans, and continued to develop our understanding of what it means to learn.

In the midst of all this work, we realized we had to embrace the idea of an outcome-based gradebook and reporting system. Our teachers and principals asked for this final step in aligning our work, and it made sense. It had grown increasingly difficult to talk with students about their learning in terms of a continuum, only to then deliver an overall percentage or letter grade in a subject. We had to honor the process by including students and parents in our shared understanding and language of how we were expressing learning. Parents learned about our rubrics at home and in student-led conferences. Our approach evolved into a consistent way of thinking about learning for all partners: teachers, students, and families. So we embraced this final step and designed a divisionwide, outcome-based gradebook and reporting system. This final step, after a very long journey, allowed us to be totally aligned with our outcome-based instruction.

The Formative-Summative Disconnect

For many teachers, the work of formative feedback was (and still is) exciting, productive, and even invigorating, especially for those teachers desperately searching for ways to help their students learn more effectively. The contrast between the formative and summative purposes of assessment inadvertently led some to the perspective that formative assessment was in fact better than summative. While formative assessment is certainly better for learning and improvement, both are essential for balance.

The evolution of the modern assessment paradigm has exacerbated the schism between how we teach and how we grade. The formative-summative experiences are now, in many places, so dissimilar that any relationship between the two is unrecognizable.

On one side there is formative assessment, where educators identify the discrepancy between students' current location on the learning continuum and the intended learning goals; both teachers and students use assessment information to determine the specific next steps to keep learning on track. The feedback teachers provide to students is specific, timely, transparent, and centered on learning.

Contrast that with the traditional summative paradigm, where grades are a commodity that students acquire by accumulating points that result from completing a series of activities. In a traditional grading paradigm, it is quite possible that the reported grade does not reflect what the student actually understands, since old evidence often combines with new evidence, and behavioral transgressions can artificially lower academic scores. Despite having the knowledge that using grades to reward and punish students decreases their motivation and damages the process of learning itself (Moss, 2013), many teachers hesitate to embrace the practice of standards-based grading. Traditional grading practices have deep roots, which makes them challenging to transform. We have decades behind us of applying penalties, assigning zeros, grading everything, and mean averaging. The threat of reduced scores for noncompliance has become so embedded that many are unwilling to question its relevance in a standards-based instructional paradigm.

Some schools, districts, and classrooms, of course, have significantly changed their grading and reporting routines; many more are at least exploring the possibility. Despite the monumental efforts of some, we have yet to reach that tipping point (Gladwell, 2000) where standards-based grading becomes the norm—where peer pressure works in our favor to realign grading and learning routines. We're closer, but we still have a ways to go.

Necessary Shifts in Tradition

In one of the high schools I worked in, our administrative team developed the slogan "Traditionally, this is what we're doing now." It was our response to the reason (tradition) many gave for their reluctance to modernize their grading practices. Admittedly, it sounds a bit cynical; however, it was our way to signal that a change in how we grade was not only coming, it was necessary, and that we were about to create new traditions of collecting evidence of learning, organizing it, and reporting it. During our year of exploration (what we called our "year zero"), we kept referencing our new traditions as our staff explored the fundamentals in preparation for implementation during the following year, or year 1.

Realigning grading practices to the now well-established standards-based instructional paradigm represents the final step of the assessment revolution. It only makes sense that teaching to standards means reporting on those very same standards. If the information we collect and report is free of any nonstandard-related distortions (such as effort, penalties, completion scores, and attitude), we can create a mutually supportive relationship and establish a seamless formative-summative experience for students, parents, and teachers. The time is now to take the first step toward changing how educators think and act within their grading routines.

Reforming our grading and reporting practices can be complicated and multilayered, and it will go nowhere if teachers don't actually take the first step forward. Educators must develop an internal sense of urgency that grading reform is more than just desired; it's required. While there is something to be said for building fluency and capacity first, we must break free from the "preparing to prepare" rut that educators can find themselves trapped in. For all of the right reasons, teachers want to get it right, but thorough preparation will never replace the hands-on experience of actually implementing the strategies and moving forward. Changes to grading and reporting practices are long overdue, which means a collective internal sense of urgency is necessary to push educators from talking to doing.

Remember, however, that urgency is not the same as panic. While simply waiting for meaningful change to occur is no longer an option, the paradox of grading reform is that we also need an external sense of patience—first individually and then with others. The urgency to act must not translate into irrational or ill-informed implementation that actually makes things worse. It doesn't mean everything should be changed all at once. Each teacher should begin where he or she is most comfortable. Begin refining the practices that already align with the new reality; learn from initial successes and challenges; and seek feedback and input from students, parents, and others so that practices can evolve. Offset internal urgency with external patience that allows everyone the necessary space to make and embed changes at a reasonable pace.

For teachers, perfection won't happen immediately (or at all). No one will snap out of habits that they have cultivated for years. Be patient and know there is an unavoidable process to establishing a new grading mindset. Some things can't be rushed, and some old habits are difficult to break. People learn more from errors in execution than from theory, so be internally driven while remaining externally patient.

Administrators should provide teachers a reasonable amount of time to establish new routines without making them feel rushed. A focus on results instead of methods will allow teachers to manage the nuances of their individual classrooms for themselves as they set the overall direction and tone for how summative assessment will regain its place in the balanced assessment system. This doesn't mean they should develop the direction and tone in isolation; rather, it is best for everyone to own a piece of the journey by using a cohesive process to develop a shared vision. Shared leadership is not the same as no leadership; principals can't be afraid to take definitive positions that support the research and sound assessment fundamentals. They should clarify which practices they can and can't support—not as a way to be authoritative, but as necessary to identify those grading routines that are no longer useful.

Mandy Stalets (@MandyStalets), Thomas Metcalf Laboratory School, Normal, Illinois

When my coworker April returned from a professional development session on accurate grading practices held at our regional office of education she was excited to share with me the new idea of standards-based grading. Despite her enthusiasm, I didn't buy it. I had a system that worked, and I was comfortable with it. This new system seemed unnecessary, subjective, and time consuming. Our students and parents understood letter grades and what they meant—at least I thought they did.

A couple of months later, April and I had the opportunity to attend a professional development session about differentiation and grading practices. After participating in two activities, my grading perspective would be forever changed. The first activity was on the meaning and usage of grades. We were asked, as groups, to define the letter grades A, B, C, D, and F on a poster board. This task proved not only challenging but quite frustrating as my group was made of teachers from my school as well as other schools. I was surprised at how different April's definitions were from mine. We had taught together for two years, shared the same philosophy on several aspects of education, yet we still had completely different views of grades and assessment.

The second activity was an even greater source of frustration. We were asked to make a list of all of the different components that make up the grades we assign. Our list included participation, graded homework, quizzes, tests, effort, projects, and extra credit, among others. During the activity, April shared that her grades only represented students' most recent understanding of the content, a reflection of her switch to standards-based grading.

I was starting to realize that the grading procedures I had grown up with and had been using for years might no longer be what was best for students. I had been assigning my students letter grades that had no meaning and little connection to how I was teaching. After the training, I was sold on the idea of standards-based grading and was a little embarrassed that I had been assigning meaningless grades for so long. I knew that I would have to make a change.

After returning to school the next fall, I assigned a test the following week. I knew I was contradicting my new understandings and beliefs by giving a traditional test, but I also knew I would have to do more research to better understand how to implement a standards-based grading system. After grading the test, I experienced my most eye-opening moment. I was looking at scores two students earned: a 100 percent and a 98 percent. I found myself reflecting on whether there truly was a difference in their understanding and why one student was higher than the other. Both had mastered the content, but one student made a small error; he had forgotten a negative sign. However, both of their explanations of their work were amazing. So, I thought, why would these students receive different grades? My mind kept going back to my new beliefs about standards-based grading. This test covered three standards, and the test result was supposed to reflect students' ability to meet those standards. Both students had completely mastered all of the standards.

Soon after, I again found myself reflecting on the meaning of test scores when two students received the grades 72 percent and 74 percent. This time, the circumstances were very different. One student did not make one error when answering the questions; rather, he left almost the entire section on solving by graphing blank. The other student was beginning to grasp all of the concepts, but was still making many errors throughout, some of which were significant. I reflected on how fair it was that I was sending both of these students home with a grade of C. Would parents understand what their child's strengths and weaknesses were, or would they just see the C and be disappointed? I realized that my grading practices had to catch up; I was teaching to standards, and I determined grades through averages and percentages, and these practices were no longer compatible.

I could never go back to the one hundred–point letter grade system. My grades now speak for themselves. What I communicate about student learning is more meaningful; my students' report cards now represent their most recent progress toward mastery of the intended learning.

How to Bring Parents on Board

Informing parents about the modern assessment paradigm begins with making it clear that their children's school experiences will not mirror their own. Many parents expect school to be just as it was when they attended, even as we recognize that so much has changed. We have the good fortune to be immersed in the system and have experienced the changes (both large and small) on an incremental basis. For some parents, their last school experience was high school, so when their children enter the school system, their only point of reference is what they experienced decades ago.

Be intentional about helping parents learn that teaching to standards has replaced the conventional routine of activity completion and that there are some assessments used for instruction as opposed to grading. Parents understand the practice–games dynamic in sports (or the rehearsal–performance dynamic in the arts), so using simple analogies and layman's terms will put them at ease during conversations that can easily slip into edutalk and acronyms. They need to understand that learning can and does happen in the absence of grades and scores. What is ideal is balance; talking down to parents or over their heads is equally problematic.

Accepting new ideas, even for educators, can take time, so be willing to engage parents in the conversation, allow them to process the information, and provide them a forum to ask questions about why certain changes are necessary and important. While parental permission is not required, it is good practice to inform parents of the changes to grading practices in a timely manner. It is prudent to take the necessary time to craft the messages so they are easily consumed and processed so that we work with parents through our transformation instead of informing them after the fact.

Conclusion

The modern assessment paradigm demands that our grading practices evolve. Teaching and learning are now focused on the achievement of standards rather than on the simple completion of activities, and while the completion of activities is still important, the priority is now on progressing toward meeting curricular standards. The standards movement was a game-changer for how students are to be assessed, how the evidence of learning is organized, and how achievement levels are communicated. Since we teach to curricular standards it only makes sense that we now organize and report evidence of learning by those same standards.

Grading doesn't occur in a vacuum, so any conversations about grading must be embedded within a larger conversation about sound assessment practices. The work on using assessment more formatively to advance the learning has moved teachers to a place where grading everything is no longer seen as the most advantageous way to advance student learning. The focus on and application of more formative assessment practices since the mid-1990s have created a misalignment between how assessment information is used in the formative paradigm versus the summative paradigm. The much-needed mutually supportive relationship between formative and summative assessment is fractured when traditional grading practices compromise the integrity and accuracy of determined levels by including nonlearning factors (such as punctuality) in one experience (grading) but not the other (learning).

Making space for learning is not an indictment of the summative paradigm, and while the way we report learning to parents (and others) may fundamentally change, the requirement to summarize learning will never leave us; what we need is balanced assessment. The urgency of grading reform is about realigning the teaching and reporting processes to create a natural flow between assessments used to advance learning and assessments used to report it. Sound grading practices are about grades that reflect student proficiency rather than grades as a reward or commodity; teachers don't *give* grades, students *earn* them.

QUESTIONS FOR LEARNING TEAMS

1. What is your biggest takeaway from chapter 1? What immediate action (large or small) will you take as a result of this takeaway? Explain both to your team.

2. Has the formative assessment work in your school or district created an atmosphere more open to considering standards-based grading? If yes, explain; if no, what more needs to happen before engaging in that conversation?

3. To what degree are grades and effective feedback still confused within your context? Is there any particular stakeholder group that needs clarity on the distinction between the two?

4. How balanced is the assessment system in your classroom? In your school? In your district?

5. What grading traditions do you think will be easiest in your context to move away from? Which traditions will be the most difficult?

6. Given your intimate knowledge of your context, how will you establish the balance between internal urgency and external patience?

*Visit **go.solution-tree.com/assessment** for free reproducible versions of the questions for learning teams.*

CHAPTER 2

Accuracy and Confidence: Our Grading True North

We can replace the emotional dynamics of fear and vulnerability with those of academic self-efficacy and eagerness to learn as the driving emotions for academic success.

—Rick Stiggins

rue north is north according to the Earth's axis. It sits at the geographic North Pole. Unlike magnetic north, which transforms over time due to magnetic changes in the Earth's core as well as local magnetic variances, true north remains constant. While much about Earth constantly changes, true north remains stable and unaffected as a geographic focal point.

In the metaphorical sense, establishing a true north for grading provides a guide for the ideal conditions. While there are some definitive non-negotiable grading fundamentals, most decisions about when to grade, how to grade, and what to grade vary from teacher to teacher. What one teacher perceives as ideal may not be ideal for another. Establishing a true north increases the likelihood that grading practices remain consistent and aligned. The grading true north prevents teachers from losing sight of the big ideas that align assessment, instruction, and grading paradigms.

Philosophy Is Insufficient

Teachers take their grading practices seriously and personally; the emotional response that grading conversations elicit is unrivaled. Often linked to a personal philosophy, grading (more than any other aspect of teaching) is a topic that frequently results in visceral reactions, creating a polarizing discourse between those involved.

Being grounded in a personal philosophy of education is fine; however, philosophical debates about grading can be counterproductive to a consistent notion of what grades actually mean. If everyone creates their own grading rules based on their own personal philosophies (Is homework graded, is late work penalized, do effort and attitude contribute to a grade?), students and parents will have to keep track of what grades mean from one class to the next. This is not to discredit or diminish the importance of having a philosophy of education, as all teachers should reflect on this throughout their careers. Reflecting on our work helps shape the kind of learning cultures we hope to establish in our classrooms.

Philosophical differences can lead to healthy conversations, but they can also fester into internal division, hurt feelings, and accusatory undertones that create tension and contaminate relationships—maybe permanently. Grading traditions run deep, and educators are often resolute in their philosophies, so it's easy to slip into philosophical debates about the purpose and practice of grading that digress into a cynical exercise during which each accuses the other of being out of touch.

Without a grading true north, teachers must create their own grading routines from their own personal philosophies. They often implement these routines in isolation, rather than growing them from a particular focus or set of collective agreements. Then teachers retroactively tie them together to manufacture a philosophy that also includes elements of behavior management, in which they use grades as a way of discouraging behavioral transgressions.

Whether it's the use of zeros, the overemphasis on grading homework, or the resistance to any reassessment opportunities, it is easy for teachers to justify why they grade the way they do. If individual teachers determine their own practices via personal philosophies, then it's likely that those within the same school (or worse, the same subject) could have diametrically opposed philosophies. Then what? One teacher applies late penalties while another doesn't; one teacher allows second chances, while another assigns extra credit. When the individual philosophies among a group of teachers misalign, students must at best navigate several different sets of grading rules; at worst, teachers render grades meaningless as students struggle to keep straight the endless combinations of what goes into a grade. A teacher's professional responsibility is to ensure the validity of what he or she reports rather than backpedal toward a philosophy designed to link and defend a random collection of practices.

Balancing the individual autonomy of the classroom teacher with the known benefits of grading consistency is difficult. While uniformity is an unlikely (even undesirable) outcome, teachers can establish alignment with grading practices by mutually agreeing on a true north. A grading true north establishes the collective lens through which all teachers examine their grading practices. This does not mean that everyone does the same thing; rather, everyone makes individual grading decisions in light of their specific circumstances but based on a similar perspective. Establishing the specifics is ultimately an individual, school, or district decision, but anchoring grading practices with a true north through which all grading decisions flow should be the goal.

The Need for Accuracy and Confidence

Anchoring grading practices with a focus on accuracy and confidence leads to grading decisions that are on point and aligned with what we know to be in the best interest of student success. First, grades need to be accurate. If teachers and schools continue to report student achievement in a summarized fashion, the data need to accurately reflect students' level of proficiency. This means that all grading decisions need to pass the accuracy test. The important question becomes, Do the grades I report accurately reflect my students' true level of understanding?

Grading practices must also serve the big idea of establishing, sustaining, and growing student confidence about potential successes; students must emerge from any grading experience with an increased sense of optimism. The question for the confidence test is, Do my grading practices contribute to student confidence, or do they raise anxiety? How teachers grade either contributes to or takes away from the overall culture within the classroom. That is not to suggest that one misguided practice will wipe out an otherwise positive learning environment—it won't. But how teachers grade is a large part of what students experience, which means teachers' grading practices have either a positive or negative impact. With all of the progressive work rooted around standards-based instruction, formative assessment, descriptive feedback, differentiated instruction, peer assessment, and self-assessment, it's puzzling that any teacher would willingly choose grading practices (such as giving zeros, averaging, and grading practice work) that might serve to dismantle students' beliefs about their potential success.

The Case for Accuracy

The accuracy of grades depends on the quality of assessments (Moss, 2013) and the teacher's ability to accurately interpret results (Bonner, 2013). Understanding the fundamentals of assessment accuracy, while not the focus of this book, is an important undertaking for teachers. Low-quality assessments have the potential to produce inaccurate information about student learning. Inaccurate formative assessments can misinform teachers and students about what should come next in the learning. Inaccurate summative assessments may mislead students and parents (and others) about students' levels of proficiency. When a teacher knows the purpose of an assessment, what specific elements to assess, and what assessment method is the best fit, he or she will most likely see accurate assessment information. In short, knowing the specifics of the why, what, and how of assessment increases the likelihood that the resulting information about students is as accurate as possible (Chappuis et al., 2012).

Reflection, Not Reward

Grades must be a reflection of student proficiency, not a reward for compliance. As such, teachers must prioritize the validity of grades. Grades are fundamentally flawed if the achievement information they report is inaccurate (O'Connor, 2011). The findings in the professional literature are mixed on whether teachers can consistently interpret assessment results accurately to avoid potential misinformation (Gittman & Koster, 1999; Meisels, Bickel,

Nicholson, Xue, & Atkins-Burnett, 2001). Consistency in interpretation also becomes more difficult with increased student diversity (Darling-Hammond, 1995; Tiedemann, 2002). With these mixed results, teachers should infer that accuracy is possible, but it will require continual focus, attention, and practice.

The validity of assessment interpretation and results begins with an alignment between assessment and instruction. As such, one could conclude that a standards-based instructional paradigm requires a standards-based assessment paradigm. Poor alignment between the two not only impacts validity, but also negatively impacts student attitudes and motivation, as well as the classroom climate (Bonner, 2013). The gap is closing between those teachers who claim to grade based only on the achievement of standards and those who actually do, but it is still significant (McMunn, Schenck, & McColskey, 2003). Once assessments align with instruction, teachers must continually work to ensure their interpretations of the results are accurate so that the ensuing response (feedback or reporting) is as productive as possible.

The advent of standards-driven instruction has made it increasingly possible for teachers to accurately report student achievement. But traditional grades are not a comprehensive description of student achievement; teachers typically summarize the information into a combination of symbols and anecdotal comments that others must correctly interpret. If not correctly interpreted, students' achievement levels are not clear. Remaining mindful of grade accuracy and validity ensures that what teachers report corresponds with what the student has actually achieved. Validity can be questionable when grades are a mixture of achievement and nonachievement factors (Brookhart, 2013b). Teachers may find this concept tough to wholeheartedly endorse as many do not agree that they should grade students exclusively on achievement (Cross & Frary, 1999). I explore the reasons for this disagreement in subsequent chapters.

Meaningful Grades

When schools allow an endless number of combinations or interpretations in grading, the reported data become ambiguous. If schools ensure that grades are only about achievement, they are more likely to convey a clear and consistent message. While teachers have much work ahead to consistently recognize the various levels of proficiency in student work, at least they can begin the process of aligning their interpretations of evidence to send consistent messages about learning. As doctors are compelled to "first, do no harm," teachers should begin to formulate their grading mindset by vowing to "first, ensure no distortions"—that is, to exclude factors unrelated to achievement from grade determinations.

The Case for Confidence

Researchers have thoroughly documented the relationship between assessment and student motivation over the years. That relationship is complex and ultimately mitigated by students' self-perception, which is mainly formed by their most immediate experiences (Crooks, 1988). Studies have established the impact that evaluation and assessment have on students' conceptions of ability, self-efficacy, and even the effort they're willing to put forth (Crooks, 1988; Natriello, 1987), and that influence still holds even as theories of motivation continue to advance (Brookhart, 2013b).

Grading Dilemma: The Art and Science of Grading

Sometimes the goal of accuracy is easier to declare than accomplish. The challenge for teachers is to accurately report student proficiency even though some assignments might be missing. Our dilemma is determining the difference between essential and nonessential assignments. Does everything have to be handed in, or is it possible for a teacher to accurately report student proficiency without a student completing every task? Teachers often determine "workarounds" for students who are absent for extended illnesses, vacations, or even disciplinary reasons. From a behavioral perspective, the distinction between an excused and an unexcused absence is relevant, but from an academic perspective it's not; if the student is not at school, there is no evidence of learning.

When grades are calculated through strict adherence to weighting formulas and distribution functions, missing assignments can increase the mathematical significance of the assignments that have been completed. In other words, the completed assignments carry more weight since the data set is incomplete. If teachers use professional judgment to work around empty boxes in the gradebook, then accurately determining essential versus nonessential assignments becomes a critical step. Grading is as much art as it is science, so relying solely on calculations or judgments is likely an incomplete process. Balance is needed, but achieving a balance between the art and science of grading (while remaining focused on accuracy) can be daunting.

How do you balance the art and science of grading?

A focus on confidence is not about inflated self-esteem, a sense of entitlement, or an arrogant approach to learning. Self-efficacy perceptions contribute to the amount of effort students are prepared to put in (Brookhart & Peretin, 2002) and are a strong predictor of achievement (Rodriguez, 2004). Confidence is about real optimism that develops from a sense that success is possible, even if it's not immediate. Too often, teachers assume that discussions of confidence mean that students are soft or being coddled; nothing could be further from the truth. As readers will see throughout this book, having definitive expectations and building confidence are not mutually exclusive.

The Growth Mindset

In *Mindset: The New Psychology of Success*, Carol Dweck (2006) helps us understand that if we nurture a growth mindset we can increase motivation and help our students improve in school. Dweck outlines the difference between a *fixed mindset* (the belief that a person's qualities are carved in stone) and a *growth mindset* (the belief that a person's qualities can be cultivated), and why the growth mindset is something all adults (including teachers) must nurture within children. The link between mindset and confidence is undeniable. Students with a growth mindset gain more self-confidence (Robins & Pals, 2002); students with a fixed mindset have more delicate confidence levels.

> People with the fixed mindset have just as much confidence as people with the growth mindset—before anything happens, that is. But as you can imagine, their confidence is more fragile since setbacks and even effort can undermine it. (Dweck, 2006, p. 51)

The fragility of the fixed mindset comes from the notion that if students believe they are born smart, they believe they are smart in perpetuity. As a result, the sudden need to try harder in order to achieve the results they are used to presents the illusion that their fixed abilities are in decline. Dweck (2006) makes it clear that "the fixed mindset stands in the way of development and change" while the growth mindset is simply the starting point from which everyone can advance (p. 50). Nurturing a growth mindset means students are more likely to feel confident about their potential success. As such, we would be wise to avoid grading practices that undermine a growth mindset and the resulting confidence. One has to wonder, for example, how any teacher could think that withholding a reassessment opportunity or implicitly expecting all-at-once learning through immediate efforts (in other words, homework) builds confidence. Choosing grading practices that have the potential to subvert a student's confidence is shortsighted if the teacher wants students to develop a sense of real optimism about their eventual success.

Personal Reflection: Confidence Building

Building confidence was an outcome I had not expected when I implemented my revised grading procedures over a decade ago. At the time, I was an assistant principal in a middle school with a 50 percent classroom teaching assignment. I was in the midst of exploring new strategies for assessment, instruction, and grading, and I had taken a fairly clinical approach to implementing those practices. In other words, my focus was implementing the new ideas with high fidelity; I had little regard for the impact the practices might have on student confidence. It was only after the fact that I realized that the implementation of sound assessment and grading practices could not only accelerate student learning, but it could also positively influence student disposition when the inevitable challenges emerged. It was only after I saw students reengage with learning they had once dismissed, take more care when they used to rush through, ask more questions instead of sitting in silence, and tackle greater challenges instead of giving up that I realized I was on to something.

I saw students who would otherwise have given up begin to re-engage with learning and persist when things got tough. When Jennifer (a high-achieving student) told me that Chris (a low-achieving student in Jennifer's peer group) had called her one evening about the assigned practice work, I was floored; I would never have expected Chris to do that a few months earlier. I knew my newly implemented practices would improve the learning environment in my classroom, but I had no idea how far they would reach or how important a professional discovery I had just made. Even so, it was enough for me to set a new priority of establishing, nurturing, and expanding my students' level of confidence about learning. I was determined to be a *confidence builder*; subject-specific content proficiency would follow suit.

Winning Streaks and Losing Streaks

In *Confidence: How Winning Streaks and Losing Streaks Begin and End*, Rosabeth Moss Kanter (2004) identifies *confidence* as the fundamental principle that makes the biggest difference in determining success and failure. Kanter illustrates that the level of confidence employees, professional and collegiate athletes, or business people feel about their eventual success relates directly to their individual success and the success of the organization; why wouldn't this hold true for students as well? Why would confidence be important to adults but not students?

One thing essential for teachers to consider is that Kanter's research did not center on schools, teachers, or students, though she mentions the education context periodically. Her research concludes that adults need confidence to thrive in the workplace and contribute to successful organizations. While the book is chock-full of relevant examples that connect nicely with the school experience, three significant lessons emerge that all educators should take note of.

The first lesson is that success and failure are contextual and connected to both past and future experiences.

> Failure and success are not episodes, they are trajectories. They are tendencies, directions, pathways. Each decision, each time at bat, each tennis serve, each business quarter, each school year seems like a new event, but the next performance is shaped by what happened the last time out, unless something breaks the streak. (Kanter, 2004, p. 9)

This notion of trajectories reminds us that to view each assessment and grading experience as an isolated event is erroneous. Each assessment experience links with the one before and the one after; how a student has done is how he or she will do, unless something breaks the streak. When teachers think about trajectories, the importance of setting students up for academic winning streaks takes precedence and the grading practices teachers choose are more likely to align with that goal.

The second lesson is the impact of anxiety on the decisions students might make about school. The grading practices teachers use have the potential to positively or negatively impact students' overall experience.

> It's not mistakes that cause winners to lose, it's panic. Panic is a sudden, anxious feeling of loss of control, and panicking can make a small fumble worse, by causing people to lose their heads and forget to think clearly. . . . Panic is the enemy of good decision making under pressure. (Kanter, 2004, p. 68)

Panic does not bring out the best in students either. Anxiety drains students emotionally and interferes with their memory, concentration, and ability to pay attention (Chan, 2001). Clearly students with diagnosed anxiety disorders require the attention of mental health professionals who can develop a comprehensive treatment plan; the implementation of new or different grading practices will not be sufficient to help these students. However, for those students whose anxiety relates more to stress than a disorder, teachers have the potential to reduce at least some of this anxiety through the instructional choices they make, including the use of grading practices that maintain confidence. While teachers may have limited influence over students' internal stress, their goal should be to ensure that increased anxiety doesn't result from any external source, including chosen grading practices. Grading practices have to pass the confidence test (will they contribute to a student's sense of optimism?) in order to remain an integral part of how teachers grade students. If they don't, it's best to discontinue those practices immediately.

The final and most important lesson is the link Kanter (2004) establishes between the expectations of eventual success and how people (students) respond to challenges and obstacles.

> Expectations about the likelihood of eventual success determine the amount of effort people are willing to put in. Those who are convinced that they can be successful in carrying out the actions required for a successful outcome—who have the "self-efficacy"— are likely to try harder and to persist longer when they face obstacles. (p. 39)

All of us want our students to try harder when they face obstacles; they are more likely to do so when they develop a heightened sense of self-efficacy, which is the expectation of eventual success. So many of our conventional grading practices fail to send the message that eventual success is possible. Teachers undermine the expectation of success—the growth mindset—when they don't fully recognize students for their current levels of proficiency, regardless of where they began. The same happens when teachers choose to use grading practices that are counterproductive to building confidence. Students must emerge from the grading experience feeling more optimistic about their potential achievement than they did going in.

Garnet Hillman (@garnet_hillman), Deerfield Public Schools 109, Deerfield, Illinois

Three years ago, I recognized a problem with my grading practices. Having spent a significant amount of time studying and implementing differentiated instruction, I realized my grading practices did not align with my instructional routines. I felt compelled to change my grading practices to better align them with my teaching to focus on what I felt was most important: learning. After a year of researching, reading, and planning, I made the move to standards-based grading, which meant that student grades were directly connected to standards while behaviors, attributes, work habits, and life skills were no longer assessed with academic achievement and growth. Over the years since this move, I have seen a collective shift in both my students' behaviors and their mindsets about learning, which has been one of the most professionally rewarding experiences of my career.

My conversations with students have changed significantly. We now talk about learning, proficiency, and mastery rather than points, percentages, and grades. Their motivation and confidence have skyrocketed as we no longer waste valuable class time on homework compliance, questions about points, or whether an assignment is necessary for their grade. Their increased confidence and motivation stem from my descriptive feedback on their formative work, which allows students to know where they are in relation to the standards I assess and what they need to do to improve. My students are inspired by more meaningful practices that contribute to their learning rather than threats for not doing what they're told; their confidence in the learning process is further developed when formative practice leads to success on summative assessments, which in turn, leads to grades that accurately report what they understand.

My students have also found learning to be less stressful. Allowing them to reassess, for example, as a natural part of the learning process decreases anxiety and allows them to perform at their highest levels. Test anxiety, a common problem for many students, is almost nonexistent in my standards-based classroom. The sense of urgency to practice, prepare, and perform has motivated my students to strive to do well on their first attempts, even though they know another opportunity is available.

There is also now a perpetual sense of hope in my classroom. Students have the right to learn and demonstrate proficiency in a positive environment that fosters student ownership. My students frequently comment on how productive the atmosphere we've created is. Without competition amongst classmates or for grades, my students collaborate more effectively and encourage each other to keep learning. They are more confident about taking risks and trying something new since they know there is a safety net. Even those who are the toughest to reach and have every reason to give up remain motivated. We've managed to change the ongoing question from "Can I?" to "How can I?" This small change has been extremely influential in the learning process.

Transitioning to standards-based grading has transformed both my teaching practices and my students' approach to learning. I am developing confident, motivated students who now view learning as a never-final process. Standards-based grading has also allowed me to be more accurate when reporting my students' proficiency levels. My students inspire me to keep progressing and learning, to accurately report where they are in relation to the standards, and to lead them forward by providing them a guiding hand.

Your True North

Establishing a collective true north is both simple and complex. It's simple because most will support the need to agree on the principles of accuracy and confidence. It's complex because agreeing on the practices that serve those principles is likely to be more contentious. This underscores the reasons why healthy discussion is essential.

Healthy conversations begin with trust and an agreement that the focus is on moving forward, not on rehashing the past and declaring anyone wrong in retrospect. As I discussed in the introduction, grading practices that people agreed were right in the past may be wrong in the present. To establish a grading true north, respectful, healthy conversation among colleagues is necessary—blaming and embarrassing others is not.

How to Bring Parents on Board

When it comes to grading and the way teachers report achievement at school, parents usually expect their children's report cards to closely resemble the ones they received when they were in school. And while parents typically support progressive, forward-thinking approaches to teaching, they often stop short of embracing changes related to the way teachers determine and communicate grades, as well as what they mean. Our conventional grading system (letter grades A through F) is so ingrained in our society that it's often used in noneducational contexts (for example, when we grade a restaurant or a politician). Because most know—or at least think they know—what each letter means, people collectively accept their use both in and out of school, which makes communicating the changes to parents that much more challenging.

Whenever teachers change grading practices, it is prudent to communicate those changes clearly to parents, especially if they make changes midway through a school year. If we use our collective true north to guide us in terms of accuracy and confidence, we will go far in helping parents understand why we have made changes. The goal with every grading practice is to ensure that parents receive the most accurate information regarding their children's achievement and that they feel teachers build, maintain, and grow their children's confidence. No parent will argue for inaccurate information or grading practices that induce anxiety, so including accuracy and confidence as part of the message is judicious.

The message should clearly communicate to parents that the changes to grading their children are about to experience represent an improvement to current grading routines and experiences. At minimum, parents should expect to know why educators are introducing new grading practices and how the changes are better for them and their children. This helps ease parental anxiety about effects on their children's long-term success, college entrance, or career readiness. Without full awareness of the grading true north, parents are more likely to fall victim to the myths surrounding standards-based grading, something we'll explore further in chapter 3 (page 33).

Conclusion

The challenge with moving to more sound grading practices is that grading is—and to some extent always will be—a personal exercise. The goal of any change effort is not to eliminate any sense of autonomy but to create alignment and consistency so that teachers, while exercising their personal professional judgments, are consistent with how they assess and report student proficiency. Establishing the true north of accuracy and confidence allows a school or district to be prescriptive of the end (grading practices that lead to accurate grades and confident students) without prescribing the means.

Again, grading occurs within the context of sound assessment practices so the issue of accuracy is paramount. The validity of our assessments, whether formative or summative, has to remain at the forefront; our assessments must always assess what we say they assess. Whether summative assessments are valid is not an option, but a requirement. If our assessment is intended to measure proficiency in mathematics, for example, then that is what the grade should reflect; the fact that a student submitted that demonstration late should have no bearing on the proficiency grade.

Likewise, maintaining student confidence is non-negotiable. Teachers' continual use of practices that have a greater potential to undermine student optimism is incomprehensible. Grading is as emotional as it is clinical for students so the residual effect of any assessment experience must be one that nurtures the growth mindset. Even if an assessment results in a student not yet reaching proficiency, the student must know there is a path to recovery. The use of the assessment true north will ensure that individual teachers, schools, and even districts will make on-point decisions about the grading practices that build a culture of learning.

QUESTIONS FOR LEARNING TEAMS

1. What quote or passage represents your biggest takeaway from chapter 2? What immediate action will you take as a result of this takeaway? Explain both to your team.

2. Compare your grading practices in your first few years of teaching with how you grade now. Which practices are the same? Which practices are moderately different? Which practices are significantly different?

3. Why can discussions about grading practices become so emotionally charged? What can you do to mitigate this potential tension within your specific context?

4. Does using the lens of winning streaks and losing streaks change how you view your current grading practices and how they potentially impact your students? Why, or why not?

5. Can you identify any grading practices you currently use that may not pass both the accuracy and confidence tests? Are they practices you could tweak, or should they be eliminated?

*Visit **go.solution-tree.com/assessment** for free reproducible versions of the questions for learning teams.*

CHAPTER 3

Five Myths of Standards-Based Grading

In the "real world" timelines are frequently negotiated (real estate, legal matters) or adjusted to circumstances (contractors and consultants); deadlines range from fixed to considerably flexible. . . . We prepare students better for the real world when we offer a variety of deadlines in school.

—Ken O'Connor

The good news about standards-based grading is that there is more local control over grading decisions than teachers may first realize. The downside of local decision making is the potential to lose sight of the core fundamentals that ensure standards-based grading is an effective and accurate way of reporting student proficiency. With so many possible variations in implementation, standards-based grading could take on multiple forms that result in misalignment between schools or even within the same school.

When any idea is unsuccessfully executed, it is typical to find fault with the idea, not with implementation. Educators often judge standards-based grading on interpretation and implementation of the ideas in the classroom, not on the merits of the ideas themselves. Unfortunately, this can lead to false indications of what standards-based grading actually is and how successful it has been for the individual teacher. For example, if the practice of reassessment is unsuccessful, some would blame the practice rather than its implementation, even when other teachers do implement it successfully. This can spawn myths that eventually lead to the dismissal of otherwise sound practices.

I intentionally explore these myths up front in this book. Addressing them first allows me to explore the topics in subsequent chapters without *what if*s and *yeah, but*s to taint readers' perceptions of a new grading paradigm. These myths can quickly take hold within a school or district and make the implementation of sound grading practices exponentially more difficult. Remember, standards-based grading is about accurately reporting levels of proficiency, regardless of how long it took for students to master a skill or how slow they started out. It is up to the teacher, school, or district to determine how to get to accuracy. Context, the nature of the subject, and the students' ages will drive the systems, routines, and processes for getting to accuracy.

Whether teachers purposefully defend the status quo or get caught up in a myth-based narrative, it is critical that those seeking to implement more effective grading practices be clear on what sound grading practices are and are not. Despite what some might think, standards-based grading is not about making it easier for students to pass. It's not about creating more work for the teacher. It does not ask teachers to grade identically. It still holds students accountable, and it aligns with what students will experience after graduation.

Researchers have only begun to study standards-based grading, but their work does reveal two things. First, it has shown that the emergent standards-based learning culture has largely succeeded in changing teachers' attitudes about grading. Second, it reveals that maintaining the scrutiny with which we examine standards-based grading is necessary since even teachers who claim to grade only on achievement still employ practices that don't entirely meet those criteria (Brookhart, 2013b). Because of a lack of published research, the common grading myths that follow have emerged from my own experience, my observations of others' implementation efforts, and the personal experiences of implementers at the classroom and school levels.

Myth 1: Standards-Based Grading Makes It Easier for Students

It's true—standards-based grading can result in more students reaching proficiency, but a collective movement to standards-based instruction has nothing to do with making school easier for students; it's about more students reaching proficiency through authentic demonstrations of learning. Rather than simply accumulating the requisite number of points or averaging out to a passing grade, students must now reach a minimal level of proficiency on a maximum number of subject-specific standards. If anything, passing has become *more* rigorous as teachers look beyond the numbers to identify the specific areas of strength and weakness as they relate to the standards of learning within each subject.

Mediocrity Is Not Acceptable

The identification of standards and their specific components has allowed teachers to see more clearly where students are along their individual learning progressions. Some teachers have simply stopped accepting and grading substandard work. Don't confuse this refusal with being punitive; instead think of the work as simply not being ready for summative grading. If we accept mediocrity, then we send the message that mediocrity is acceptable; it's not. Those who refuse to accept mediocrity promote continual growth by asking students to keep trying and learning in order to bring their assignments up to an acceptable level. That's not easy.

Standards-based grading also has nothing to do with dumbing down or lowering standards. At some point, not good enough has to truly become *not good enough*, with the expectation that learning is never finished. Timelines, deadlines, grading periods, and reporting cycles are the realities of the system, so we know that learning cannot, in a practical sense, go on forever. That said, within those recognized restraints, refusing to accept subpar demonstrations of learning by students raises the standards of rigor within a classroom. Teachers should expect nothing less than the best from students, and while each student has an individual best, the only way students will learn that teachers expect high-quality performances from them is to hear "Not yet" when they turn in assignments that need more time and attention.

Failure Is Still Possible

Another aspect of the myth that standards-based grading is easier is the notion that no one fails. We must address this topic, but I do not mean it to become a distraction. Failure is still technically possible, and this section is in no way an endorsement for retention.

Students earn a passing grade when the teacher determines they have presented a sufficient amount of evidence (at a sufficient level) to justify a passing grade. If a student has not submitted enough evidence or has ultimately not reached the defined minimal level of proficiency, then the student doesn't pass. How this is handled depends on the age of the student and the extent of the failure.

This is especially tricky for elementary and middle school students since research favors nonretention policies. At best, retention has no positive effect on student outcomes (Jackson, 1975; Jimerson, 2001; Roderick & Nagaoka, 2005); at worst, retention produces negative academic and personal outcomes (Holmes, 1989; Holmes & Matthews, 1984; Jimerson, 2001; Westbury, 1994). High school educators must also be aware that retention late in a student's academic career can have a significant impact on academic attainment (Jacob & Lefgren, 2007). So if students technically fail but are socially promoted with peers, what are teachers and schools to do?

One possibility would be more effective communication that the student hasn't technically passed; educators must obviously do this with care and finesse. It is counterproductive for students and parents to assume a student has met the majority of standards simply because he or she has reached the next grade level. Teachers already know this information on an intimate level; what's missing is an efficient and effective process for communicating it. The local school culture and the established routines of communication largely dictate how this might unfold.

No-fail policies are one reason some push back against standards-based grading. Predetermined no-fail policies might seem to pass the confidence test, but they fall short of passing the accuracy test. Even when teachers do everything to prevent failure, some students still fall short of expected performance levels. The standards-based instructional paradigm does make it easier to identify the specific standards with which a student is struggling, but the sheer number of standards, along with the variety of proficiency levels students display at the next grade level, can challenge teachers. Eliminating failure is always our goal, but it's important to know that the elimination of failure is not a given of standards-based grading. If no one fails, it's because each student reached the minimal level of proficiency, not because the teacher wouldn't allow it.

Grading Dilemma: Handling Failure

So how do you handle failure in your own context? While learning is continual, the school year, as it currently exists in most schools and districts, is finite. At the end of the year, what happens when a student clearly has not turned in the requisite number of assignments or falls short of proficiency on the minimum number of standards required to justify a passing grade? The age and maturity of the student dictate the established routines to communicate this lack of success. Still, it is important to continually reflect on how we can improve the clarity of our communication with both students and parents. This is a challenge, since students may lose hope over communication that is too direct and misunderstand a message that is too cryptic. Again, we know that this message is likely more direct in high school settings as it becomes more obvious through our methods of reporting (as discussed in upcoming chapters). While failure may be easier to identify in a standards-based culture, students have the potential to react negatively regardless of age. Here are three items to consider.

- *Do you communicate failure with finesse to avoid diminishing or shattering student confidence?*

- *How effective and efficient is your internal communication regarding students who move from one grade to the next without sufficiently meeting the majority of grade-level standards? Is your communication more or less efficient and effective with external transitions (such as elementary to middle school or middle school to high school)?*

- *What steps could you take to ensure that your communication of students' lack of proficiency is more effective, efficient, and productive?*

Myth 2: Standards-Based Grading Is More Work for the Teacher

If implementing standards-based grading is more work, then teachers might not be implementing it correctly. Admittedly, it's easier to refuse late work, use zeros, calculate averages, and disallow reassessment, but conversations about what *more work* means need some contextual interpretation. It's important to recognize that the best interests of students and the best interests of teachers' workloads can, at times, be at odds; what is most *efficient* for teachers is sometimes not most *effective* for students.

It's Different Work, Not More Work

Once the dust settles on the implementation of standards-based grading, many teachers find it's no more or less work; it's just a different routine. On the one hand, teachers might offer students reassessment opportunities (more grading) but they may have also moved away from grading everything students produce in favor of more formative assessment work (less grading). It really is a question of how teachers want to distribute their time. If the workload is skewed in the direction of the teacher, then it's likely students aren't involved enough in the process of grading. While students shouldn't be grading themselves, teachers can most certainly ease their workload by teaching them how to self- and peer-assess, especially during the formative assessment process.

It is prudent to examine students' assessment and grading practices holistically. Grading practices are just one part of a teacher's overall instructional paradigm, and they can consider them contextually. We know that the middle of any implementation effort always feels messy. Until the new practices become habit, they will feel forced, artificial, and like more work, especially for teachers with many years of established traditional grading practices under their belts.

New Practices Need New Routines

If four of thirty students submit a required assignment late, the teacher is not doing more work. When the assignments were originally due, we might say that the teacher was four short; the late assignments only bring the amount of work to the same level it would have been had every student met the deadline. However, what can inadvertently become more work is the process the teacher goes through to finally receive those late assignments.

The successful implementation of any new practice is often only as effective as the routines, processes, and systems designed to support those using it. Without a new routine, the new practice is doomed to fail. Creating sustainable routines for teachers is important to ensure long-term success of a new grading paradigm. These new systems begin with the teachers identifying what they need to sustain implementation of the new practice. From there, conversations shift to grade levels, departments, and even the staff as a whole. At some point, school administration must be part of this process in order to create a cohesive system that effectively responds if, for example, students miss deadlines and don't respond to the teacher's initial efforts.

Shifting to a standards-based culture of grading is much more than implementing one practice in isolation; it requires a comprehensive approach. Expecting immediate, sweeping shifts from one practice (such as no zeros) is unrealistic. Teachers can't simply implement a no-penalties policy and then back away and watch it unfold (or unravel). Each new practice needs a replacement routine, which I explore throughout this book. Many of these replacement routines will be acceptable alternatives that bridge the gap between the teacher's current grading mindset and a desirable one. These alternatives are especially helpful in the early stages of implementation when teachers may feel daunted by the emotional commitment of leaping to any new practice.

Stephanie Harmon (@StephHarmon41), Rockcastle County High School, Mount Vernon, Kentucky

So often when I talk with other teachers about standards-based grading, they say "It's a good idea but I don't have the time," or "Aren't you doing a lot of extra work?" Nothing could be further from the truth! Once I implemented standards-based grading, I found that I have *more* time and there is no "extra work" because how I spend my time has completely changed.

Now my time is spent designing assessments and planning instruction that is focused on clear learning targets, which are congruent to the standards for the course. I am focused on what is necessary for students to show mastery of the learning targets—as are my students—and standards-based grading practices allow this to occur more easily.

I used to spend hours every night grading homework. Much of that time was spent trying to determine if I was being consistent in how I assigned points. I was more focused on what I thought was fair and what the numerical grade should be, rather than providing the feedback students really needed to improve. I also allowed behaviors to be part of the grade; did the student participate or was the assignment submitted on time? While these things are important, I decided their grades should be based on whether or not the student had mastered the content.

Now, I no longer assign a point value for homework; I provide feedback using comments and a non-numeric coding system, which I share with parents and students at the beginning of the semester so that all stakeholders understand that the grade is based on what the student knows. The non-numeric coding has allowed me to track student behaviors, which do influence learning, so I can discuss issues and successes with my students. This actually takes less time and is easier than when I assigned points. I'm focused on individual student work, and the feedback is specific to the needs of that student.

The grading of tests is easier as well. Now I'm focused on whether the student has mastered the intended learning and what evidence I have to support that claim. If a student hasn't mastered the learning yet, then he will have other opportunities to practice, retest, and show me his learning.

Another myth is that retesting creates more work. With my retesting policy, the student, not me, does the work. In order to show mastery, some students will need more practice and more experiences with the content than other students. These experiences may vary from more time in the lab to talking with me about a concept or how to solve a problem. Instead of a one-size-fits-all approach to teaching, I provide feedback and guidance to each student. The time I spend facilitating the practice and retesting is much less than the time I used to spend assigning points to homework.

For me, standards-based grading is much easier, less time consuming, and more specific to the needs of the individual student. Students get multiple opportunities to show me that they have mastered the learning. This has been very liberating as I find myself having more time to spend working with my students than I did in the past!

Myth 3: There Is Only One Way to Implement Standards-Based Grading

So much of what educators call standards-based grading is the cumulative effect of local decisions that eventually became the norm. Don't always take the commonalities between schools as hard and fast rules for standards-based grading. Statements like, "You can't ever grade homework," or "The most recent evidence is always most accurate" sound correct and may represent how the vast majority implement standards-based grading, but they are not definitive rules to follow; there is some nuance to this process that we must explore.

Our goal is to accurately report student proficiency while maintaining students' confidence in their continued growth. Beyond that, the decisions about grading practices are more local than universal. The end result may be universal—accurate grades—but the practices to achieve accuracy vary according to context. This is good news for teachers; especially those who resist standards-based grading because they believe that the goal is to standardize grading practices. There is no question that consistency among teachers teaching the same students or subject is beneficial, but uniformity is unnecessary.

Every grading decision we make has consequences. Decide to grade homework and there will be a resulting consequence; decide not to grade homework and there will be a different resulting consequence. As teachers audit their grading practices to uncover those that support the true north of accuracy and confidence, the important question to consider is whether each grading practice enhances or diminishes the ability to accurately report proficiency. I identify the consequences of these decisions throughout the book as I explore specific practices and acceptable alternatives.

As long as grading practices don't undermine accuracy and confidence, teachers should autonomously choose the practices that they believe work in the best interest of the students they're working with. Anchoring grading decisions with accuracy and confidence insulates teachers from making grading choices that have the potential to undercut a student's self-efficacy.

Myth 4: Students Are No Longer Held Accountable

What exactly does it mean to hold students accountable? Educators use the phrase often, but they rarely reflect on what it actually means. Standards-based grading still holds students accountable, but with a new definition of accountability. I explore how teachers can redefine accountability more thoroughly in chapter 7; here it is only important to know that the notion of students not being held accountable is a myth. Accountability is redefined, not eliminated.

Accountability can be carried out through different avenues, so having a working definition of accountability is crucial. Two teachers might agree that students need to be held accountable, thinking they are on the same page, and yet, for each, *accountability* means something different. One may think of accountability as consequences for behavioral missteps while another may view accountability as the belief that all learning is essential: same word, two different working definitions. Being held accountable for irresponsible behavior does not have to equate to experiencing a punitive consequence.

The focus on learning brought about by the standards movement encourages educators to examine evidence of learning holistically and in its totality rather than mathematically combining tasks that represent part of the same standards. The task completion paradigm focuses on students completing all tasks in order to earn the necessary credit, points, and percentages teachers use to calculate a grade. They emphasize getting it done in order to fill empty spots in the gradebook. The focus on learning shifts teachers from a task completion paradigm to a learning paradigm.

The *learning* paradigm recognizes that many tasks represent overlapping standards. Rather than emphasizing completion of every single task, teachers focus on identifying necessary evidence. This is a different way to prioritize. If students are likely to address missing evidence in an upcoming assignment, the teacher could decide that the missing task students haven't completed is unnecessary; alternatively, the teacher might consider the missing task critical and take every step to ensure the students complete it.

What teachers see as consequences may not actually be such for students. Most teachers would see a zero as a consequence, but the zero may actually allow the student to opt out of the assignment, especially if the net result of the zero is a grade that is still acceptable; that's not accountability, that's just punishment. Real accountability means teachers deem no essential evidence or demonstrations optional and that students are responsible for all of the learning.

Again, in standards-based grading, students are still held accountable, responsibility is still important, and deadlines still matter. It's a different kind of accountability, one that I explore in more depth in chapter 7.

Ken Mattingly (@kenmattingly), Rockcastle County Middle School, Mount Vernon, Kentucky

"But they won't do the work if it's not for a grade." I've heard that statement ad nauseam during my teaching career. There was even a time when I believed it, too. Now I know better because my students do their work without receiving a grade.

In fact, it is rare for a teacher to give an assignment just for a grade. Teachers assign work for practice, to assess current student understanding, and to prepare for the next day's lesson. However, somewhere along the way, we've stopped communicating this to our students.

I began to tell my students why I was assigning the work—to help them master the targets! I began to change my classroom culture so that mistakes were expected and even celebrated as learning opportunities. And, I changed my classroom culture by holding students accountable for completing the work. I had to show them how the work I assigned gave me valuable information on what they understood and where they were struggling. I had to show them there was value in the work. Students will do work when it has value for them. Many fail to see the value and so decide, Why do it?

Still, not every student gladly completes the work. The question then becomes, How do I hold them accountable? Traditionally, the answer would be to punish them with a low grade, or better yet, a zero. However, that doesn't help anyone. It lets the student off the hook for doing the work, and it doesn't tell me what they do or do not understand. So, in my classroom, the consequence for not doing the work is to do the work! If they haven't done the work, students lose their break or incentive time or they eat lunch in my room until they complete the work. This is non-negotiable.

What I have found is that these behavioral consequences mean a lot more to my students than any academic ones. They pay the penalty with the most valuable commodity they have: their time. While this approach hasn't made all of my students complete 100 percent of their work, I now have less trouble with work completion than ever before. I also have students who understand that the work (the practice) is designed to get them ready for the target assessments (the performance).

Myth 5: Students Will Be Unprepared for the Real World

The debate among educators about what students experience after graduation is both inevitable and the reason some are cautious about a standards-based approach to grading. As the argument goes, all of the second chances, the so-called lack of accountability, and the disregard for deadlines leave students unprepared to tackle the realities of life in the real world. If we ignore deadlines as adults, they argue, we will eventually be fired. While that may be true in some cases, the argument is futile because the idea that deadlines don't matter in standards-based grading is a myth, one that turns some teachers against standards-based grading. The concern among teachers about real-world preparation, however, is very real.

A Real Concern

The truth is we should all be concerned. School is not a way to make students experience an early version of adulthood, but we would be remiss if we didn't pay some attention to the potential impact our practices have on a student's ability to succeed after graduation. The limitation of the real-world argument is that students cannot learn every life lesson before graduation and that our human stages of development prevent us all from fully grasping the content and context of these life lessons prior to experiencing them.

As well, if teachers are going to proclaim the importance of these life lessons, habits, and characteristics, then they need to be purposeful about it rather than waiting for arbitrary student stumbles to provide an opportunity. If these skills and habits are so critical to the success of our students after graduation, then leaving it all to chance seems odd. The way we teach and assess proficiency is also the way we can teach and assess important life skills. We would never leave argumentative writing to chance, so why would we do it with something as important as the lesson of responsibility? We should intentionally teach the habits and attributes that ensure students are ready for life after high school, then assess them with accuracy and develop them through support and instruction.

The Illusion of the Real World

In the business world, great managers capitalize on individual strengths, pull the triggers necessary to activate those strengths, and tailor their coaching to employees' unique learning styles (Buckingham, 2005). The most productive growth environments are the ones where employees see constructive feedback as a source of empowerment rather than criticism (Walker, 2002). From their perspective, the most productive work environments are supportive, strength-based, and often personalized. That doesn't look at all like the real world described by many educators. In their descriptions, the real world is cutthroat and heartless, but a closer examination of some major corporations (such as Google) reveals a different story. If educators aren't careful, their depictions become more a threat of an unknowable future than a real guide to life after high school—more illusion than reality. Sure, not all work environments are ideal, and less-than-desirable managerial practices certainly exist, but that doesn't mean students are guaranteed to experience them after graduation.

In fact, much of the so-called real world is standards based. Whether it's a driving test, the bar exam, a pilot's license, or a whole host of other personal and professional hoops, credentials for employment are often grounded in the same principles as standards-based grading; one either meets the standard or doesn't. As well, when one finally meets the standard, the new result does not typically mingle with any previous results. Standards-based grading accurately reflects a student's level of proficiency without interference from other sources. The evaluator must separate unrelated, nonstandard aspects to ensure the clarity of what's being determined and ultimately reported. What's interesting is that some who push back against standards-based grading feel the separation reduces the significance of the important, real-world attributes that students need to develop to be successful as adults; the truth is it doesn't.

To become successful adults, students need to learn how to manage their time, be respectful, maximize their efforts toward a task, and be dependable members of a team; no one disputes this. The real question is, How? How do teachers most effectively instill these important attributes in their students? Again, if these characteristics and attributes are critical, then we must be willing to give them the attention they deserve, something I will discuss in more depth in chapter 9.

Personal Reflection: Making Predictions

I admit it—I have been guilty of making predictions about what a student will be like as an employee. It seemed logical that I could examine a student's academic results and corresponding attributes and know what kind of adult he or she would be. On more than one occasion, however, I've been proven wrong not years later, but in the same moments I was making those predictions.

Many high school students are employed part time, and what we find out about their work life outside of school might surprise us. Sometimes the student whose writing assignments are always late is the same employee who never misses a shift at the local grocery store. Sometimes the student who is less than enthusiastic about using the quadratic formula just got promoted to assistant manager at the local fast food restaurant. While these circumstances may not be true of every student who falls short of expectations, I have found that they are not as rare as we might think either.

Some of our students are already in the real world and are actually quite successful. We risk our credibility when our predictions don't match the student's current reality. When our predictions are grounded, thoughtful, and provide missing information that the student is not yet aware of, then they can serve a productive purpose. However, if our predictions are simply designed to scare students about their potential failures going forward, then they're misguided. This constant look to the future distracts us from our primary responsibility of ensuring students' success. The best preparation for success *tomorrow* is success and confidence *today*. Scaring students about the future is counterproductive.

Children Are Not Wired Like Adults

In his October 2011 *National Geographic* article "Beautiful Brains," David Dobbs explains that our brains undergo what he refers to as a "massive reorganization between our 12th and 25th year" and that "as we move through adolescence, the brain undergoes extensive remodeling, resembling a network and wiring upgrade" (p. 43). This massive reorganization helps make clear why teenagers often engage in behaviors adults would rarely consider.

The truth is that the teenage brain is not simply an early version of the adult brain; it's different. As such, it's difficult for teenagers to see the world the way adults do. If the twenty-fifth year is the end of the reorganization of the brain, it's no wonder most teenagers can't truly relate to adult life responsibilities. By the twenty-fifth year, most adults are at least seven years removed from high school, which means adult-referenced conversations during high school, while noble and well intentioned, are often premature.

What About College?

The most immediate real-world concern for students typically involves college and university attendance. Will students who experience standards-based grading face disadvantages after graduating from high school? Many adults recall their own grading experiences while in university and worry that standards-based grading is too soft and will leave students unprepared for the rigor of the collegiate learning and grading experience. I would argue that the granular nature of standards-based grading and the separation of important attributes could result in students being *more* prepared, as they would have a clearer picture of both their academic proficiency and their behavioral readiness. A student with high proficiency but low-level attributes would know that more attention, effort, focus, commitment, and even organization could be necessary for success at the next level. A student with lower proficiency (still high enough to gain acceptance into college) but high-level attributes would know that the habits and skills are there, but more focus on content proficiency and mastery will be required as workloads increase.

If standards-based grading leaves students unprepared for college or their careers, then it's an implementation issue. Those who argue unpreparedness only succeed in fear mongering, making others so anxious that they are unable to thoughtfully examine any idea—including standards-based grading (Kotter & Whitehead, 2010). It's one thing to raise authentic concerns over the long-term implications of any change in practice; it's quite another to raise anxieties to irrational levels through fear about what students might experience in the future.

At the Massachusetts Institute of Technology (MIT), freshmen are graded only on a pass or no-record basis during the first semester; the second semester allows for A–C or no-record grading. Regular A–F grading begins in a student's sophomore year. More details on MIT's grading policies can be found on their website (http://web.mit.edu/registrar/reg/grades/policies.html). Wellesley College (Wellesley, Massachusetts) uses shadow grades for first-year students. Similar to MIT, first-year students will, on their transcripts, receive a pass or no pass in all of their courses. However, students are given a report of the letter grades they would have received, but this information is only for the student and will never appear on the transcript or be released under any other circumstances. For a full description of Wellesley College's shadow grade system, visit their website (www.wellesley.edu/registrar/grading/grading_policy/shadow_grading_policy).

MIT and Wellesley College are just two examples, and while so many other universities and colleges may still use traditional grading systems, these examples do show that some schools—even prestigious schools—are willing to rethink the grading paradigm to best serve their students.

How to Bring Parents on Board

Sometimes too little information is worse than no information. Too little information can leave parents uniquely susceptible to the myths of standards-based grading. Since parents are not directly involved in the day-to-day decisions made in classrooms and schools, information reaches them through unpredictable and atypical means. Once a myth about standards-based grading takes hold in a parent community, it can be especially difficult to uproot. It doesn't take long to figure out that the most efficient means of derailing the implementation of any new idea is to rally the parent community against it.

Myths usually develop from misinformation and exaggerations, so teachers and principals would be wise to include parents at all discussion points along the implementation continuum, as well as prepare for any questions or concerns they might have. The key to this is a simple message.

Simple messages are sticky, memorable, and contagious (Gladwell, 2000), so the more confused parents are about the proposed changes, the stickier our messages need to be. We can neutralize misinformation with clear and simple messages that make the potential changes less daunting and more accessible. Teacher-talk won't cut it; parents need layman's terms and commonsense examples. Educators can easily forget how complex the language of education is. Faced with unfamiliar acronyms and terminology, parents can feel inept as they attempt to navigate proposed changes. Commonsense examples—like the relationship between practice and games or how employees are typically given full credit for their growth within a company—often help establish a happy medium between talking above parents and talking down to them.

Conclusion

This chapter focused on the myths of standards-based grading that can hijack meaningful conversations about grading reform. Rather than letting these myths fester, it is wise to address these issues head on to ensure they are kept in perspective. Each of the myths represents a real concern that needs attention; being mindful that the myths don't inadvertently become a reality is essential. The myths shouldn't stop discussions before they start, however, they can be used as a guideline for what teachers don't want their new grading practices to produce.

No one wants students unprepared for life after high school, nor does anyone want students to be irresponsible, though this can happen with a haphazard approach to implementing more modern grading practices as well. The intent of more sound grading practices is to create a culture of learning that yields accurate information about student proficiency; the myths put forth in this chapter do not represent the end goals of grading reform. Those who resist can use the myths as a way of keeping the grading reform effort in check. *If* the new practices and procedures begin to look as though the myths are coming to fruition, then a system of checks and balances is needed to stay on track.

Teachers are entitled to their perspectives, and no one should be surprised by the differences of opinion that are expressed during grading discussions; these opinions and perspectives cross an unnecessary line when, in advance of any productive conversations, the myths of standards-based grading are used to undercut productive conversations.

QUESTIONS FOR LEARNING TEAMS

1. What quote or passage represents your biggest takeaway from chapter 3? What immediate action will you take as a result of this takeaway? Explain both to your team.

2. Which of the five myths is the most serious hurdle your school or district will have to overcome?

3. Have you ever been involved in the implementation of a good idea that failed to take hold because of a poorly executed implementation plan? If so, what was it about the implementation plan that derailed its potential success?

4. How can we ensure that the implementation of new grading practices doesn't result in simply making school easier for students?

Continued →

5. Have you and your colleagues within the same subject, grade level, or department allowed for individual grading decisions while maintaining the consistency and accuracy of what you report?

6. How do you (or can you) strike the balance between preparing students for the future as adults and honoring where they currently are in their development toward adulthood?

*Visit **go.solution-tree.com/assessment** for free reproducible versions of the questions for learning teams.*

CHAPTER 4
The Standards-Based Mindset

I cannot emphasize strongly enough that getting sidetracked with details of scaling or policies before you tackle the question of what grades mean in the first place will lead to trouble.

—Susan Brookhart

The symbols we use to communicate student achievement are just that: symbols. More critical to the grading conversation are the meanings behind those symbols. While the *no letter grades* mantra is a popular approach in this era of standards-based learning, replacing letter grades with other scales or symbols is not something that can be determined through an identical traditional process. In other words, if we replace letter grades with another system that is still a function of predetermined percentage increments calculated primarily through weighting and mean averaging, then the no-letter-grades movement has failed to deliver on the promise of significantly changing the role of summative assessment to a more meaningful method of communicating achievement.

How we report learning to parents and others will continue to evolve, but the need to do so will always be a necessary and important part of our responsibility. Letter grades alone are not the issue; the real issue is the juxtaposition of how we traditionally determine letter grades with our current standards-based instructional paradigm. We can neutralize this incongruence by developing a standards-based mindset, which aligns with the standards-based instructional paradigm and allows teachers to approach the reporting of achievement from a standards-based perspective, even if traditional symbols and constructs still exist.

Why a Standards-Based Mindset?

Many of us have started, and then subsequently stopped, a new exercise plan. When the mental commitment to be fit is strong, people tend to find reasons to exercise and go out of their way to make time for the gym, a run, and so on. No matter the day-to-day obstacles that emerge, the mental focus is so strong that they make time for their workout.

On the other hand, when motivation fades, people make excuses. Suddenly work is too busy, family commitments are too important, and other so-called priorities get in the way. While some of the obstacles may actually be priorities, the excuses can create a new reality that makes exercise something only other people have time to do.

The lesson for educators is that our actions typically follow our thoughts. Like the fitness plan example, when teachers think and feel differently about grading it changes how they grade. When the mental commitment to change grading practices is strong, teachers will find every reason to make it work despite the limitations of the report card, the grading program, or the lack of buy-in from colleagues. It won't matter that no one else in the department is doing it or that the parents might not like it; if it's right for kids, we'll forge ahead. On the other hand, without this change in mindset, we will find every excuse why it can't or won't work. Suddenly, the fact that no one else is doing it or that the parents won't like it will cause us to hesitate (even resist) changing anything. This is why sustainable grading reform must begin on the inside with the development of a standards-based mindset and work its way outward.

Developing a standards-based mindset accomplishes two things. First, the prospect of actual standards-based reporting becomes less daunting. Developing a new report card template is the low-hanging fruit of grading reform, but having a standards-based report card doesn't guarantee actual standards-based grading. An Internet search produces thousands of templates to use or adapt; however, the report card should be the last thing to change, and it should only change to realign grading and reporting practices with a standards-focused instructional paradigm. Second, the standards-based mindset allows the flexibility some teachers need if they work within a school whose shift toward standards-based grading is incomplete or not yet started. We can't wait for the system to be perfect before we begin making important changes to our grading practices.

Grading with a standards-based mindset is not contingent on a system of standards-based grading and reporting. In fact, teachers can grade with a standards-based mindset even when they work in a context that uses traditional systems of reporting. Teachers who develop a standards-based mindset will find an eventual move to standards-based grading and reporting much easier to navigate.

Standards-Based Mindset Defined

Essentially, a standards-based mindset represents a way of thinking about grading that does not actually change the symbols or methods used to communicate achievement. The first task in developing this mindset is to reach consensus on the purpose and foundation of the grading process (Brookhart, 2011). This allows us to think about grading from a standards-based perspective even if the report card template or the existing symbols haven't changed. Figure 4.1 illustrates the gap that can often exist between the paradigms of traditional and standards-based grading.

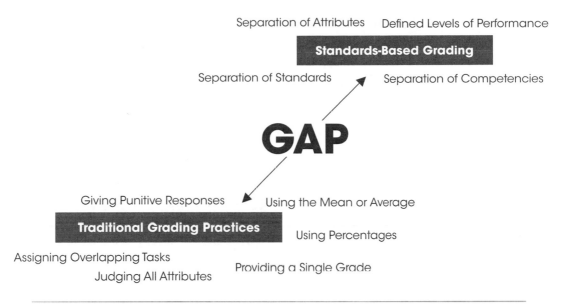

Figure 4.1: Traditional grading versus standards-based grading.

On the one hand, we have traditional grading practices that essentially require teachers to determine a single grade based on the entirety (learning and behavior) of what the student has done. They typically organize evidence of learning by tasks (such as quizzes, tests, and projects) that overlap the same standards, and achievement levels are often the result of the mean averaging of these weighted tasks. Teachers use predetermined percentage increments to distinguish between traditional levels of achievement (A through F) and include nonachievement factors (such as late work and extra credit) in the grade determination, artificially increasing or decreasing an overall grade. It's a traditional system that most of us are familiar with, experienced as students, and maybe even used ourselves.

On the other hand, a standards-based grading and reporting system requires teachers to organize evidence by standards and factor out all nonachievement attributes. They assess these attributes separately from proficiency grades, against their own standards of achievement. These standards outline, often in rubric form, the characteristics of the strong work habits and attributes students need to be college or career ready. Rather than using traditional letter grades and percentages, standards-based grading involves *levels of proficiency* that illustrate a natural progression of quality. Even more recently, schools have established a third category of reporting on achievement against certain cross-curricular competencies now emerging as another area of emphasis where competencies (such as critical thinking or creativity) are assessed through performance assessments and frequency scales (for example, How frequently does the student think with creative intent or demonstrate original thinking?).

Here's the rub: the gap between these two grading paradigms is often too wide to simply move from one to the other. Teachers find there are too many layers, nuances, and specific grading practices that they must implement, examine, revise, and rework to simply flip a switch and move from traditional grading to standards-based grading. This is why establishing a standards-based mindset is the necessary first step to long-term grading reform. In many of the schools I've worked in and with, the failure to establish a new, collective mindset about grading impedes real progress toward grading reform.

Figure 4.2 illustrates how a standards-based mindset can be the first step toward fully establishing a standards-based approach to grading. By allowing teachers to separate the determination of grades from the reporting of grades, the standards-based mindset encourages them to take a standards-based approach to evidence of learning and not definitively choose sides between traditional and standards-based reporting. Teachers can grade with a standards-based mindset even when the process for reporting hasn't caught up; it simply changes *how* they determine single, traditional symbols.

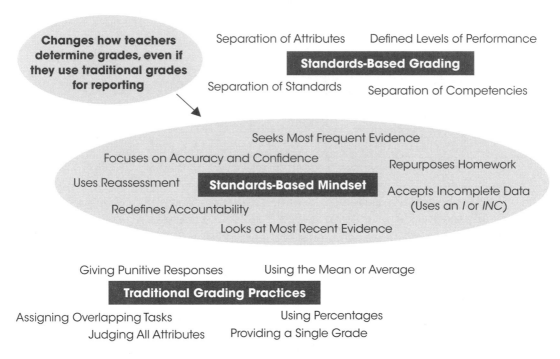

Figure 4.2: The standards-based mindset as a first step to establishing a standards-based approach to grading.

By rethinking how we organize and examine evidence of learning, repurposing the role of homework, redefining accountability, and creating opportunities for reassessment, we are more likely to report accurate grades and create a grading experience that leaves students feeling optimistic about their future success. The move from traditional grading to a standards-based mindset (from the bottom left corner of figure 4.2 to the center) represents the heavy lifting of the grading conversation and is the requisite first step for teachers, schools, and districts whose long-term goal is standards-based grading and reporting.

A standards-based mindset will engender an increasingly productive grading paradigm, even if a formal standards-based reporting system is not the eventual outcome or goal.

Teachers can determine required percentage grades (such as 80 percent) through a more accurate and commonsense process that thoughtfully examines evidence instead of just deferring to a mean average. Again, when we are mentally committed to grading reform, we'll find reasons to do it; when we're not committed, we'll make excuses.

Establishing a standards-based mindset allows for the gradual introduction of individual, standards-based grading practices that teachers would feel uncomfortable and overwhelmed to deal with simultaneously.

Darin Jolly (@drjolly), Former Principal, Mabank Junior High, Mabank, Texas

At Mabank, our journey toward standards-based learning and grading began in the spring of 2008. Our teachers and school leadership team began reflecting on our practices to determine our beliefs, purpose, and the role of grading in our school. We realized inconsistencies in our grading practices, and it was obvious that learning was not always reflected in our student grades. Instead, our grades were mostly determined by behaviors, punitive measures based on deadlines, grade caps, inflation, and averaging. We needed to shift our grading practice to *grading for learning* instead of *learning for grading*.

As a principal facilitating this reflective process, I quickly saw that we were all over the map as educators, bringing so many different experiences and years of practice to the table. Throughout this experience, we learned so much about our campus team, our individual values, core beliefs, and practices. We had several great debates about the differences between learning responsibility and teaching responsibility. Simple questions from our traditional routines as educators became increasingly challenging to answer as we progressed toward determining our beliefs and purposes for grading in our school. Not only did we have our individual preferences and ideas of how to grade and why we grade, but we could also not agree on the foundational purpose of grading. We also realized we had students who were failing as a result of our ineffective grading system.

The more we dove into the pool of grading questions and procedures, the deeper the pool became, with new questions emerging as we explored grading practices. We attended assessment conferences and presentations and referenced the relevant literature. Our districtwide Instructional Leadership Team, comprised of representatives from our six campuses, collaboratively initiated the process of developing a grading manifesto, which we anticipated taking three years to fully implement.

Even though we did not fully transition to standards-based grading, we were able to establish healthy grading practices. We now grade for learning; we call it *standards-based learning*. We found that the grading discussion never ends and is a truly formative process that has us continually reflecting on our grading practices to meet the needs of our learners.

Hybrid Grading

Integrating a standards-based approach with a traditional system may allow teachers to develop their own form of *hybrid grading*. The system may still require traditional numbers and symbols (A through F), but teachers can determine them with a standards-based mindset. In essence, hybrid grading is a combination of traditional and standards-based grading. While some might view this hybrid as "standards-based grading lite" or yet another excuse to stop short of a full commitment to standards-based grading, it does offer teachers a way to methodically change their approach to grading without a complete overhaul. It's easy for authors and education consultants to demand that certain aspects of grading change immediately, but many of those aspects are not within teachers' sphere of influence and, therefore, will not change overnight. A more productive approach is to explore what *can* be done to bridge the gap between what is desirable and what is possible. Hybrid grading is not an attempt to create a new buzzword, program, or label. Hybrid grading is about what teachers do and relates more to grade determination than grade calculation.

The difference between grade *determination* and grade *calculation* is the professional judgment of the teacher. Calculated grades often result from a mathematical algorithm (a mean average), and the only point of discretion is the weight teachers assign to each task type. This method gives little (if any) consideration to timing of student demonstrations of proficiency or how frequently they perform at their highest levels. Deferring to calculations does provide some cover from potential criticism as teachers can remain at arm's length of how the numbers played out, leaving students isolated in owning their results, despite the fact that the teacher was solely responsible (through the grading rules he or she determined) for how he or she manipulates the numbers in the first place.

On the other hand, when teachers *determine* grades, they also consider the elements of timing and frequency. I will cover the specific practices a teacher might use for a hybrid approach in subsequent chapters. For now, my point is that teachers must learn to be comfortable with determining a student's proficiency not just by how the numbers play out, but by when (and how often) a student performs at his or her level of proficiency.

There is a great deal of professional judgment in grading (O'Connor, 2009). Unless grades are simply a ratio of questions answered correctly to questions asked, teachers already judge the organization of evidence and the aspects of greatest importance. The advent of electronic gradebooks makes the science of grading quite alluring for some teachers. With spreadsheets, graphs, trends, and class averages, teachers can produce a slew of "evidence" to support the grades they report, but it's almost as though the computer determines the grade.

What gets lost in all the calculations is the art of grading, where we embrace our professional judgment, experience, and agreed-on performance criteria to determine the most accurate level of proficiency. The art of grading is to use the numbers but not let them be the final judge. It's about understanding growth trajectories—that some students take longer to reach high levels of proficiency than others. It means understanding where students finish, not where they started, and recognizing that some previous evidence of learning may interfere with the accuracy of what teachers ultimately report. It is about finding a balance.

Personal Reflection: The Art of Grading

As the assistant principal of a high school, I found myself in a meeting with an English language arts teacher. While we'd had a number of brief conversations about the idea of alternative grading practices, she was still not convinced and wanted to dedicate some time to exploring the concept a little more deeply.

After meeting only a few minutes, we agreed that our conversation would be more productive if she could see what the alternatives might look like, so we took her active gradebook, saved a duplicate copy, and began to use a mock gradebook to experiment with a variety of approaches.

We focused on one student—Tina—who was one of the English teacher's most challenging students, both academically and behaviorally. Tina's scores were littered with zeros for work that she had not submitted, despite being capable of completing (something Tina herself would later acknowledge). I took control of the keyboard and began to remove the zeros from Tina's grade profile in preparation to explore the potential alternatives. As I removed each zero, Tina's overall grade began to go up. (As with most electronic gradebooks, the program we used at the time only included entered scores, so any empty spaces did not count in final grade calculations.) The removal of a zero eventually pushed Tina's grade over the threshold from a fail to a pass. Even though I hadn't finished the process of removing zeros, the teacher interrupted and declared, "You see, this no-zero thing doesn't work. Now Tina's passing!"

Admittedly, I was caught off guard by her reaction. She was leaving the pass-or-fail determination to the computer program. I immediately stopped what I was doing, turned to her, and said, "Tina doesn't pass until you decide she passes. That's not the computer program's decision; that's yours." The teacher had lost sight of the art of grading, something that's easy to do when we become overly clinical about our manipulations within an electronic gradebook.

The rest of my time with the teacher focused on the art of grading and how important it is for teachers to honor their professionalism by using their expertise and experience to make the final decisions about achievement. The lack of sufficient evidence alone would, in the end, result in a poor grade or level. The need to calculate a poor grade or level through the use of zeros during a semester is an unnecessary step. Grading programs can help make those decisions more efficient, but the final decision must come from the teacher based on student demonstrations, established standards, and agreed-on success criteria.

Figure 4.3 (page 54) provides an example of a common traditional gradebook to illustrate what a hybrid process might look like. The purpose of this example is to juxtapose a grade calculation and a grade determination. With the latter, the teacher employs a hybrid approach by using the numbers with the potential of looking beyond to consider the student's progression and learning trajectory. The numbers are a starting point but not necessarily a finishing

Grade Scale	Mathematics Department Weighting
A = 90–100 B = 80–89 C = 70–79 D = 60–69 F = <60	Tests = 40% Quizzes = 30% Assignments = 20% Homework = 10%

Jennifer's Mathematics Grade Spreadsheet

Unit 1: Standards 1 and 2				Unit 1: Standards 3 and 4							
HW	HW	Assign	**Quiz**	HW	HW	HW	Assign	Assign	**Quiz**	**Unit 1 Test**	**Final Grade**
58%	62%	64%	**69%**	65%	74%	68%	77%	75%	**85%**	**83%**	**74% C**

HW = Homework; Assign = Assignment

Figure 4.3: Hybrid grading example.

point. Since not every assignment is worth one hundred points, to simplify, all scores have been converted to percentage equivalents.

Keep in mind, however, that figure 4.3 does not represent any kind of recommendation. Aspects of it counter what I will discuss later in the book. The example is an oversimplified version of what most teachers typically manage at the end of the term, semester, or school year, and I have kept the weighting of each task type at an unsophisticated delineation. It is an example to show the basics of a hybrid process only.

Let's take a closer look at Jennifer's grade profile and explore three options and ideas.

1. If Jennifer's teacher deferred to the grade calculation and the predetermined weighting scale, Jennifer would have earned a C (73.9 percent), which is displayed in figure 4.3.

2. However, if Jennifer's teacher were to extract the quiz and test results, it's clear that Jennifer performed at a higher level, which may indicate that Jennifer starts slowly but does progress through the standards. This might cause her teacher to emphasize those results more than the others. Jennifer's average quiz result is 77 percent, and her test result is 83 percent; both are clearly higher than her overall final grade.

3. Averaging the quiz scores (77 percent) with the unit test score (83 percent) results in a grade of 80 percent, which not only is higher than her calculated grade but also represents another grade category.

Imagine if Jennifer's teacher chooses option 3 (a form of hybrid grading) and reports a B instead of a C for Jennifer. The teacher still uses a traditional form of reporting (B) but has determined the grade with a standards-based mindset. She may consider that Jennifer's homework results represent old evidence that becomes invalid once Jennifer demonstrates a higher level of understanding. She may also recognize that the unit test is comprehensive, more than adequately samples the curriculum, and represents a culmination of the learning through the unit which allows her to increase its emphasis in the overall process of grade determination.

The standards-based mindset allows Jennifer's teacher to increase the weight the unit test carries when Jennifer demonstrates a high level of proficiency; she didn't declare that ahead of time to avoid pressuring the students but did so once the evidence presented itself.

Clearly this is a simplistic hypothetical designed solely to emphasize the point that the standards-based mindset can function within a traditional reporting system. The grading program or the report card template need not change for Jennifer's teacher to take a standards-based approach to determining Jennifer's mathematics grade. Rather than overanalyzing this one particular hypothetical, I just want readers to see the big idea of a hybrid approach as a possibility. Students are not hypothetical; they're real people who have real experiences and real relationships with their teachers. Really consider the possibility that the numbers don't always tell the whole story and that it's up to teachers to make a final decision about proficiency.

Teachers and the Rules

In his book *Outliers: The Story of Success*, Malcolm Gladwell (2008) challenges the conventional ways in which society views success. One of his arguments is that we collectively pay no attention to external influence on successful individuals; we have romanticized the notion that individual merit is what determines success. When discussing the consequences and flaws of this idea as it relates to established cut-off dates for participation in most youth sports organizations, Gladwell (2008) writes:

> We make rules that frustrate achievement. We prematurely write off people as failures. We are too much in awe of those who succeed and far too dismissive of those who fail. And, most of all, we become much too passive. We overlook just how large a role we all play—and by "we" I mean society—in determining who makes it and who doesn't. (pp. 32–33)

By "we" Gladwell means *society*; by "we" I mean *educators*. Rules that frustrate achievement exist within traditional grading paradigms as much as they do in youth sports organizations. Whether individually or as a team, teachers determine most of the grading rules that students experience. Teachers must often abide by established school and district grading policies, but these tend to focus more on ends than means. In most cases, teachers decide how to handle late work, reassessment opportunities, or what learning evidence is essential. These decisions greatly influence how teachers determine and ultimately report grades. A student consistently at a minimal level of understanding (passing) could end up with a failing grade if he or she consistently submits assignments a few days late. If the report card indicates failure, then the grade isn't accurate because the quality of the work was at a minimally acceptable level.

Let's go back to the example of Jennifer in figure 4.3. Professional judgment and rule making in grading are easier when students show a linear growth trajectory with stronger end results, as was the case with Jennifer. Most teachers are comfortable with dismissing early results when later quiz, test, or project scores reveal a much higher proficiency. But what about when the opposite happens? What if the early results are stronger than the more recent results? What if the smaller assignments are strong, but the larger demonstrations fall short? Or worse, what if there is no recognizable pattern and the results can only be described as inconsistent across time and scope? Does one just defer to the average, or is there another way?

The process for determining a student's grade is different and possibly easier in a standards-based reporting system, but again, the standards-based mindset alone can help. For now, assume a traditional system of reporting and use a standards-based mindset to consider another student's final grade: Jason (figure 4.4). Assume the same A-to-F grading scale and the same weighting scale (40/30/20/10) as in figure 4.3.

Grade Scale	Mathematics Department Weighting
A = 90–100 B = 80–89 C = 70–79 D = 60–69 F = <60	Tests = 40% Quizzes = 30% Assignments = 20% Homework = 10%

Jason's Mathematics Grade Spreadsheet

Unit 1: Standards 1 and 2				Unit 1: Standards 3 and 4							
HW	HW	Assign	**Quiz**	HW	HW	HW	Assign	Assign	**Quiz**	Unit 1 Test	Final Grade
75%	52%	72%	**66%**	80%	75%	80%	62%	85%	**90%**	63%	70% C

HW = Homework; Assign = Assignment

Figure 4.4: Hybrid grading example with nonlinear growth trajectory.

According to the distribution and grading scale, Jason's final percentage grade would be 70.44 percent. Is that the grade Jason should receive? Here are three questions to consider.

1. Is it significant that seven of the eleven results in Jason's gradebook are above the 70 percent final grade?

2. Is it significant that Jason's unit test (the result that carries the heaviest weight) is 7 percent below the final grade?

3. Hypothesize how a student could score 90 percent on a quiz, but then 63 percent on a test in which potentially half the questions cover the same standards (3 and 4) as the quiz.

With Jason's gradebook, there are some details missing. If the homework and assignments focused on meeting targets, but the quizzes and test focused on meeting standards, then greater emphasis may be placed on them; however, if all assignments focused on meeting standards, then the weighting distorts achievement levels. In this example, given the inconsistency of results, the teacher may decide that the calculated grade is, in fact, the most accurate grade. The point of hybrid grading is not to always go against the calculations; rather, it is to be thoughtful about when the calculation is accurate and when it is not.

It is naïve to think that the grading rules teachers make don't influence students' success. This is not to say that when students are unsuccessful it's the teacher's fault; it's not. But the rules do make a difference, and teachers do have a choice in how they respond to grading decisions they face. Different responses, systems, or routines could produce different grades, even when the student's actual level of proficiency remains constant. When a student's grade drops as a result of tardiness, the student's proficiency level remains the same. If we report a drop based solely on tardiness, then accuracy is questionable.

The good news is we can write different rules using a standards-based mindset. We can protect the integrity of what we report by avoiding the nonachievement factors that have distorted grades for decades. Teachers are more than just number crunchers; our professional judgment of quality is essential to a productive summative grading system. Students are ultimately responsible for their achievement, or lack of it, so long as we don't nudge nonachievers below the passing threshold with an overly punitive grading decision; first, ensure no distortion.

How to Bring Parents on Board

Another critical step to changing the grading culture is to help parents develop a standards-based mindset. Without it, parents may struggle to distinguish between their children's behavior and their grades. Three common misunderstandings parents have about grading relate to their children's work ethic, work completion, and overall behavior. When teachers clarify these potential misunderstandings, they give parents much greater insight into both the purpose and process of grading.

"But my daughter worked really hard." A strong work ethic is admirable, but this attribute is unrelated to a student's level of proficiency. Now, students who work hard are likely to achieve higher levels of proficiency, but the proficiency grade shouldn't get an extra boost. Parents need to know that grades are not linked to how hard a student has worked; some students don't have to give maximum effort to achieve maximum proficiency. It's essential, on the other hand, to find other ways to honor students' work ethic to avoid diminishing its importance to the development of the whole child.

"But my son did all of the work." Here we focus parents on quality versus completion. Teachers and parents share the same goal of encouraging students to complete all essential work. However, the grades students receive do not correlate directly to compliance. Like work ethic, completing all assignments is a minimal expectation, but it doesn't indicate a student's level of proficiency in relation to the standards. Again, for most students, fully participating in all essential assignments will likely result in at least a higher than normal performance, but it's no guarantee; doing the work and understanding the work are two different things.

"But she's such a good girl." Adults perpetually try to instill compliance and being good in children. The reference to compliance should not be mistaken for *control*, which has a much more cynical connotation. We all have to comply on some level. Obeying stop signs, merging into traffic, or sitting in assigned seats at a concert all represent a level of compliance; it's the same in school. Students who follow directions, act respectfully, and take responsibility elevate the culture of any classroom, but having a strong character and earning an A are two separate issues.

Educators must ensure that parents can distinguish between attributes and proficiency. That separation may not have existed when parents were in school, so it's understandable that they expect their children's grades to include behavioral attributes. They don't necessarily resist progress; it's just that they don't know any different. Once parents have adopted a standards-based mindset, educators will be one step closer to establishing a more meaningful grading and reporting routine.

Conclusion

This chapter focused on developing a standards-based mindset as an essential first step toward meaningful, long-lasting changes to grading practices. Our mindset about grading is powerful. When our minds are fully committed to more accurate and sound grading practices, we find reasons to make whatever changes we deem necessary regardless of any limitations (such as grading policies) that may be in front of us; when we're not, we make excuses.

Moving toward standards-based grading is not an all-or-nothing endeavor; the journey toward standards-based grading has several steps and involves many teacher, school, and district decisions. Some schools or districts may never move to a standards-based reporting process, yet, they can achieve significant enhancements in terms of establishing criteria, creating more accurate assessments, reorganizing evidence, and developing a culture of learning. Taking a standards-based approach through a different mindset will undoubtedly make that move to more formal standards-based procedures, policies, and processes easier, but it's not necessary.

Eliminating the nonlearning factors that inadvertently—or intentionally—distort achievement will restore the integrity of grades, whether those grades are traditional letter grades or descriptive levels. The standards-based mindset is the necessary foundation from which schools and districts can develop more meaningful grading practices that align with the realities of standards-based instruction.

QUESTIONS FOR LEARNING TEAMS

1. What quote or passage represents your biggest takeaway from chapter 4? What immediate action will you take as a result of this takeaway? Explain both to your team.

2. Can you identify one or more aspects of your current grading practices that already embody a standards-based mindset?

3. If your school or district announced tomorrow that it is changing to a standards-based gradebook and report card, would the overall reaction be positive or negative? Do you think most would find excuses or reasons?

4. Can you now identify any rules that frustrate achievement within your own grading practices and routines?

5. Will it be easy or challenging to develop a standards-based mindset within your parent community? If easy, what steps need to be taken? If challenging, where is the best place to begin?

---

*Visit **go.solution-tree.com/assessment** for free reproducible versions of the questions for learning teams.*

CHAPTER 5

How to Give Students Full Credit for What They Know

Our world is full of redos. Sure, most adults don't make as many mistakes requiring redos as students do, but that's just it—our students are not adults and as such, they can be afforded a merciful disposition from their teachers as we move them toward adult competency.

—Rick Wormeli

Once one knows something, one knows something. That may seem obvious, but that isn't always the case for students in school. With traditional grading practices, teachers often combine what a student knows with what he or she used to *not* know (typically via mean averaging) to calculate a grade. Schools stuck in the rut of traditional grading practices use formulas of weighting and averaging to arrive at grades that often don't reflect students' actual levels of proficiency. Giving students full credit for what they know, regardless of how slowly they got there, is fundamental to developing a standards-based mindset.

The idea passes both the accuracy and confidence tests. First, giving students full credit for what they know is clearly accurate, as teachers either dismiss or contextually reconsider old evidence. New levels of proficiency related to foundational knowledge and skills emerge, rendering the previous evidence invalid (Guskey, 2015). Teachers can reconsider old evidence contextually when students demonstrate new levels of proficiency that add to the sample size and potentially impact their trajectory. What we determine and report must be accurate; it doesn't get any more accurate than giving students full credit for what they know. I further highlight the consideration of evidence later in this chapter.

Giving students full credit for what they know also increases their confidence, especially that of struggling learners. In a traditional system, starting low or starting slow leaves a student mathematically disadvantaged. When teachers combine initial low scores with newly earned higher scores, the result is usually somewhere in the middle. This means that students must outperform themselves considerably to have any impact on their final grade. Nothing is more frustrating to a struggling student than finally scoring well on a significant assignment only to have his or her overall level of proficiency increase by a minuscule amount, or feeling pressure to earn an A on a final exam just to pass the class.

On the other hand, teachers can protect students' confidence by assuring them that initial setbacks are not set in stone and can disappear from any grade determination once they demonstrate a more sophisticated level of understanding. This seems straightforward, yet this idea continues to elude teachers who are unwilling or unable to make the connection between grading practices and student hope, optimism, and efficacy. Consider the following grading dilemma.

Grading Dilemma: Mean Averaging

Sierra and Kylie earn almost identical grades on a fractions unit test. Whether adding or subtracting, multiplying or dividing, solving word problems involving fractions, or interpreting and using fractions in real-world applications, Sierra and Kylie correctly answer virtually the same number of questions within each section of the test. At the end of each unit, Sierra and Kylie's teacher routinely sends home a unit summary to inform parents of their children's overall achievement levels as well as the specifics of each individual assignment that led to the summative grade. Despite finishing the unit at the same level of understanding, Sierra and Kylie do not receive the same overall grade for the fractions unit.

Sierra has always been a strong mathematics student who grasps new concepts quickly. Her early results on smaller assignments are usually strong, and she maintains that level of consistency for the duration of the unit. Mathematics doesn't come as easily for Kylie. While she typically reaches high levels of understanding, it often takes her longer than others to reach the intended learning goals for any given lesson. As such, Kylie's early results on smaller assignments tend to be mediocre, at best. Kylie attends the extra study sessions her teacher holds once per week, receives extra help from her older brother, and creates a methodical study plan a week in advance of any test. In the end, Kylie's results on most unit tests are strong and reveal that her slow starts don't stop her from high achievement.

Sierra and Kylie's teacher uses a system that combines weighted task types with mean averaging, so Kylie's poor early results weigh heavily on her final grade while Sierra's strong early scores tend to buoy her results throughout the unit.

Consider the following questions.

- *Should Sierra and Kylie receive the same grade for the fractions unit? Why or why not?*

- *Why might the teacher think Sierra deserves a higher grade than Kylie? Do you agree?*

- *Why might another teacher think Kylie deserves a higher grade than Sierra? Do you agree?*

- *Have you encountered a similar scenario in your career? How did you respond?*

- *Have you ever been Kylie or Sierra? How did you respond?*

The Mean Can Be Mean!

Calculating the mean average can indeed be meaningless. Here's an example: if LeBron James (estimated to have earned $65 million in 2014) walked into a room with three teachers, the average salary per person in that room would be approximately $16 million per year. While mathematically precise, this mean salary calculation comes nowhere near providing a clear picture of the salary situation among the four people in that room; early or extreme scores (like zero) can have the same effect in a traditional gradebook. No one denies the validity of calculating a mean; the debate lies in its accuracy in summarizing evidence of learning. For decades, teachers have relied on the mean average to calculate grades, yet the mean rarely reflects what students know in the end, as it is vulnerable to extreme or atypical results. The mean can, in fact, be *mean* by not giving students full credit for where they are along their continuum, even when the calculation itself is spot on.

The pure mathematics of mean averaging is that every score of 40 needs an 80 to reach an average of 60. Practically speaking, students who start slow or low are immediately disadvantaged in their prospects of earning full credit when they reach their highest level. But if teachers apply a standards-based mindset to the situation, a student who *used* to be a 40 but is now an 80 is an 80, not a 60. This notion becomes slightly more complex when the assignments used to determine overall proficiency levels cut across multiple or unrelated standards within the same curriculum or when a single grade for an entire subject is required. But within the individual standards or even units of study, the need to offset early setbacks with exponentially higher results just to average out to a pass is an unreasonable and unfair expectation. The standards-based mindset is not about establishing flawless formulas, but rather a way for teachers to think as they examine the evidence of learning students produce.

The process of reporting levels of learning may never be entirely free of mean averaging, especially at the middle or high school level. All three measures of central tendency—mean, median, and mode—are valid mathematical calculations. That said, it is critical to recognize the imperfections of each to make thoughtful decisions about when and when not to incorporate each into our grade determinations. The mean can be mean, but it can also be the most accurate when we assess multiple standards via a large sample size.

The issue with averaging is not the calculation itself but the range that it covers (for example, 0–100 percent). Outlier scores carry significant weight. In the LeBron James example, we could triple each teacher's salary and the mean would still be $16 million because LeBron's $65 million carries significantly more weight. The median neutralizes outlier scores, but the increments between the scores within a data set are not regular, which can skew its accuracy. The mode is the simplest to determine, but when considering a wide range of potential scores, it can end up being significantly different from the mean. Figure 5.1 demonstrates the variations that can emerge via the three measures of central tendency within the same data set.

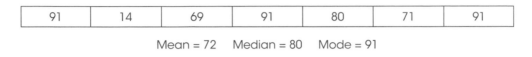

| 91 | 14 | 69 | 91 | 80 | 71 | 91 |

Mean = 72   Median = 80   Mode = 91

Figure 5.1: Mean, median, and mode.

Figure 5.1 is a raw data set. Clearly if teachers interpret it as a gradebook then they must factor in the nature of the assignments resulting in the scores as well as the standards involved within each assignment. Most would likely consider the mean (72) to be the most accurate, yet by simply reordering the identical data set (figure 5.2) a different view emerges, leaving the mean (72) less accurate as a reflection of proficiency.

| 14 | 69 | 71 | 80 | 91 | 91 | 91 |

Mean = 72   Median = 80   Mode = 91

Figure 5.2: Mean, median, and mode reordered.

The point is not to dismiss averaging in its entirety but to thoughtfully use it to summarize when it makes the most sense. Mean averaging along 101 levels of performance (0–100 percent) has the greatest potential for distortion. Like the LeBron James salary example, the zero has significantly more influence over the data results than any other scores. Figure 5.3 demonstrates this impact by adding a zero to the existing data set in figure 5.2.

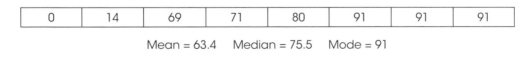

| 0 | 14 | 69 | 71 | 80 | 91 | 91 | 91 |

Mean = 63.4   Median = 75.5   Mode = 91

Figure 5.3: Mean, median, and mode with the effect of a zero.

One zero and the mean drops by 8.6 percentage points while the median drops 4.5 percentage points (the mode is unaffected). It's important to see the mathematical impact an outlier score can have on a data set and why simply deferring to the average is a practice that falls far short of passing the accuracy test and leaves the art of grading out of the equation.

Numbers can make our grading decisions more efficient, but the numbers shouldn't decide the levels of proficiency—teachers should.

The Subversive Pressure of Speed

Most of us accept and understand the notion that some students take longer to learn. On any given day in any given classroom, some students reach the intended learning goals on their first attempt, while other students need extra time and support; a third group may require further instruction. Despite this widely accepted truth, our traditional grading practices send a different message.

Conventional grading practices mathematically hamper students if they start slow or low. When students fail to receive full credit for what they know, the real message from teachers is to learn quickly. Even when two students (Sierra and Kylie, for example) reach the same level of proficiency, it's the student whose early results were higher who will receive the higher grade. Few (if any) curricular standards even tangentially reference the speed at which students attain proficiency, yet speed can be the biggest factor in determining student grades.

Of course, we all prefer students learn as quickly as possible, but when they don't, we should not saddle them with penalties or other disadvantages because of it, even when the student isn't putting forth his or her best effort. Effort is important, but it's a behavioral attribute and has no place in the determination of a proficiency grade; it matters, but how much the student knows and how hard the student worked are two different things.

We must factor speed out of the grade determination equation. On the one hand, we tell students that learning is all that matters, but then we allow how quickly they learned to influence our final decisions.

The Distraction of Weighting

Another distraction in grading is the practice of *weighting*—having certain tasks contribute more to final grades than other tasks. First, it focuses on task types (tests, quizzes, labs, and so on) instead of learning. Weighting can be relevant when the scope of one demonstration is far greater than some others. A research paper clearly carries more weight than correcting the subject-verb agreement or understanding irony. But weighting becomes a distraction when it's applied within the same standard and the only distinguishing factor is the nature of the task itself. Figure 5.4 illustrates this distraction by taking the same algebraic problem and giving it two different task titles.

Quiz	Test
$2x + 6 = 16$	$2x + 6 = 16$

Figure 5.4: The influence of weighting.

With traditional weighting, the question on the right is worth more than the question on the left. It's not worth more because it represents a deeper, more sophisticated level of understanding or requires the student to apply a multitude of standards in an authentic situation. It's worth more because of the nature of the event. By focusing on the event, we lose sight of learning and proficiency. If students answer the questions proficiently on the quiz but less so on the test, they receive a lower grade than if the reverse happened.

Weighting should only occur when the task clearly involves a deeper level of complexity and represents a more thorough assessment of the student's overall achievement. It's a distraction when the same questions are worth more simply because there were more of them, or the event took longer because the teacher gave students a thicker packet. Some standards are more important than others and, therefore, carry more weight or emphasis within the overall curriculum; but weighting within standards becomes an unnecessary, artificial, inaccurate, and misguided process of distinction.

Reassessment

Reassessment is both the most important and most misunderstood practice of grading reform. It lies at the heart of the notion of giving students full credit for what they know or understand. Reassessment is far more than a simple do-over; it represents a moment of recertification when teachers suspect (or understand) that students have reached higher levels of proficiency. As well, the term *reassessment* helps us focus on what it really is; to call it a retest, rewrite, or retake is to focus on the event itself, rather than the newly achieved levels of learning.

Reassessment passes both the accuracy and confidence tests. When students know or understand more than they once did, the reassessment opportunity allows teachers to measure (and report) students' current level of proficiency; without reassessing, the reported grade is no longer accurate. Students' confidence increases since they know they will be able to learn from their mistakes, engage in some targeted learning or practice, and then have the opportunity to demonstrate a new level of understanding.

What If Students Blow Off the First Assessment?

One concern many teachers have is that some students won't take the initial assessment seriously if they know there will be a second chance. Further, they can see what's on the first assessment to better prepare for the second one. While this concern is real, it is also largely within our control. If there is a loophole in our reassessment practices or policies, then it's hardly fair to blame the students for finding it; it's our job to close it.

Students can only blow off the first assessment if we let them. There must be solid, predictable routines in place to offset the potential for students to exploit a reassessment policy. The options for those routines are plenty, but teachers need to settle on *one* routine that allows the reassessment opportunity to fulfill its promise of accurately measuring students' current levels of proficiency.

For example, I referred to my reassessment policy as a *social contract*. It was an agreement between my students and me about how the reassessment opportunities were to take place. This social contract was born of necessity, since my first attempts at implementing a reassessment policy went predictably sideways. After that, I realized that my reassessment policy was only going to be as effective as the routines that surrounded it.

When I first began to allow reassessment opportunities, several students did not take the first assessment seriously. I still remember when Doug, an eighth-grade mathematics student, walked into my classroom the day of our fractions test and told his buddy, "No, I didn't study. I'll just take the retest." While Doug was not the only student over the years to act in such a manner, I remember Doug specifically because he is one of the few to phrase his motive in exactly the way most of us fear students will. Doug's comment made me realize something had to change.

A week or so later, I re-introduced the reassessment process as a social contract that, in the end, mitigated almost all of the issues. The social contract represented a 50-50 agreement that allowed the process of reassessment to fulfill its potential of giving students full credit by verifying any new levels of proficiency. The feature box summarizes how I explained my revised reassessment policy to students.

Social Contract

Here's how reassessment is going to work from now on. If you know more, can do more, or understand more, I will give you every opportunity to demonstrate more. Two times, three times, four times, doesn't matter—you will have every opportunity for a reassessment, but it's not automatic. Reassessment is contingent upon two things.

First, reassessment hinges on an authentic effort on the previous assessment. The whole process is about you learning from your mistakes via my feedback on what you did well and what you need to continue working on. Do everything you can to prepare, and I promise to help you. If you blow off the first assessment thinking you'll just do the retest, the whole process breaks down. I will have nothing to say to you—no feedback—in order to help you improve, since what is on paper doesn't really represent what you know.

Second, it is contingent upon you advancing your understanding. Something has to be different the second time (or third) so as to make this a productive experience. I will provide you with some targeted instruction that you will work on between the first assessment and the second. That is our social contract; you have to hold up your end of the bargain for this to be a productive experience. Otherwise, we're just wasting each other's time.

This is not a do-over; this is about keeping you moving forward. Come in and tell me you still don't understand, and I can work with that. Come in and tell me you're not ready, and we can tailor the experience to support you. Do this every single time, and I may suspect that you are trying to work the system. Remember, I see you every day. I know how you work, and I watch you practice. It will be easy for me to compare what I see every day with what I'm being told about your level of preparedness. This has to be a good-faith process. I want to focus on learning and not get distracted by how long it takes you, but you have to meet me halfway to get the most out of the experience.

If I suspect that you are not holding up your end of the bargain, we are going to have a conversation and I will remind you of our social contract. If it persists, I may end up calling your parents and letting them know that it's becoming increasingly difficult for

Continued →

me to offer reassessment opportunities to you. It's not because I want to deny you the opportunity or make you "earn it," it's because the process of reassessment is becoming a waste of time and there are too many other students who want or need my assistance. We all get distracted when you worry more about working the system than learning and when I spend more time trying to catch you than help you. If we act in good faith, then the process of reassessment will allow you to maximize your levels of achievement. Does that seem reasonable?

No students objected. Sure, some may have silently objected, but no one said I was being unfair. I didn't just ask once, either. We had a small discussion about how this would work in practical terms. When I took the time to explain the spirit of my reassessment policy, my students understood and I had very few issues with them blowing off assessment opportunities. There were a few who tried—Doug being one of them—but my routine made it easier for me to intervene early enough to redirect them back to our social contract.

Something Has to Be Different

The key to ensuring that reassessment is a productive part of the learning process is to make sure (or at least strongly suspect) that the student has achieved a new level of proficiency before extending the reassessment opportunity. For some teachers, that means building the targeted instruction that must occur between assessments into their instructional routines. That way, teachers can directly monitor students' focused study and be available when they need support. This is often the approach with elementary and middle school teachers who often have more time to ensure students keep learning. This doesn't preclude elementary or middle school students from working outside of school time (morning, lunch, after school) or at home, but it is less common with younger students.

As students move into high school, targeted instruction between assessments happens more often outside of class time. In this case, either the student attends a tutorial (before school, at lunch, or after school) or the teacher provides specific direction on what the student should complete at home. The students most in need of further learning and reassessment would most likely benefit from a tutorial, which is why teachers often choose this option. Rather than providing assistance to individual students repeatedly throughout a week, a daunting prospect for teachers with multiple sections, they can provide efficient, targeted support within the tutorial at a set time.

Charity Stephens (@differNtiated4u), Spanish Teacher, Liberty, Missouri

In 2006, I was stuck in a rut of ineffective instructional practices. Both my office referrals and student fail rate were at an all-time high. I was a one-and-done teacher. My cycle was teach, test, and move on with no room for reteaching or retesting students. I avoided colleagues and hid behind closed doors. This naturally resulted in little to no changes to my instructional practices and limited opportunities for student success.

In a powerful TED Talk, Simon Sinek (2009) discusses "why, how, and what." This talk really resonated with me. Sinek says that "when we communicate from the outside in, people can understand vast amounts of complicated information, but it must drive behavior." If we have lost sight of why it is we are teaching, how will we ever get students to want to join us in learning? In order for change to truly occur, we must turn within and ask, "Why am I teaching?"

My response was, "To help students learn how to learn." It was evident, however, by the high fail rate in my class that my instructional practices were creating learning roadblocks. I realized that how I was assessing student understanding was misrepresenting student knowledge. I was simply using textbook tests, tallying points, and determining a percent. After examining Bloom's taxonomy and Webb's Depth of Knowledge charts, I decided to give my unit tests a massive overhaul. I realized that if I built my tests in order from recall to application to creation then I would be able to clearly see what students know and can do with the learning objectives.

Of course, rebuilding unit assessments was just the beginning of many practices I changed. I realized that to help students learn how to learn, I had to abandon one-and-done assessments. My new test format allowed me to clearly see what I needed to reteach; it also allowed me to see who was ready to move on. I was then faced with the dilemma of retesting students, something I had never done in the past. What became clear is that if my goal was to help students learn how to learn, then I could no longer continue preventing them from doing so. After the first time I retested students, I struggled with how to capture their grades. I grappled with capping the grade versus allowing full credit. At first, I capped the grade, but that practice quickly fell by the wayside as a thought kept nagging at me: was I committing educational malpractice by capping student grades when in reality their knowledge and understanding reflected a higher grade? Ultimately, I stopped capping grades and never looked back.

There are many educators who will read this and say, "Yeah, but students should have listened the first time. Students just take advantage of reassessments by not studying the first time. They need to learn responsibility." While responsibility is important, for me, assessment came down to creating wide-open opportunities for students to learn; there was no room for roadblocks in my instructional practices.

Simon Sinek's (2009) final words are, "It's those that start with the why that have the ability to inspire those around them or find others that inspire them." I knew if I taught from the inside out I could inspire my students to discover their whys.

I realized I had the choice to move beyond being a one-and-done teacher to create a more authentic learning experience through my assessment routines. My reassessments could branch out beyond paper-and-pencil tests to more differentiated opportunities that focused on meeting standards as opposed to completing inflexible tasks. I found my why, and once I did, I was able to overhaul my instructional practices, including reassessment, to create a more inspiring and motivating experience for my students.

Two Keys to Effective Reassessment Practices

To effectively reassess, teachers can first have students reflect on their current levels of proficiency based on the most recent demonstration, and second have students address the areas of deficiency with some targeted learning. Remember, new practices (reassessment) require new routines (personal reflection and targeted learning) in order to be sustainable in the long term.

Figure 5.5 shows an example of a personal reflection sheet. Upon completing a test, for example, teachers can ask students to review their results in three specific categories.

1. The standards and targets on which they were proficient

2. The standards and targets that would benefit from some extra practice

3. The standards and targets for which more learning is necessary

In addition, with the two latter categories, the students (with their teacher's help) would contemplate how to prevent simple misunderstandings from affecting their results again and how they will continue their learning within their identified areas of deficiency.

The reassessment reflection sheet in figure 5.5 ensures that the student has thought through his or her subsequent learning and is targeting the specific areas in need of more attention. Vague and unhelpful directions such as "Go over the chapter again" or "Study harder next time" don't specifically address the issue at hand. The process of reassessment is about learning from mistakes and reassessing once students have reached new levels; to reach those higher levels more efficiently, students would be well served to reflect on *what was* in order to reach *what will be.* This metacognitive exercise—thinking about their thinking—will facilitate their eventual success.

It is important to note the difference between a personal reflection and asking students to apply for a reassessment. Students have the right to learn; having them fill out an application to beg for a reassessment goes too far. Learning should neither be capped nor arbitrarily cut off. Teachers too often make their decisions to allow or not allow a reassessment opportunity based on student behaviors such as attitude, participation, and attentiveness. These attributes are important, but teachers should keep them separate from learning.

That said, it is not unreasonable to ask students to reflect on subsequent learning goals. There is no one way to do reassessment, but there are five fundamental aspects that ensure a teacher's reassessment practice is effective.

1. **Learning matters:** As we've discussed, new learning leads to a new assessment. Just scheduling a do-over produces similar results to the first assessment. Student reflection is essential. We reassess when students reach new levels of proficiency, not just when they want to give it another shot.

2. **Standards matter:** Most teachers will repeat the event (retest), but that isn't necessary. There are often multiple ways in which students can show proficiency within a standard or collection of standards. In a standards-based instructional paradigm, the standard is what matters. For some students, adjusting the assessment format could result in a clearer and more accurate measure of what a student really knows.

Reassessment Reflection Sheet

Name: _____ Assignment: _____ Date: _____

Directions: Please look at your assessment results and organize them into three categories: (1) the standards and targets you are proficient with, (2) the standards and targets you need a little extra practice with, and (3) the standards and targets for which you need more learning.

Part A: Areas of Strength

1. The standards and targets for which I've reached the proficient or advanced level are:

Part B: Areas for Improvement	
2a. The standards or targets I need a little extra practice on due to simple misunderstandings are:	3a. The standards and targets that require more studying since I'm not sure where or what went wrong are:
2b. I will overcome these simple misunderstandings by:	3b. My learning plan to improve my proficiency within these standards is:

Source: Adapted from "You Be George" activity, CASL Training (Chappuis, 2005).

Figure 5.5: Reassessment reflection.

*Visit **go.solution-tree.com/assessment** for a free reproducible version of this figure.*

3. **Timeliness matters:** The more space there is between the first assessment and the second one, the more likely the reassessment exercise becomes just something to get done. Reassessment is most effective when the learning is fresh. But reassessing sooner rather than later doesn't mean teachers should limit students' opportunities to keep learning.

4. **Flexibility matters:** Sooner is better than later; however, enforcing time limits (for example, five days) might inadvertently affect students negatively. The scope of the standards may require more time and so might a student who predictably struggles within the given subject area. Teachers would be wise to stop short of a one-size-fits-all reassessment routine. Flexibility doesn't mean the student tells his or her teacher when the reassessment happens; the student and teacher collectively decide on what's necessary for real improvement and a reasonable timeline to allow that to happen.

5. **Accuracy matters:** An important question teachers should consider is how to respond to students' newly demonstrated levels of proficiency. In some cases, new evidence trumps old evidence, leaving the student at a higher level of proficiency within the standard. In other cases, new evidence prompts teachers to contextually reconsider the standard, since the demonstrations are more complex and involve multiple aspects of quality. (I explore this in greater detail in the next section of this chapter.)

Following these principles allows teachers to create reassessment routines that fit with the ages and maturity levels of the students with whom they work.

Grading Dilemma: Reassessment Policy

Following is a sample reassessment policy based on the policies of real schools; City Center is not a real school. Read through it and then answer the subsequent questions. If you are working with a team, consider a group discussion about each of the questions.

CITY CENTER SCHOOL REASSESSMENT POLICY

At City Center School, the practice and policy of reassessment provide students with additional opportunities to demonstrate proficiency or mastery over standards and subject-specific content.

Reassessment policy specifics:

- All students will be given the opportunity to reassess on summative assessments.

- All reassessments will cover the same material as the original, however in most cases, the questions will be different. It is also possible for the format to be changed. The focus is on the demonstration of learning, not necessarily the replication of assessment events.

- Students must apply for a reassessment (in writing) within two weeks of the teacher notifying them of the failing grade. The entry of the failing score into the online gradebook is considered sufficient notification; it's the students' responsibility to monitor their grades as they are determined.

- Before reassessing, students may be required to attend a tutorial, are expected to complete corrections on the original assessment, and complete any other task as directed by the teacher.

- Students caught cheating will receive a zero, are ineligible for a reassessment, and will be subject to school discipline as per the code of conduct; cheating on a reassessment will also result in a zero with no opportunity to reassess and discipline.

- If a student scores lower on the reassessment, the original assessment score will stand.

- If a student scores higher on the reassessment, the maximum score awarded will be 70 percent. Even if the reassessment score is 100 percent, the final grade will be 70 percent on that particular assignment or standards. This policy is for all content areas and all classes.

- Students will not be permitted a reassessment on final exams or culminating year-end projects.

Consider the following questions.

- *Which aspects of City Center's reassessment policy do you think are favorable?*

- *Which aspects of the reassessment policy do you think are misguided?*

- *Which specific aspects of the reassessment policy are in direct conflict with one another?*

- *If this were the reassessment policy in your school, how would you handle the tension between what you believe to be in the best interest of students and those elements of the reassessment policy that you disagree with?*

How to Give Full Credit

Unavoidable in the process of giving full credit is our professional judgment in our final determination of proficiency levels. Again, our goal is to accurately report student proficiency, regardless of how low or slow the student started, and this requires us to accurately interpret the evidence at hand. In some cases, teachers might surmise that the most recent evidence of learning is the most accurate; in others, the most frequent evidence is the most accurate. Much of this depends on the number of variables within standards and the level of complexity in each demonstration of learning. Distinguishing between the two is the teacher's call, and while this distinction may challenge them at first, by following the subsequent guiding principles, collaborating with colleagues, and practicing a little, teachers will soon find the process less onerous than first thought.

Most Recent Evidence

When teachers assess students on standards with few variables in how they demonstrate their proficiency, the most recent evidence is the most accurate. For this to be true, the evidence should also represent a somewhat linear learning trajectory. To be clear, few variables doesn't mean students can't demonstrate their learning in a variety of ways—they can. But it does mean the path to proficiency is fairly straightforward. Recent evidence is most accurate on standards related to foundational knowledge and fundamental skills.

New evidence trumps old evidence, since what the student used to know is no longer relevant and *slip back* (not knowing) is highly unlikely. That is, once students understand the definitions of key terminology, formulas, or processes, they are unlikely to slip back and suddenly not know. Proficiency is not perfection, but mistakes are the exception, not the rule. When teachers determine that the student's progression toward meeting a standard is relatively linear, then the most recent evidence is the more accurate option.

This method is simple because teachers can take the most recent results at face value. The line between most recent and most frequent is not always definitive, so professional judgment is still important, not just with interpreting the evidence, but with the decision between most recent and most frequent. To be clear, this is a guideline, not a formula, and it is ultimately up to the teacher to make the final determination.

Most Frequent Evidence

The most frequent evidence is the most accurate when assessing standards with a number of variables that contribute to the overall demonstration of proficiency. In these cases, teachers would not dismiss old evidence but contextually reconsider it given the most current demonstration by the student. With a complex standard, the most recent evidence falls short of providing a clear picture of where students are along their path to proficiency, so it is better to consider the entire sample to determine the overall level.

When assessing writing, for example, teachers must consider the entire sample. Significant variables include the topics, the student's background knowledge, the student's level of interest, and the order in which he or she completes writing assignments. Consider the following example of two students who take the same English language arts class (from the same teacher) in subsequent years as outlined in figure 5.6. The teacher assessed both assignments on a four-point scale.

In the first year, David's results appear to show a linear trajectory of improvement. To take the most recent evidence as the most accurate would earn David a 4 as a writer. He started low, but consistently grew as a writer to reach the advanced level—or so it seemed.

Year 1	Writing Sample A	Writing Sample B	Writing Sample C	Writing Sample D	Writing Sample E
David	1	3	3	3	4
Year 2	**Writing Sample B**	**Writing Sample A**	**Writing Sample D**	**Writing Sample E**	**Writing Sample C**
Allison	3	1	3	4	3

Figure 5.6: Evidence from one year to the next.

In the second year, Allison's teacher decided to reorder the assignments. While Allison earned the same results as David, they emerged in a different order, not because Allison had a different trajectory of improvement than David, but because her teacher reordered the assignments. In this case, Allison would earn a 3 since the most recent evidence is a 3. But is this accurate given David and Allison earned the same results on each of the writing assignments? The answer is both yes and no.

Three is likely the most accurate level for Allison, not because it's the most recent result, but because it's the most frequent. When one considers all of the writing samples, it becomes clear that 3 is the most consistent result for both Allison and David. It would be inaccurate to simply defer to the most recent result, especially since there are so many contributing variables, including the teacher's decisions about the order and nature of the assignments. Table 5.1 provides a brief summary of the guidelines for accuracy when considering the most recent or the most frequent evidence.

Table 5.1: Most Recent Versus Most Frequent Results

Most Recent Is Most Accurate When . . .	Most Frequent Is Most Accurate When . . .
• There are few (if any) variables in how students demonstrate proficiency. • Student growth toward proficiency is fairly straightforward. • Teachers are assessing foundational knowledge and fundamental skills. • Teachers are assessing building blocks for deeper learning and understanding. • New assessment takes precedence over previous demonstrations of learning.	• There are a number of variables in how students demonstrate proficiency. • Student growth toward proficiency is complex, given all the elements that contribute to the demonstration of learning. • Teachers are assessing deeper understanding of strategies and processes. • Teachers are assessing applications of foundational knowledge and skills in a variety of circumstances. • New assessment evidence leads to a contextual reconsideration of previous evidence.

Again, the line between most recent and most frequent is blurry. Teachers are the ultimate decision makers as they consider the standards, learning goals, success criteria, and progression toward proficiency. Teachers would be wise to work together with their colleagues to make consistent, aligned decisions about the most accurate evidence of learning.

A Team Decision

The work of Richard DuFour, Rebecca DuFour, and Robert Eaker on professional learning communities (PLCs) can be most helpful when considering whether to use the most recent or most frequent data. Not only do teachers need to consistently reach the decision itself, they also need to consistently identify critical learning goals and interpret the evidence in each level from novice through advanced. While the human element of assessment and grading will always slightly vary along the edges of these levels, teachers can achieve better alignment when they collaborate on the decision.

The first two (of the four) critical questions for PLCs (DuFour, 2005) provide an anchor for this discussion. First, being clear on *what students need to know or be able to do* helps focus on whether the intended standards cover foundational knowledge and skill levels or whether they are more complex. The second question of *how we will know when they've learned it* addresses the interpretation of evidence, and whether the most recent evidence takes precedence or whether it adds to the overall sample size. While many experienced teachers may deem the collaborative process an unnecessary step, working together builds an inherent system of checks and balances to ensure that they both effectively elicit and accurately interpret evidence of learning. The collaborative process aligns a collective view of proficiency and also ensures that everyone accurately interprets the performance criteria. In the end, the process increases the likelihood that students receive full credit for what they know and can do.

How to Bring Parents on Board

Few parents will argue with the notion of giving their children full credit for what they've learned. That said, it is still important for teachers to explain *how* they will determine full credit. The process for determining grades must be transparent so parents understand how teachers apply their professional judgment to results. Simply telling parents that professional judgment will determine grades will not be enough; while they don't need a class on constructing criteria, they do need to understand the success criteria, the process used for final determinations, and why the mean average often falls short of providing an accurate picture of their children's learning.

Parents most likely have the least experience with reassessment, since this practice was not as common when they were in school. Anchoring this conversation on the true north of accuracy and confidence will go a long way to help parents understand why this is an important practice for meaningful grading. Also, make sure parents see that this is not meant to allow children to take a laissez-faire approach to assessment, but to accommodate the fluid nature of learning. Parents must know that their role at home is critical to successful reassessment policies. Parents who know when assessments are scheduled can ensure their children are prepared, and avoid the habit of blowing off assessments that some may slip into. When teachers create a reassessment policy buoyed by a strong teacher-parent connection, it will more often fulfill its potential.

Finally, using the most frequent evidence may require some explanation as well, particularly when it comes to contextually reconsidering old evidence. Parents want to know where their children are in relation to the intended learning, but what we send home often challenges them. Wherever possible, let parents know which standards fall into the most-recent category and which ones into the most-frequent category; this is especially helpful if parents are viewing summative assessment results online and attempting to determine their children's true level of proficiency. The concept of most recent versus most frequent won't challenge parents to understand as long as they are aware ahead of time how teachers will apply each. With the most-recent approach, parents need to know that teachers may remove old evidence from the gradebook if it's no longer relevant; with the most-frequent approach, they must understand how teachers will combine and summarize results given the most recent demonstration of learning.

Conclusion

The notion of students earning full credit for their learning seems like a no-brainer, but so many of our traditional grading practices focus more on when learning occurred or on what sized event. Differing to the mean average, emphasizing speed, and using weighted task types all represent ways in which the accuracy of grades is potentially compromised. Once a student reaches a level of understanding, it is irrelevant that the student was once at a lower level. Giving full credit is the first step to realigning the learning-grading paradigms.

Within the mindset of full credit is the practice of reassessment, which, to be productive, can't digress into a "come in tomorrow and guess differently" opportunity. While some might argue semantics, the preference of the term *reassessment* places the emphasis squarely where it belongs: on the learning. Terms like *retest*, *redo*, and *retake*, while not egregious by any stretch, do focus more on a repetition of an event rather than the reassessment of the standards. Regardless of label, for reassessment to function within a learning-focused culture, it must be about continual learning, which means something has to happen between the first and second opportunities. The targeted learning is anchored on what's next and serves to move the student along a positive growth trajectory.

Once the evidence is made clear, the decision then is how to most accurately report that learning. The most recent evidence of learning is usually most accurate with foundational knowledge and skills, while the most frequent evidence may be more accurate for those standards at a greater depth of knowledge; still, a teacher may emphasize the more recent evidence since the sample size is robust and was collected over a longer period of time. The big idea here is that there is no formula for making this decision; it's up to the teacher to make this distinction. More advantageous still is when departments or teacher teams make this decision collectively to ensure alignment with how evidence is organized and examined. This decision won't always be easy, clean, or perfect, but it will lead to more thoughtful decisions and will restore the art of grading that no formula or flowchart can satisfy.

QUESTIONS FOR LEARNING TEAMS

1. What quote or passage represents your biggest takeaway from chapter 5? What immediate action will you take as a result of this takeaway? Explain both to your team.

Continued →

2. Have you ever used the median or mode to determine an overall grade or a grade within a standard? If yes, explain to your team the specific process you used and the specific subject or topic you applied it to. If no, would you now?

3. What is more present in your current grading routines—the subversive pressure of speed or the distraction of weighting?

4. If reassessment is currently part of your classroom routines:

   a. What has been the most challenging aspect to implement?

   b. Have there been any unexpected successes? Explain.

5. If reassessment is not currently part of your classroom routines:

   a. What is the main source of your hesitation?

   b. What would make you more comfortable with implementing a reassessment policy?

6. How do you distinguish between targeted instruction and students earning their reassessment opportunities through behavioral compliance? In other words, how do we prevent learning from becoming accessible only through behavioral compliance?

7. When it's not clear, how do you anticipate deciding between the most recent and most frequent evidence to determine grades? Is this something that you could apply universally, or does it depend on subject or age?

*Visit **go.solution-tree.com/assessment** for free reproducible versions of the questions for learning teams.*

CHAPTER 6

How to Repurpose Homework

Having students do homework out of fear of negative consequences turns a situation ideal for building intrinsic motivation into one that implies the teacher thinks external contingencies are required to get it done.

Harris Cooper

Educators have long engaged in a spirited debate about whether homework is a necessary part of an effective instructional process, and while that debate continues, teachers must make individual decisions about the role and impact of homework in their classrooms. My focus in this chapter is not to definitively support or oppose homework; rather, I examine how to repurpose homework for teachers who decide that homework will be a part of the overall learning experience for their students.

Discussions about homework often lead to pivotal questions: Should homework be assigned in the first place? If yes, then how much, how frequently, on what activities, and with what content? Teachers face the question of what to do with the evidence of learning students produce as a result of homework; that's my focus in this chapter. While traditional homework practices typically include scoring the homework and including those scores in the overall grade determination, a standards-based mindset means repurposing homework to pass the accuracy and confidence tests.

The tension between routines of homework and their accuracy and confidence comes from how early teachers introduce the majority of homework into the learning.

When teachers use homework as part of their grade determinations, it can distort early results. Students often surpass those results with more practice, time, and concentrated study. As well, early results can have a detrimental effect on a student's level of optimism going forward. Rather than paying attention to learning from their mistakes, students fixate on poor results that, for many, reinforce pessimistic views about their potential to succeed. By repurposing the role of homework, teachers can create an environment where mistakes are instructional (rather than judgmental) and early stumbles no longer compromise the integrity of what teachers ultimately report about student proficiency.

The Homework Debate

In their 2004 article "Villain or Savior?: The American Discourse on Homework, 1850–2003," Brian Gill and Steven Schlossman examine the role of homework in K–12 schools. Among their conclusions was the realization that homework has consistently elicited strong emotional responses both in favor and against. They sum up the passionate arguments on both sides of the homework debate in their opening paragraph:

> Too much or too little; too easy or too hard; a spur to student achievement or student alienation; a marker of enlightened or lazy teaching; a builder of character or a degrader of self-esteem; too demanding or too dismissive of parents; a stimulus of national economic vigor or of behavioral conformity. The range of complaints about homework is enormous, and the complaints tend—as much today as in the past—toward extreme, angry, often contradictory views. (Gill & Schlossman, 2004, p. 174)

Gill and Schlossman conclude that both supporters and opponents of homework tend to exaggerate their positions, drowning out more moderate voices.

In her book *Rethinking Homework: Best Practices That Support Diverse Needs*, Cathy Vatterott (2009) emphasizes the homework dilemma teachers face when she writes, "The attempts of researchers to answer that basic question [does homework improve achievement] have led to conclusions that are inconsistent at best and contradictory at worst" (p. 58). As well, Vatterott points out that the overall research on homework is limited, as only a small number of researchers have given significant attention to this complicated topic.

The Call for Homework

The call for homework, and especially the call for *more* homework, centers on the notion that the more time students spend on their school work, the more they will learn (Epstein & Van Voorhis, 2001). In their 2006 study "Does Homework Improve Academic Achievement?: A Synthesis of Research, 1987–2003," Harris Cooper, Jorgianne Civey Robinson, and Erika Patall conclude that "with only rare exceptions, the relationship between the amount of homework students do and their achievement outcomes was found to be positive and statistically significant" (p. 48). While they suggest more research to fully cement the relationship between homework and academic achievement, Cooper, Robinson, and Patall nonetheless conclude that doing homework increases student achievement.

Generally speaking, research does indicate a positive, meaningful association between homework and achievement at both the class level and the student level (Trautwein, 2007). Researchers associate this positive relationship more with the nature of the homework (Hattie, 2009) than the amount of time spent completing homework tasks (Cooper, 1989; Hattie, 2009; Trautwein, Köller, Schmitz, & Baumert, 2002). That said, the effect of homework seems to increase significantly as students get older; the effect for high school students is twice as high as that for junior high (middle school) students, and again twice as high for junior high (middle school) students as that for elementary students (Cooper, 1989).

The Call Against Homework

The call against homework hinges on the notion that homework is potentially harmful to students' emotional well-being as well as intrusive in valuable family time at home (Bennett & Kalish, 2006; Kohn, 2007). In their 2006 book, *The Case Against Homework*, Sara Bennett and Nancy Kalish, along with citing the usual criticism, go so far as to suggest homework, as a sedentary activity, is an overlooked contributor to child obesity similar, at least physiologically, to watching television.

In his book *The Homework Myth: Why Our Kids Get Too Much of a Bad Thing*, Alfie Kohn (2007), like Bennett and Kalish, challenges the research findings that show positive correlations between homework and increased achievement, especially with elementary and middle school students. Kohn (2007) forcefully asserts that homework is a burden to parents, stressful to children, creates family conflict, reduces the amount of time children have for other activities, and reduces children's interest in learning.

Homework can have a counterproductive effect when teachers assign a lot of it, don't or barely monitor the work, allow students to practice incorrect methods or procedures, and undermine a student's motivation to keep learning with the nature of the assignment (Trautwein et al., 2002). As well, the positive association of homework and achievement, which often results in teachers assigning copious amounts of homework, seems to disadvantage lower-ability students by reinforcing their belief that they cannot learn since early results are often poor (Hattie, 2009). Finally, while many teachers cite the development of time-management skills and responsibility as justification for regular homework assignments, presently there is no evidence that regular homework routines develop the time-management skills of students (Hattie, 2009).

The Need for Balance

The layered, complex, even conflicting research about homework can leave even experienced educators unsure of how to move forward. Despite significant research that points to the negative consequences of many traditional homework routines, educators also know that they cannot realistically expect students never to produce evidence of learning at home. None of the research calls for inordinate amounts of homework, as it more likely produces positive effects when teachers distribute practice in small doses (Marzano, Pickering, & Pollock, 2001). Research supports the introduction of moderate, age-appropriate homework routines as students get older (Cooper, Robinson, & Patall, 2006). So what are teachers to do? Homework often feels like a lose-lose idea that leads teachers to make isolated, individual decisions.

Cathy Vatterott (2009) offers a third alternative, which is to take a commonsense approach to the issue of homework, when she writes:

> The value of the research is in the broad strokes it paints, not in the minutiae. Its value comes as we reflect on the *logic* of its conclusions—do they make sense for *our* population of students? Are they consistent with what we have come to know from experience about our type and age of student? The other value of research is to dispel the myths behind some of the most strongly held beliefs about homework. (p. 71)

The most favorable course of action is to juxtapose research and experience by closely monitoring student responses. If students are motivated, engaged, productive, and progressing, then it's likely the established homework routine is a positive one; counterproductive responses mean the teacher would be wise to reconsider some or all homework practices.

It also appears that it's best to find balance between an aggressive approach to homework and no homework at all. The following six guiding questions provide a universal litmus test should a teacher deem homework an essential part of his or her students' learning experience. I've arranged the questions in a linear progression, meaning an answer of no to any question means teachers should not assign homework.

1. **Is it learning centered?** At minimum, the work we ask students to complete at home should cover the essential learning or standards. Homework should never be busywork.

2. **Is it necessary?** We should ask ourselves if it is necessary for students to take time out of their home lives to complete an assignment.

3. **Is it reasonable?** Can we reasonably expect students to complete the assignment within the time available, and is it a reasonable amount of work given the age of the students?

4. **Is it high quality?** We should not ask students to complete tasks like word searches and crossword puzzles in lieu of other activities or family time.

5. **Are the students ready?** Students need to be ready to work independently in order for homework to be a productive experience; otherwise, frustration and discouragement will result. This leads to the need to differentiate homework depending on the typical clusters of readiness within a classroom.

6. **Were the students involved?** Homework is typically more productive when students have input on the purpose of the homework, what it entails, and how much is necessary to complete. Wherever possible, we should give students a choice in what we expect beyond the instructional minutes.

While decisions about homework are up to the individual classroom teacher, these guiding questions help them create productive experiences for their students. We should not take lightly the expectation for students to complete work beyond instructional hours, so the core of any decision about the need for homework should be about ensuring the experience is worthwhile.

Homework as Practice

In the remainder of this chapter, I speak to teachers who have decided to include homework as part of the essential instructional routine; the focus here becomes what to do once students have completed the assignments. We must also consider the important question of how to respond if students do not complete their homework (or any other expected assignment), but I will save that question for chapter 7 and my exploration of redefining accountability.

Traditional homework routines typically include homework results when teachers determine final grades. While the contribution from the homework column would be relatively small, homework nonetheless would still be a primarily summative experience. Remember, teachers can distinguish formative and summative assessment by how they use the resulting assessment information, so if they use homework as even part of grade determination, it serves a summative purpose.

Repurposing homework essentially means solidifying it as a formative exercise that focuses more on the process than the final result and on feedback and improvement rather than the accumulation of points and percentages. Repurposing homework is about introducing (or reinvigorating) the notion that practice is an essential part of learning; we focus on feedback and growth, not immediate mastery and fear of falling behind in the gradebook. We can't imagine a musician, an athlete, or an actress improving without practice, yet the concept of practice still eludes some teachers who've created a grade-everything paradigm within their classrooms. It is difficult for any assessment to serve both a formative and summative purpose simultaneously. If the focus is feedback, it's formative; if the focus is verification and reporting, it's summative. According to Dean, Hubbell, Pitler, and Stone (2012), "Providing feedback (rather than grades) on homework can encourage students to take risks and show teachers aspects of their conceptual understanding that they might not have revealed on a graded assignment" (p. 108).

Practice Versus Games

After athletic or musical practice, parents never ask their children, "What was the score?" We accept the concept of practice as an integral activity on the road to improvement. Every parent knows that practice is critical to improvement, despite the fact that coaches never score it. Practice is practice, games are games, and while there is a clear relationship between the two, their purposes are inherently different. Practice is for improvement while the games verify expectations and validate the decisions made during practice.

In his book *Outliers*, Gladwell (2008) writes, "The idea that excellence at performing a complex task requires a critical minimum level of practice surfaces again and again in studies of expertise" (pp. 39–40). We accept the idea of practice for improvement everywhere except school.

In many classrooms, everything students produce receives a score or grade, which makes everything a performance. While we've learned that grades and the judgment of scores may interfere with the positive impact of our feedback on students (Butler, 1988; Elawar &

Corno, 1985; Wiliam, 2011), many teachers resist the idea of not grading practice assignments because they believe if they don't grade it, students won't do it. This unfortunate view suggests students have no inherent interest in learning and reduces the school experience to an exercise of point acquisition. And it assumes that what teachers ask students to do for homework is not worth doing unless they get something tangible out of it, like points.

Personal Reflection: Turning Homework Into "Home*learning*"

I remember the first time I told my eighth-grade students that I was no longer going to grade homework. I was still going to assign homework, check that students completed it, and review the correct or most appropriate responses, but I was going to stop short of assigning an overall score to go into my gradebook. Homework would now be about practice, feedback, and improvement, and would play no part in their overall grades.

We talked about how important practice was using the practice-games example. I didn't just proclaim the new routine, I explained why and took the time to discuss the spirit of this new practice. I told students, "Come to class with a page full of incorrect answers and eraser holes in your paper, and I can help you. Come to class with a page full of correct answers that you copied from a friend, and I'm not sure what I can or should do." Once I stopped using homework in the gradebook, my students quickly realized there was no point in dishonesty because there were no points to earn.

I knew this was the right change but was unsure whether it would produce the desired results. Two specific outcomes emerged; one was a surprise and one I anticipated. The surprise was that nothing changed. The students who previously had always completed their homework still did their homework, whether there was a grade involved or not; the students who struggled to complete their homework still struggled to complete their homework. The promise or threat of high or low scores wasn't the motivating factor for my students.

The anticipated outcome was that I now got a more honest look at where my students were in their learning. They were more honest with me about what they did and didn't understand. Learning had replaced point chasing, and we were now able to work in service of learning without the distraction that scores so often produce. While it was admittedly risky, it was one of the most important changes I ever made to my teaching practices. As Daniel Pink (2009) writes in *Drive*, "Let's not waste our kids' time on meaningless exercises. With a little thought and effort, we can turn home*work* into home*learning*" (p. 186).

The Inaccuracy of Grading Practice

While the practice-games dynamic may be enough for some to alter their practices, there are more reasons to move away from grading homework. Again, whether any teacher assigns or expects homework is an individual decision. The question at hand is what to do with the evidence of learning that students produce. Grading homework not only distracts many students from working independently, it also has the potential to significantly distort the students' true level of proficiency through a number of factors that I outline in the following eight questions.

1. **Whose work is it?** As I mentioned in the previous example, we can't control who actually completes the homework or how much help they receive. As a result, we can't know the degree to which any grade represents the students' levels of understanding. By removing the grade as a factor, we free students to seek assistance—something we should encourage them to do—when they are struggling to understand or finish the assignment.

2. **Are you that flawless?** The notion that a lesson need only be taught once and a class of diverse learners will all master the concept is absurd. Even the most effective teachers aren't *so* good that some students won't need more or different instruction and support.

3. **Are you sure they know what to do?** Sometimes what looks like a lack of effort is actually a lack of clarity. Students may not be clear on directions, or, occasionally, we may not have been as clear as we should have been, especially for more complex tasks. Grading the homework results would prematurely measure proficiency and a student's ability to decipher our instructions.

4. **Are you emphasizing learning or completion?** Grading homework tends to put unnecessary pressure on students to get it done at all costs. The more attention we give to grades, the less attention we have for learning. If homework is to play a formative role, then grades have no place in this process.

5. **Will your feedback matter?** We know how important effective feedback is and how scores and points distract students from making good use of that feedback. Simply put, grades distract from the process of learning.

6. **Where is the risk?** We discourage risk taking in a grade-everything paradigm. While teachers might say they want students to take risks, students won't do so if it proves costly to their overall grades. We need to give students the space to practice without penalty.

7. **Are they ready?** Some students take longer to learn and may not be ready to work independently. This is often the case with new learning where students' familiarity with the topic at hand is limited.

8. **Is it too early?** The early measurement of proficiency puts students at a mathematical disadvantage. Even if they improve, they often do not receive full credit for this improvement. As well, teachers rarely remove early evidence from gradebooks, resulting in overlapping evidence that combines to produce a meaningless overall grade or level. When teachers combine old evidence with new evidence (within the same standard), the result is rarely an accurate picture.

Unless they have older siblings, students enter the school system in kindergarten with little or no understanding of what grades are or what they mean. It's adults who introduce the concept of grades to students, then turn around and blame the students for becoming grade obsessed. Adults have to accept that they have trained students to anticipate a score on everything they do; what adults pay attention to is what children learn to believe is important. The good news is that if we have trained students to be grade obsessed, we can retrain them to focus on learning. We want students to feel a sense of satisfaction from reaching a deeper level of understanding; we want improved assessment results to help students realize that practice really does help (O'Connor, 2011).

Grading Dilemma: Practice Work

What do you do when the nongraded formative work shows a level of proficiency that's above the levels demonstrated on summative assessments? The practice-games dynamic is easier to embrace within the most desirable trajectory of learning where the student struggles early on, but with increased practice and attention is able to reach higher levels of understanding; what if the opposite occurs? What if formative work is promising but summative assessment results fall short? Assuming you've controlled for the validity of the formative work (you *know* the student did the work independently) or any identified diagnoses (such as test anxiety), how do you handle the organization and reporting of evidence? On the one hand, evidence is evidence, so if you've seen real evidence of understanding, should it matter if the assessment is formative or summative by label? On the other hand, formative assessment is often more granular in focus while summative assessment often asks students to combine the discrete skills into more complex demonstrations of learning, so using a formative assessment for summative purposes may not be plausible or accurate.

We've all seen it: students who do well in practice but fall short in the game. Consider the following questions.

- *What do you do?*

- *How do you determine whether formative work can be used for summative purposes without compromising the confidence of the students or the accuracy of what ultimately gets reported?*

Alternative Homework Routines

If a teacher has shifted his or her mindset about homework but still considers it an important part of the instructional process, the question becomes what to do instead of grading it. It's not enough to just stop grading homework; what we need is a replacement routine that allows us to actually do something different. Students who exhibit challenging behaviors need replacement behaviors that honor their feelings but encourage them to act in a prosocial rather than antisocial way. Similarly, it's important to identify replacement routines that honor the teacher's approach to homework while increasing the likelihood that he or she can productively use its results. With that, here are six alternative ways teachers could handle the issue of homework without relying on the grading process to (falsely) motivate their students.

1. **Make it optional:** Nothing empowers students more than having a choice about whether the homework is necessary. If the homework is for practice, then there is no immediate concern about whether every student does every question. As assessment results emerge, homework may no longer be optional for some students, but it lends the teacher a little more credibility when he or she insists that individual students who need more practice should do their homework.

2. **Differentiate the homework:** Differentiation is primarily about readiness (not ability) so teachers would be wise to ensure that the assigned homework matches each student. Too difficult and the homework becomes frustrating; too easy and the homework becomes a chore. Differentiating the homework is respectful and reveals to students that teachers understand them as learners.

3. **Differentiate the pathway:** My friend and colleague Cassandra Erkens (2014) recommends starting from a point of inquiry and exploration that uses three pathways. The homework teachers assign to the students is the same, but their responses, or pathways, will vary: (1) students who, upon completing the homework, feel confident that they've mastered the content generate three potential quiz or test questions; (2) students unsure of their level of mastery attempt three to five more problems to extend the practice; and (3) frustrated students stop working on the homework and generate a list of questions about their specific struggles so the teacher can better assist them on the following day.

4. **Differentiate the response:** This strategy can stand alone or be an extension to differentiating the pathway. Once homework results are clear, teachers can divide students into three groups: (1) students who've mastered the content can work on extension activities independently; (2) students unsure or short of specific content mastery can work together with another student at a similar level to overcome their current hurdles; and (3) students who remain frustrated work directly with the teacher in a small group. An atypical distribution within any of these groups would signal that teachers may need to do something else (such as reteaching the lesson).

5. **Peer correctives:** Upon entering class, students work in pairs to reconcile any unresolved issues that emerged while they completed their homework. It is likely most beneficial to strategically organize these groups. While there are times when heterogeneous partnerships add real value, in this case homogeneous pairings are optimum. The goal is for each student to offer something to the other; if teachers pair students at opposite ends of the learning spectrum, then the student at the low end is unlikely to contribute anything of substance.

6. **Distribute homework strategically over time:** Frequent, short practice sessions early in the learning are most beneficial (Dean et al., 2012). Over time, as students deepen their knowledge and understanding, teachers can stagger practice sessions (homework) further apart and require multiple sessions (days) to complete. Immediacy of feedback is critical during the early stages of learning; later, students may be ready to self-regulate and provide themselves with feedback (self-assessment) prior to the teacher's input.

If the purpose of homework is to further students' learning, then grading that work is counterproductive. Using homework as formative assessment means the results of the assignment or activity have an instructional, not judgmental, impact. As we've discussed, grades neutralize feedback, so to make productive use of homework assignments, teachers should save the grading process for later when verification is necessary. If we are to accurately report where students are in their learning and bolster their confidence going forward, then grading their early attempts clearly misses the mark.

Cindy Warber (@CindyWarber), Teacher, Swartz Creek, Michigan

After nineteen years of scoring everything my students did, I decided to take a risk and only use final assessments such as group presentations, tests, and lab reports to determine my students' grades. I was no longer going to grade homework, class notes, or warm-up activities. I wanted students' grades to communicate the skills they had developed and their level of mastery of course-aligned science standards.

The tipping point came when I was examining the final semester grades for my biology and physical science students. As I looked at each of their grades, I realized I wasn't confident about what their grades were actually reflecting; one student had a B when I knew she really struggled to understand the material and repeatedly performed poorly on assessments while another student, who added such depth to class discussions and who went on to get a five on the AP exam, came close to failing the second semester. Did I really calculate the grades correctly? As a high school teacher in a traditional public school, I recognized that final grades determine a student's GPA, which directly impacts college admissions, scholarships, and class rank. For years, students in my class who maintained a straight A were those who excelled on unit assessments and turned in all the homework and daily assignments on time. Lower grades (Bs, Cs, Ds, and Fs) resulted from either a combination of missing assignments and high test scores or low quiz scores with bonus points to inflate the final percent. I began to wonder, What should a grade communicate to the student? What does a grade actually represent about a student's knowledge and skills?

When I collected student work to grade for accuracy, I often questioned where students found their answers. Some would confess to cheating, and others admitted to just filling in the answers without ever using their book or available resources. I began to question the value in giving points on any assignment completed outside of the classroom. The feedback was essential, but the points sent a false message that students were performing at a high level when there were obvious gaps in their understanding. I wondered if homework should even count toward students' final grade when it was meant as a tool for learning, not grading. That's when I decided to use homework scores as part of my process for determining final grades.

Despite the questions, concerns, and challenges that came from both parents and students, the turning point happened when my students realized that the purpose of homework and class assignments was to aid in their learning process; that's when I knew this change was here to stay.

Although homework was optional and not scored, I still tracked assignment completion to provide parents (and even coaches) with evidence of student homework choices and their connection to test results. Though I felt positive about the changes I was making and was validated both by research and practical insights from other educators, I desired feedback from my students to be certain these changes were beneficial. I didn't know if the message that assignments were for learning and not points was getting through until I received a letter from a tenth-grade student who admitted to copying an assignment from an answer key found on the Internet. When I read her letter I thought, "She gets it!" and I knew I was finally getting through to my students. Here's an excerpt from her letter:

"Everything you said in class today was absolutely right from my point of view and situation. You made me finally realize that the 'game' is over. To be completely honest, I knew this day would come sooner or later. Because playing the game was exactly what I was doing. I would always turn in the homework that was being graded then fail every test and quiz. I would find ways to earn points without knowing all the material. So when you told us that you'd only be grading tests and quizzes, I knew that I needed to do whatever it took to finally understand what we had to know. Just during this first marking period, I've stayed after school to get help and a better understanding in all my classes because of you. Part of the reason I think I played the game is because I never really thought of myself as smart or capable. But you've helped me actually believe in myself."

This student did some reassessments and still struggled to get the grade she wanted. As the year progressed, she finally figured out what questions to ask during review sessions. I still remember that breakthrough moment when she whispered, "Oh, so that's all you have to do to find the answer." This connection didn't come by turning in a homework assignment for points but rather from a sincere desire to fully understand the concept and not give up. As educators we long for encounters like this, when our dedication and student effort combine for a rewarding outcome. These moments are never about the grades; they're about learning what grades were meant to celebrate.

Homework as Extension

It is unrealistic to expect students, especially older students, to produce essential evidence of learning at school. Not all work they complete at home is necessarily practice; some is essential and designed to verify achievement (summative assessment). As Ken O'Connor (2011) writes:

> Sometimes homework requires students to show what they know by extending or integrating their knowledge and understanding through projects or assignments done partially or completely outside the classroom. This is clearly summative assessment and is

legitimately part of grades as long as there is careful monitoring to
ensure that it is the student's own work. (p. 110)

This is why a simple mantra like "Don't grade homework" is not specific enough. "Don't grade practice"? Sure, but "Don't grade any work completed at home" goes too far.

The challenge facing us when grading homework as an extension of classroom work is to ensure the accuracy of what we ultimately report. We cannot monitor the work that students complete outside of school hours as closely, so we have the added task of ensuring its authenticity. It may be impossible to be 100 percent sure, but there are some ways teachers can validate the levels of proficiency students demonstrate on work done outside the classroom.

Sometimes It's Necessary

With limited instructional time, it is often necessary for students to work at home. As well, many of us are using authentic assessment to create more essential learning and assessment experiences that require noninstructional hours. Whether it's a research paper, a first-person interview and write up, an experiment, a real-life application, or real conversations, we attempt to immerse students in authentic experiences that will lead to students doing more work outside school.

Accuracy is the critical element of grading, so while out-of-class summative assessments may be necessary, it is still important that we take steps to corroborate students' demonstrated levels of proficiency. In other words, we need to verify in class demonstrations that occur out of class, because otherwise we risk reporting inaccurate grades. With writing, for example, it may be necessary to collect an in-class writing sample to verify the level of the work completed at home. Clearly, the teacher would have to be mindful of the difference between an in-class assignment (often assessed as a first draft) and an assignment written over the course of several days or a week (assessed as a final product). That said, the teacher could check structure, vocabulary, development ideas, tone, and other writing attributes to potentially expose irregularities that could compromise the accuracy of the assessment.

We must at least attempt to verify that work completed at home is the students' original work. With frequent formative assessment and periodic summative moments, we become more familiar with our students' current levels, making it much easier to detect any anomalies within the evidence they submit.

What About Group Work?

With teachers moving toward more project-based learning and the renewed emphasis on collaboration as an essential competency, the prospect of students working together for a singular purpose has never been more relevant. But this increase in collaboration also increases teacher responsibility for delineating individual achievement from group results. Again, the issue is accuracy, and while collaborative learning experiences may be desirable—even necessary—we have to protect the integrity of the individual student's proficiency grade.

Assigning group scores is wrought with accuracy issues (O'Connor, 2013). To be clear, it is possible for students working within the same group to earn the same score, but that should occur only after the teacher has verified that each student has *earned* that score; simply defaulting to a group score and entering it under each student's name can lead to inaccuracies. The work in collaborative efforts is often not evenly distributed, and while fair is not always equal, we expect that overall, students will contribute equally to the task.

But we know that doesn't always happen, and what's worse is that we can't always detect these inequities. One student might complete the majority of a project (or all of it) in exchange for an invitation to a party the following weekend; another student may take it all on for fear that the others will negatively influence her overall grade. Defaulting to group scores compounds the issues of inaccuracy since many group projects carry significant weight within the gradebook. Without verification, students could receive inflated or deflated credit for factors beyond their control.

The separation of individual achievement is easier said than done. There are two ways we can account for individual achievement within a group result.

1. **Require an individual component:** While the result of the group work may be a collaborative product, teachers could also require students to submit an individual component to supplement the group project. This could be a reflection paragraph, a specific explanation, or a summary piece that allows the teacher to collect individual evidence of student understanding.

2. **Assess individuals separately:** Remember the goal is to assess standards, so teachers could create assessments that verify and validate the group score. Rather than making these individual assessments a part of the project, have them stand alone (maybe do them in class) and cover the same standards as the group work.

It also makes sense sometimes to just ask students about individual roles in group work, although we can never be sure if a hidden agenda or pressure is at play. The bottom line is to avoid group scores wherever possible; where it's not, then we should consider supplemental assessments to validate the group score.

Accurate Inferences Through Clear Criteria

With the onset of more authentic assessment experiences and project-based learning, students are, more than ever, receiving permission to show what they know in a wide variety of formats. This allows them to capitalize on their talents and pursue their passions, and it often removes the hurdle of assessment format from the process of accurately determining proficiency. However, determining proficiency is still a challenge. With ratio-based assessments, it's easy to determine the number of questions correct to the number of questions asked. With performance assessments (such as projects), teachers must infer proficiency—that the student's demonstration meets the established criteria, as there is no ratio involved.

The key to making these inferences is twofold: (1) establishing clear criteria and (2) practicing. First, with the wide variety of formats students use to demonstrate their knowledge, we need to be clear on what the success criteria are and communicate them to students. Students must know what they're demonstrating. In fact, we could go a step further and have students identify where they demonstrate proficiency. By requiring a script for a video project, for example, we can ask students to highlight where in the video they address each standard. We still need to make inferences, but this helps us know where to look.

The second aspect is practice. Working in teams can be especially helpful as teachers develop their skills in making inferences about student demonstrations. At first, it may be prudent to limit the number of available options for students to demonstrate their learning—not to stifle creativity, but to keep the options within a range the teacher is comfortable with. As the teacher becomes more comfortable, he or she can expand the number of options; collaboration can help those with limited experience.

How to Bring Parents on Board

Parents often use homework as a litmus test to measure the quality and rigor of an academic program. They may be perplexed—even disappointed—when their children come home without any homework or with homework that will not receive a grade. They may think the teacher is too easygoing and compromising their children's education; this is especially true for parents of younger students who may not understand the consequences of overburdening students with homework. As well, the notion that homework is mostly practice and rarely contributes to the report card grades is another mystifying difference between parents' experience in school and their children's.

When talking to parents about repurposing homework, remind them of the practice-games dynamic. Too many parents see grades and scores as evidence of learning and, therefore, assume that the lack of grades means nothing is happening in school. Remind them that volleyball practice doesn't count in the standings, but it's clear that their children are doing something at practice and that practice is critical for improved performance. Point out that practice is where their children have room to risk, experiment, and even fail without fear of penalty. Stress that expectations are no less rigorous, despite the absence of grades or scores, and that the idea is to turn the spotlight squarely on learning and away from point accumulation. It will take some time, but eventually parents will disconnect rigor and scores and see that repurposing homework creates a more engaging and fulfilling experience for their children. Beyond that, here are three specific elements to emphasize with parents.

1. **Emphasize quality over quantity:** The goal is to provide their children with quality assignments that enrich their experiences, establish a link between home and school, not to create the illusion of rigor by focusing on the quantity of homework assigned.

2. **Emphasize purpose over time:** Time is a distraction on par with quantity. Homework purposefully addresses their children's needs, development, or readiness. Students may not all need the same amount of practice, nor will they all put in the same amount of time. Required homework serves a purpose and will never be compulsory busywork.

3. **Emphasize external support:** With grades and scores off the table for a formative assignment, students are now free to access support from parents, siblings, or friends without compromising accuracy. In fact, we encourage them to seek support, and while our eventual goal is for them to work independently, initially that may not be possible. Practicing the wrong way is not helpful; we need students practicing their new learning the right way so parents (and others) can play an important role in ensuring this happens.

Parents know practice is a critical element to success, but we need to retrain many of them to understand how repurposing homework eliminates the acquisition of points from the process. Just as coaches don't keep score in practice, teachers who refocus their collective attention squarely on learning don't either.

Conclusion

This chapter was about repurposing homework so that it serves a more productive purpose within a learning trajectory. The question about whether homework serves any purpose at all is one for another day. If teachers make the decision to assign homework, then repurposing homework as practice to be used more formatively—thereby leaving grading out of the equation—makes the most sense. There are times where homework serves to extend or deepen the learning, which leads to using this work for summative purposes. As was the case in chapter 5, the fundamental question about homework is whether it increases or decreases the accuracy of what ultimately is reported about student proficiency.

The fundamental question about homework is purpose. Once teachers are clear on purpose then all processes and practices follow. If the purpose of the homework assignment is practice, then the focus should be on descriptive feedback that advances the learning. If the purpose is extension and verification, then the focus should be on inferring quality through the established performance criteria to determine (and record) proficiency levels. Grading practice work creates the assessment oxymoron of *formative grades* where the intention and the resulting action are misaligned.

Once grading is off the table, teachers can explore and implement a variety of ways that make homework more meaningful. By differentiating the experience for students, teachers can align assignments to the level of readiness, which will likely be more meaningful and inviting for students. Grading homework forces teachers to standardize the assigned homework since the validity of the grades can be compromised if the cognitive complexity varies from student to student. Remove grading from the equation, and opportunities abound.

QUESTIONS FOR LEARNING TEAMS

1. What quote or passage represents your biggest takeaway from chapter 6? What immediate action will you take as a result of this takeaway? Explain both to your team.

2. What side of the homework debate do you fall on? Explain your position.

3. What is the biggest concern you expect your students to express when you repurpose homework? What about from parents?

4. With group work, how do you control the accuracy of the assessment for each student? Are there some current routines that you might consider changing? Do you create supplemental assessments?

5. How confident are you that the inferences you make about student proficiency are on point? What aspect of performance assessment is the most challenging for you?

---

*Visit **go.solution-tree.com/assessment** for free reproducible versions of the questions for learning teams.*

CHAPTER 7
How to Redefine Accountability

Some teachers consider grades or reporting forms their "weapon of last resort." In their view, students who don't comply with requests suffer the consequences of the greatest punishment a teacher can bestow: a failing grade. Such practices have no educational value and, in the long run, adversely affect students, teachers, and the relationship they share.

—Thomas R. Guskey

At the heart of the debate between traditional grading and the standards-based approach is the question of accountability. As we discussed in chapter 3, standards-based grading is about a different kind of accountability. When students don't follow through on expectations, some teachers believe that they must do something, and while that may be true, the something they choose is often misplaced: an academic consequence for a behavioral misstep.

Teachers lose focus—even creditability—when they mismatch consequences with the issue at hand. Nowhere is our true north of accuracy and confidence more at risk than with the issue of accountability. The traditional notion of accountability renders grades inaccurate and leaves many students feeling unoptimistic about their potential success. Accountability doesn't have to involve punitive consequences; instead, it can emphasize that all learning is essential and there is no loophole for opting out. Students don't understand less about a topic because they hand their teacher something a few days after it was expected, but if we lower the students' scores, that's exactly what we communicate.

The Perils of Punitive Grading

Teachers have used punitive grading for decades. Whether it's a 10 percent reduction per day for late assignments or a zero for work not submitted, teachers often lean on these practices to incentivize students to meet the expected deadlines. While well intentioned, these punitive methods rarely produce the desired results. Some students still miss deadlines and fail to submit all of the required assignments.

Some teachers feel justified in penalizing students despite the fact that no studies support the use of low grades as effective punishment (Guskey, 2004). Punishment often leaves students feeling helpless about the possibility of improving (Selby & Murphy, 1992) and disenchanted from adults who say they support positive development and relationships but whose actions are incongruent with that mission (Karson, 2014; Kohn, 2005; Lee, 2013).

Punitive Grading Is Inaccurate

While the conversation on penalties and zeros is often anchored on the issue of accountability, it really is more an issue of accuracy. While some may argue that the use of punitive practices is justified, it's indisputable that these practices place accuracy in jeopardy.

We most often use grades to indicate student proficiency as it relates to standards or learning outcomes for a subject, and since most curricular standards make no reference to behavioral attributes (like punctuality), we compromise accuracy when we combine achievement (curricular standards) and nonachievement (anything else) factors. What makes this even more problematic is the lack of uniformity in the nonachievement factors that are included. Even when there is a degree of uniformity, different teachers rarely give them the same weight. One teacher applies late penalties while another does not; one teacher factors in participation while another gives credit for completing work regardless of its quality. As Susan Brookhart (2013b) writes, "Validity is in question when grades mean different things in different schools or subjects, in different teachers' classes, and for different types of students" (p. 260).

Research indicates that teachers also include nonachievement factors such as effort in traditional grading (Feldman, Kropf, & Alibrandi, 1998; McMillan, 2001; Waltman & Frisbie, 1994). This mixture of factors makes it unclear to parents and others what the actual achievement levels of students are, and while the reported grade might be well earned (a B, for example), parents would be hard-pressed to know how a teacher determined the final grade, for instance, that a child has A-level proficiency but was downgraded due to consistently poor work ethic or tardiness with assignments.

Imagine an assignment where a student earns an 80 percent (sixteen out of twenty) according to the established success criteria, but the teacher downgrades him by 20 percent to an overall score of 60 percent (twelve out of twenty) because he submitted the assignment on Wednesday instead of Monday. The 60 percent does not accurately reflect the student's demonstrated level of understanding and is a classic example of mixing achievement with nonachievement factors. All assessments are imprecise to one degree or another (Marzano,

2010) and with teachers already challenged to accurately analyze and make appropriate inferences about student proficiency (Heritage, Kim, Vendlinski, & Herman, 2008; Herman & Choi, 2008), the last thing we need is another element that dulls accuracy; students should receive full credit for what they know.

Punitive Grading Is Misplaced

The case in favor of punitive grading is an argument that, if reversed, makes no sense at all. On one hand, applying an academic penalty (10 percent per day) to a behavioral misstep (such as submitting an assignment late) is a traditional practice that many still philosophically justify. On the other hand, applying a behavioral penalty (like suspension) to an academic misstep (such as not being able to add fractions) makes little sense and would not be a common practice; we can't have it both ways. If the latter example is incongruent, so is the former.

Behavior is behavior; proficiency is proficiency. Sure, there is a logical and accepted connection between achievement and effort, but the hardest working students do not always earn the highest grades. We must measure achievement independent of effort, since we can't be sure how much effort students have actually put forth and have no reliable way of measuring effort when students are unsupervised.

If students' behavior falls short, schools need systems, routines, and procedures (such as codes of conduct) for responding to these issues without compromising the integrity of proficiency grades. Applying an academic penalty does nothing to assist the student with meeting the expected levels of behavioral performance; punishing students for irresponsibility doesn't teach students *how* to be responsible, only that they should have been responsible. If we want students to learn to be more responsible, then we need to explicitly teach them how.

Punitive Grading and Cheating

Cheating seems to be the one exception that many cite as justification for punitive consequences; dishonesty is surely something that deserves punishment. While adults may feel fully justified in applying punitive consequences in situations where students have been academically dishonest, a closer look reveals that the result is still an inaccurate grade that loses its meaning and usefulness.

This inaccuracy can feel counterintuitive as dishonesty, especially intentional, represents a breach of trust that we do need to address. Again, no one would argue that academic dishonesty is acceptable, but where perspectives differ is how we should handle it.

For many students, cheating is a win-win. If they cheat and get caught (and get an automatic zero), then they don't have to do the work they didn't want to do in the first place; if their cheating goes undetected, they earn credit they don't deserve. The academic penalty for not doing the work on one's own should therefore be doing the work on one's own. The teacher should deal with the behavioral violation separately, depending on the severity, through school or district policies and procedures. In this way, we maintain the integrity of the proficiency grade while our behavioral response aligns with the behavioral misstep.

A word of caution on cheating is that it isn't always a malicious act on the part of the student, even though it may appear that way. Imagine what it's like to be a student who feels so desperate that the only road to success is to cheat. As Ross W. Greene (2008) writes in *Lost at School*, "Kids do well if they can," and that "behind every challenging behavior is either an unsolved problem or a lagging skill" (p. 49). Our students need compassionate adults who serve more as teachers than wardens. Even if students are intentionally dishonest, they need adults who'll help them learn to be more appropriate, more open to risk, and more confident about their abilities to succeed. This doesn't mean we don't address dishonesty; it does mean a policy of being reasonable should apply in all circumstances and students should emerge from the experience feeling hopeful.

Grading Dilemma: Penalties and Incentives

The majority of teachers implementing some form of penalty (10 percent off or a zero, for example) does so to provide an incentive for students to stay current and meet required deadlines; the problem is, penalties don't provide an incentive. Teachers who use penalties will admit that not all students submit work on time despite the existence of the penalty. In fact, those teachers typically make it crystal clear to their students that late work will result in a penalty and that nonexistent work will result in a zero, and, yet, students still don't meet the required deadlines. Could it be that the threat of a penalty doesn't actually work with all students? Could it be that the root cause of the late or missing assignment has nothing to do with desire or effort? Is it possible that late assignments happen for other reasons than pure laziness? Taking the overly simplistic position that *late* is synonymous with *apathy* could result in an unwillingness to dig deeper and find out why a student struggles to meet the expected submission dates.

- *Is it that students don't care or have they learned not to care as a way of coping with their history of falling short?*

- *Why do teachers continue to utilize punitive grading practices when they don't produce the desired results?*

Punitive Grading Holds Students *Less* Accountable

Ask any teacher at the beginning of the school year which standards or assignments are optional and the likely response is, "None of them." Despite their sincerity, teachers who employ punitive practices often overlook how their practices render whole portions of the learning optional. Students who struggle and students who settle both present situations in which what we believe to be accountability actually lets students off the hook.

Struggling students whose results are barely above passing have little incentive to submit work after a few days with a 10 percent per day penalty. Most of them realize that after a few days, regardless of quality, they will get an F on the assignment. This only undermines their motivation. Most teachers would argue that the penalty provides an incentive to meet the deadline, but for struggling students, it has the opposite effect.

The other group we rarely consider is the students who settle. Imagine a student who doesn't do an assignment and receives a zero, which results in a significant decrease to his or her overall grade. Now what? If the student is still satisfied with his or her overall grade (despite the decrease), then there is almost no incentive to complete the missing work since nothing more can happen; the grade is as low as it can go and the positive impact of completing the work may not be worth the subsequent time and effort required to do it.

Real accountability means we expect students to complete all required assignments. Combine this definition of accountability with the principle of giving students full credit for their learning and we have created an environment where students have more incentive to complete the required assignments. Using an *I* or *INC* (for *incomplete*) instead of a zero is the most accurate response to missing work since all of the required evidence to accurately determine proficiency is not available.

The key to using I or INC for important individual assignments is to ensure that the cumulative grade (either the overall score or the score within the cluster or standards domain) also changes to an I or INC. When important pieces of evidence are missing, students shouldn't have a grade. Lowering the score through punitive measures only serves to muddy the accuracy of what teachers report. If the student has not provided all essential evidence, then only by recording an incomplete can teachers pass the accuracy test. By doing so, the teacher effectively says, "I don't have all the necessary evidence so you don't have a grade." In the schools I've worked in and with, students and parents responded much more positively and productively to this approach than to any punitive measure.

A New Kind of Accountability

Redefining accountability requires a more sophisticated approach than simply deciding what to do when a student doesn't follow through. For some students, this is a one time event, while for others it's an ongoing issue. It could be the result of a lack of understanding, or it might be a lack of will. If we understand the variety of profiles, we allow for *real* accountability that takes into consideration the reasons for the academic or behavioral missteps. Again, effective practices are only as good as the systems designed to support the teachers who implement those practices. In other words, it's easy to proclaim no zeros but more complicated to identify the replacement routine necessary to support implementation; that's where many standards-based grading practices fail to fulfill their promises. Eventually teachers become frustrated because the new approach to accountability falls entirely on their shoulders. If it does, it's quite predictable that frustration—even burnout—can set in and move teachers back to a more punitive approach.

While it's not possible to preplan for every scenario, it is possible to examine the issue of accountability more closely. Table 7.1 (page 98) outlines a sophisticated approach to accountability by first distinguishing students as *can't do*s or *didn't do*s, as well as determining whether the issue is infrequent or chronic.

Table 7.1: Can't Dos Versus Didn't Dos, and Infrequent Versus Chronic: An Approach to Accountability

	Infrequent Issue	Chronic Issue
Can't-do students	These students occasionally need additional instruction and support from the teacher.	These students need regular, predictable, and more targeted instruction and support from the teacher and support team.
Didn't-do students	For these students, we must make learning mandatory instead of invitational from a schoolwide system.	These students require more targeted behavioral interventions from the teacher and administration to prevent the problem from persisting.

Can't Do—Infrequent

Can't do means the student has a skill deficiency preventing him or her from completing the required assignment. If, on occasion, a student doesn't quite understand the lesson for that day and struggles with completing any required tasks, it is the responsibility of the classroom teacher to provide the additional instruction and support. Since the student can't do the work, the teacher is in the best position to effectively address the specific learning issues. As well, since this profile is inherently unpredictable and rare, the teacher can efficiently take action without relying on a system, process, or protocol.

Teachers can respond to those within this profile as needed and will often need little time to address the issue. Some teachers may ask students to attend an extra tutorial at lunch or after school; others may simply provide a few moments of support and instruction during class time. How involved the intervention is depends on how complex the can't-do issue is. Regardless, the classroom teacher responsible for the original instruction will know best how to address the present challenge. That is not to say that the teacher shouldn't seek assistance from colleagues to determine the most favorable course of action, but it does mean the responsibility for resolving the issue rests with the classroom teacher.

Can't Do—Chronic

While these students still have a *can't-do* skill deficiency, the gap in understanding is predictable and more ongoing than a one-off (*infrequent*) situation. With these students, schools need a system or protocol that allows the teacher to work with the student support team to both understand the complexity of the learning challenge and to know what is most likely to have a long-term positive impact. Despite the chronic, repeated nature of the challenge, there is no place for student discipline within this profile; as we have discussed, behavioral consequences for an academic shortcoming are misplaced and misguided.

Students with an individualized education program (IEP) are likely to have the necessary support routines already built into their plans, but non-IEP students for whom gaps in learning are significant and predictable require a shared approach between the teacher and the support team. For example, a teacher might have a scheduled weekly appointment with a student (such as Thursday after school) to ensure that the student is organized, on track, and confident about recently covered as well as upcoming learning; these students follow the same routine as the can't-do–infrequent students for individual assignments but with an additional layer of support. That could mean a scheduled block in which the learning assistance teacher works simultaneously on deepening the student's understanding of the standards at hand as well as addressing any learning deficits that may prevent long-term success.

The intensity of any intervention must match the intensity of the challenge, so for some students, a preexisting programmed approach may be sufficient; for others, teachers need to personalize the response. A programmed approach is more efficient in terms of both planning and access. Since the system already exists, it is easier to fit the student to the system and begin the additional support almost immediately. With a personalized approach, the system must adapt to the student, so much more planning is involved to readily and reliably address student needs. When in doubt, it's advantageous to begin with a programmed approach to avoid overplanning for can't-do issues that may appear to be more complex than they actually are.

Didn't Do—Infrequent

What distinguishes a didn't do from a can't do is that the student, despite having the capacity to complete the required assignments, hasn't done so; teachers can also refer to these students as "won't dos" if it is clear that they are defiantly refusing to complete any work, though it is a challenge to determine that definitively. This category frustrates teachers the most, and as such, schools would be wise to create a system of shared responsibility that allows teachers to focus on the can't dos. Didn't-do students understand what to do but haven't done it; teachers should not refer students who require more instruction through this system since the supervising adults may or may not have the expertise to deliver it.

For didn't-do students, we must make learning mandatory, not invitational. Too often teachers simply invite them to learn when they continually request the completed work or they make themselves available for additional time and support *if needed*. Assuming the required assignment is essential, there should be no option on completing it. Teachers need to move from requesting to expecting, and schools need a predetermined protocol for how to respond to students who occasionally don't submit the required assignments. Following is a description of the system we used in one of the high schools I worked in. It is important to note that it describes one possibility, not the only choice. Schools must always consider the specifics of their own context in terms of resources, space, personnel, funding, student age, and other unique factors (such as, do the majority of the students take the bus home immediately after school?) before determining the best-suited approach. Nonetheless, the following description does provide a likely framework.

To share the responsibility within the didn't-do–infrequent paradigm, we decided to hire an education assistant to supervise a work-completion room in the library during lunch every day. This assistant was not qualified to provide additional instruction, so students referred to the work-completion room had to be clear on both content and directions; they had to know what to do, even though they hadn't done it.

If a student arrived to class without the expected assignment, the teacher would email the assistant to inform her who was assigned to the room at lunch that day along with the specific assignments. (Technology such as Google Docs could make this process even more efficient today.)

Let's say a high school student named Jason goes to the library at lunch, checks in, and then completes the missing assignment. Once completed, he hands the assignment to the assistant (so he doesn't forget to hand it in to his teacher himself). The assistant then puts the completed assignment in Jason's teacher's mail slot after lunch. If Jason doesn't show up, the assistant would immediately email the grade-level administrator (in this case, the assistant principal), who would locate Jason in one of his afternoon classes to find out why he was a no-show.

The assistant principal might discover that Jason forgot to go to the work-completion room; it's also possible Jason didn't attend on purpose. Regardless of the reason, the assistant principal tells Jason to see his teacher after school to arrange to complete and submit his work. Immediately after meeting with Jason, the assistant principal informs Jason's teacher of the situation so she will expect to see Jason after school.

Jason then meets with his teacher after school to either complete the work at school or to arrange to submit it the next day. If Jason fails to attend his expected meeting, the assistant principal will call Jason's parents to discuss not only Jason's incomplete work but his repeated refusal to follow the directions of several adults. The hope would be for the assistant principal and the parent to discuss a plan for resolving both the missing work and the behavioral noncompliance.

That's real accountability.

Didn't Do—Chronic

Students who fall within this category are those capable of completing the vast majority of expected assignments but continually fall short of that expectation. Rather than more instruction, they require behavioral interventions to support their move toward increased productivity. In my high school, they would still go to a work-completion room, but again, since it's chronic, they need additional behavioral support. To be clear, these behavioral interventions do not mean removal and isolation; this is not about punishing students who haven't completed their work. Behavioral interventions refer more to the broad category of social-skills support. A student may, for example, predictably struggle with deadlines, so he or she must learn how to pace his or her work completion or develop a habit of accessing additional support more rapidly in advance of a deadline.

The classroom teacher and the administration, possibly including guidance counselors and other support personnel, share the responsibility for these students. The necessary interventions and instruction focus more on student attributes and work habits. The counselor may assist the student in learning how to turn larger assignments into smaller, more manageable pieces. In an extreme case, the teacher may require the student to complete his or her homework at school before actually going home. Teachers, along with as many as two or three other adults, tailor the specifics to the needs of each student. Regardless of the scenario, the team works to find the most relevant, targeted solution to the student's challenge, whether it's struggling with deadlines, disorganization, or lack of efficient study habits.

If a student consistently doesn't complete work and refuses to participate in any of the interventions, then it becomes an issue of discipline. Again, discipline is not code for removal and isolation; however, issues of discipline cannot go unchecked. Schools have already established expected social norms for behavior and respectful interactions, so if students violate these, the response should align with any established discipline procedures. Student age also plays a factor in determining the response, but regardless, teachers must address inappropriate behavior. That said, remember that what looks like apathy may be a lack of understanding or increased anxiety. Be cautious in responding too swiftly from a disciplinary perspective. The line between can't dos and didn't dos can blur at times, so when in doubt, assume it's a can't-do situation until it is certain that it really is didn't do.

Sherri Nelson (@sherrinelson00), Instructional Coach, Huron, South Dakota

What could possibly bring together a mother, a football coach, a wrestling coach, a classroom teacher, and a middle school student two weeks after a grading period has ended? An "incomplete" in math and our newly created Family Day. Prior to the implementation of our Family Day, it was a daily battle to get the student, whom I will call Lucas, to complete his assignments and produce quality work. At Family Day, Lucas, along with several other students, spent an entire afternoon diligently working while his mother, teacher, and coaches offered encouragement while he completed his missing assessments.

In our school, the consequence for not doing your work is doing your work. We have redefined accountability by building an academic support system in which teachers, parents, and students work together to ensure all our adolescent learners experience academic success. We are influencing student accountability and achievement by focusing on four things:

1. Requiring all students to complete all summative assessments

2. Improving communication between parents, staff, and students

3. Allowing struggling students extra time to master the standards

4. Providing extra help to students before, during, and after school

It is difficult for teachers to move forward with new content when students do not provide evidence to demonstrate learning has taken place. Therefore, we require all students to complete all summative assessments at a quality level. Students must redo summative assessments below seventy percent as well as work not completed to the best of their ability. The names of students who have missing summative assessments are placed on a missing-assignment list that all staff members have access to.

Continued →

Our electronic database sends automated text and email messages to our parents. Parents are notified when their children have missing assignments and can reply directly to the specific classroom teacher; follow-up messages inform parents when the assignments have been completed.

Students who are capable of doing quality work, but choose not to do their work, are questioned by a variety of staff members who ask them, Who do you owe? What do you owe? What is your plan? If the work remains missing, students must complete the assessments during their own personal time. We reteach content material to struggling students before school, during lunch, during intervention period, and after school. We remove student names from the missing-assignment list once they achieve quality work. All students with missing summative assessments are issued an incomplete; no grades are issued on their report cards until their missing assessments are completed.

Our goal is for our adolescent learners to take responsibility for their own learning by transitioning from our adult-induced accountability to personal accountability. We are pleased with how Lucas and many of our other students have been able to turn things around and demonstrate personal responsibility. It is our hope that Lucas and his classmates will carry their academic knowledge and newly learned accountability skills with them to high school.

Accountability With Intent

The issue of accountability is this simple: if teachers want it, they must teach it. With academic instruction, we purposefully define learning goals, identify success criteria, and instruct students through a progression to facilitate their achievement of standards; we can do the same with desirable attributes like responsibility.

Is Responsibility Really a Priority?

Educators agree that students need to learn to be responsible, but not all are willing to devote the necessary time and attention to purposefully teach responsibility. Rather than waiting for a behavioral stumble to teach a life lesson, schools that take seriously the teaching of responsibility ensure that it's a part of the lexicon from the beginning. These lessons can be formal or informal.

Formal lessons on responsibility may be anchored around responsibility to self (for example, submitting work when it's due), responsibility to others (for example, being reliable and collaborative), responsibility to the school (for example, cleaning up after oneself), and even responsibility to the learning environment (for example, arriving to class on time and completing homework). Conducting these lessons intentionally is the only way to ensure that students learn these critical life lessons.

Some schools may choose not to create formal lesson plans but instead increase their attention to responsibility through student assignments. Teachers address what they often refer to as *general learning outcomes* or *student attributes* within the context of a particular task. For example, after thoroughly explaining the directions and assessment criteria for an upcoming project, a teacher may describe to her class what a reasonable pacing plan might be in order to ensure that they meet the deadline. As well, the teacher may set some interim benchmarks to both check whether students are on track and prevent them from waiting until the last minute to begin. The lessons don't need to be formal; they just need to be purposeful.

If individual teachers or schools declare that responsibility is a critical lesson but without any instructional intent, the declaration is nothing more than a veiled threat. If it really matters, then adults will collectively give the necessary time and attention to ensure that students develop the skills to become responsible students and citizens.

It's No Different Than Teaching Respect

Consider how schools teach respect. Every school expects its students to demonstrate respect. Through both direct instruction and modeling, teachers instill the elements of respect within their students. When students demonstrate disrespect, adults respond. The intensity of the response matches the intensity of the disrespect, and how schools respond depends on student age and the social norms established within the school.

Using the gradebook to teach respect is not necessary. When students are disrespectful, it has no impact on their grades because disrespectful behavior has no connection to student proficiency within a given subject. Somehow schools are able to expect respectful behavior, respond when students are disrespectful, and redirect them to show the appropriate level of respect, all without touching the gradebook; responsibility should be no different.

What adults pay attention to is what children learn to believe is important. If students don't take responsibility seriously (at least in school), it is because teachers don't give it the attention it deserves. This won't happen overnight, however; as adults within a school give responsibility the profile it deserves, students will eventually realize that responsibility is an important achievement.

How to Bring Parents on Board

One could argue that parents want their children to learn to be responsible as much as they want them to achieve proficiency on specific academic standards. This in no way diminishes the importance of academic proficiency; rather, it speaks to how much parents value responsibility and other characteristics that will serve their children both in school and beyond.

While parents might feel that the punitive approach is the only way to instill these valuable habits and attributes in their children, it's important for them to know that instruction and punishment are not synonymous. That could be what parents once experienced in school, and they might feel that being "soft" will only create opportunities their children will surely take advantage of. Other parents may simply not know any other way to respond. We need to make it clear to parents that the removal of punitive consequences does not mean that learning to be responsible is no longer important and in no way represents being soft on kids. Parents appreciate teachers who set clear parameters and are firm, yet fair, in enforcing those expectations without applying a punishment unrelated to the behavioral misstep.

Indirectly, teachers also model the ability to affect student behavior without resorting to punitive consequences, something parents may begin to replicate at home.

We must enlist parental support to maximize the potential success of the can't-do and didn't-do systems, especially when it comes to using noninstructional time. Make sure parents can see that we design these systems to ensure the accuracy of what we report and to instill a sense of responsibility within their children. We need to design and explain our use of noninstructional time to parents not as a behavioral consequence, but as a system of support that prevents students from falling behind or simply opting out; we're not withholding free time—we're enhancing the opportunity to be successful. How we talk about this extra support builds the necessary credibility and distinction.

In the end, the separation of important attributes from the proficiency grade provides parents with more specific, relevant information. They no longer have to infer proficiency versus behavioral competence by parsing each from a single grade. Again, it all comes down to our grading true north. Talk to parents about the importance of disseminating accurate information without distorting the proficiency grade; emphasize the importance of maintaining their children's confidence while holding them accountable to learning. As always, taking the time to thoroughly present the redefined notion of accountability will go far in preventing parents from misinterpreting the new approach.

Conclusion

Arguably the hottest of the hot-button grading issues is the issue of accountability, which some use as code for punishments administered when students don't comply with expected directions or behaviors. Redefining accountability is about moving to an alternate view where student accountability is where all essential evidence is mandatory. Make no mistake, behavioral missteps aren't ignored, they're just compartmentalized in what we might call the behavioral silo (in other words, addressed through codes of conduct). As discussed in chapter 3, the myth that students aren't held accountable can hijack thoughtful conversations and purposeful action toward real accountability. That said, if schools or districts inadvertently allow the issue of accountability to slip, they would be right to be criticized.

At its best, a redefined notion of accountability would hold students *more* accountable without the need for punitive responses. So much of what we've called accountability actually serves to let students off the hook. Our more advanced learners can absorb zeros and penalties and still reach high levels of achievement; our struggling learners lose all incentive once the zero or penalty sends them past the threshold of recovery. Real accountability addresses the specifics of the can't do/didn't do profile along the axiom of whether the issue is infrequent or chronic to ensure the most targeted interventions and supports are available to keep learning on track.

The idea that punishing the absence of a skill will produce the skill is absurd. We don't approach mathematics, ELA, or any other subject that way. As well, every school expects their students to be respectful and is able to hold students accountable for any displays of disrespect without ever compromising the integrity of a proficiency grade; responsibility is no different. Punishing students' irresponsible behavior will not teach them how to be responsible. If schools and districts are serious about teaching students to be responsible, then they will define responsibility through clear criteria and set about teaching students in a more purposeful and supportive manner; that's real accountability.

QUESTIONS FOR LEARNING TEAMS

1. What quote or passage represents your biggest takeaway from chapter 7? What immediate action will you take as a result of this takeaway? Explain both to your team.

2. On a scale of 1 to 10 (with 1 being *not at all* and 10 being *already there*), where are you in terms of removing punitive consequences from your grading practices? Explain why you chose the number you chose.

3. What would it take or what would you need to do in order to move three numbers higher from your answer to question 2? (For example, if you determined you were a 4, what would it take to move you to a 7?)

4. What is it about cheating that makes it so difficult for some (or you) to eliminate an academic penalty from the potential responses?

5. Which of the four quadrants represented in the can't-do/didn't-do approach is the one you or your school is already most effective in handling? Which one are you least effective at handling? Explain both.

6. What already existing routines (such as articulation) would make the teaching of responsibility a little more seamless?

*Visit **go.solution-tree.com/assessment** for free reproducible versions of the questions for learning teams.*

CHAPTER 8
How to Use Levels of Proficiency

Proficiency-level descriptions allow us to identify not only differences between proficient and nonproficient work, but also the degree of proficiency on a continuum.

—Tammy Heflebower

We begin our look at grading from the outside with the move from traditional grades to levels of proficiency. Until now, we've discussed how a standards-based mindset can bridge the gap between a traditional grading paradigm and the desire to be more standards based; the standards-based mindset allows for a new approach to grading and reporting even when the process of formal reporting hasn't changed. But what if teachers are ready for the next step? What if teachers, the school, or even the district is ready to fundamentally change the way they report achievement? For those who are ready for a more standards-based reporting system, the journey begins with replacing traditional grade calculations with levels of proficiency that teachers determine through a combination of data and professional judgment.

Using levels of proficiency that give students full credit for learning results in a more accurate process of reporting. I want to emphasize once more that in this book I use the term *grades* to refer to more than just letters and percentage increments. Schools can move away from letter grades as determined by percentages and mean averages, but it is naïve to think that grades as a summary of achievement that we report to parents and others are not necessary in perpetuity. As I discussed in chapter 1, the disconnect between our traditional grading paradigm and our standards-based instructional paradigm has revealed the limited (if not useless) role of traditional grades; the indispensable need to summarize achievement demands a more relevant process for doing so.

Grading Dilemma: A Tale of Two Schools

Imagine you've been invited to visit two schools and meet with their assessment teams who, among many duties, were responsible for leading a change toward standards-based grading; each school claims to have moved to standards-based grading and reporting. On paper, the first school (A) has moved to a five-point scale (0–4) while the second school (B) appears to have kept traditional grades intact.

School A	School B
4	A
3	B
2	C
1	D
0	F

Upon meeting with each team, you ask a few clarifying questions about their standards-based systems. When you meet with school A you ask them to clarify the meaning behind each of the five levels. They tell you that a 4 is 90–100 percent, a 3 is 80–89 percent, a 2 is 70–79 percent, a 1 is 60–69 percent, and a 0 is 59 percent or lower.

When you meet with school B, you are somewhat perplexed, as they use traditional letter grades, so you ask them to clarify how it's possible that they have shifted to standards-based grading. They tell you that while they kept the traditional letter grades, the meaning behind each letter grade is significantly different. An A is no longer based on a percentage (90–100), but rather indicates a student who had reached an *advanced* level of understanding; a B is *proficient*; a C is *emerging*; a D is *novice*; and an F represents *insufficient evidence*.

- *Which school is actually more standards based?*

- *What does this tell us about the importance of the symbols versus the importance of the mechanics of grade determination?*

Levels Versus Traditional Grades

It is ironic that defenders of percentage-based grades often build their arguments on their accuracy when distinguishing among 101 levels of performance (0–100) is next to impossible. The very notion that a teacher can make a clear distinction between a 74 percent and a 79 percent is absurd. Even by examining student evidence, a teacher would be hard pressed to be so precise. Teachers most often base percentage grades on calculations involving an average of previous work with the most current work; rarely does this result in an accurate determination. The traditional grades reported often do not reflect what a student actually knows.

On the other hand, ask any teacher to divide his or her students into four groups—let's say advanced, proficient, developing, and novice—and calculations become unnecessary. Teachers can do so without opening their electronic gradebooks. Teachers wouldn't actually do this to students, but my point is that they can far more easily (and precisely) distinguish among 4 levels than 101. The need to expand beyond four is based on a desire to separate and rank students in some kind of numerical order. Does anyone really believe that a student with, for example, an 83.7 percent has performed at a higher level than a student with an 81.4 percent? This desire to turn grading into a purely scientific process of calculations has pushed the art of grading aside. It's time for all of us to recapture or reinvigorate our judgment as an essential part of grade determination. Professional judgment clearly plays a role with judges, doctors, mechanics, and a whole host of other trained professionals; it's valid and relevant in education as well.

How Many Levels?

Once teachers decide to move to a system of levels, then the next question is, How many? Teachers can use any number of levels as long as the distinction between one level and the next is clear and definable. The fundamental difference between levels and percentages is that we determine levels by examining evidence for quality while we must calculate percentages through an algorithm. We must clearly define each level in terms of quality as it relates to the standards rather than a simple judgment using labels such as *excellent, very good, good*, and so on. I will discuss the specific meaning of levels shortly, but for now the question remains, How many levels?

From my experience, most teachers (and schools) tend to settle on five levels (four levels of quality plus a level for insufficient evidence). Figure 8.1 shows a five-point scale with a sampling of corresponding descriptors. A through F grades have been included in the figure as a reminder that the symbols we use to report, in this case letter grades, can be redefined to align with a standards-based approach instead of predetermined percentage increments.

Note, however, that increasing the number of levels too much can be problematic. As Thomas Guskey (2015) writes in *On Your Mark*, "As the number of levels or categories increases, so do the number of classification errors" (p. 41).

0	1	2	3	4
F	D	C	B	A
Insufficient	Novice	Developing	Proficient	Advanced
Not yet	Beginner	Emerging	Competent	Distinguished
Not there	Minimal	Acceptable	Accomplished	Exemplary
Below basic	Basic	Apprentice	Practitioner	Expert
Undrafted	Rookie	Professional	All star	Hall of fame

Figure 8.1: Five-point scale examples.

What Do the Levels Mean?

Video games offer an easy way to illustrate the distinctions among levels. As a player progresses through a game, the level of complexity or sophistication required to keep advancing also increases. Reaching the next level requires meeting certain conditions or requirements; it rarely matters how long the player took to reach that level. Some games have time limits, but many simply ask the player to reach a certain point, complete a number of tasks, or fulfill a set of criteria before advancing to the next level.

Levels of proficiency within the classroom are essentially the same. To reach each level, students must perform at a specific degree of sophistication or competence. Figure 8.2 is an example of the five-point scale with distinctions for each level. Teachers would be wise to work together to define the levels in their particular context; simply using another school's levels without meaningful discussion about what each level means could result in some inconsistencies in execution.

Level	General Description
Advanced	Students at the advanced level have reached a level of mastery over the grade-level standards. They are able to apply and adapt to authentic, atypical, or unpredictable situations or circumstances. These students can draw upon their conceptual understanding to solve real problems that show a level of creativity and sophistication. These students are able to accurately self-assess and have a depth of understanding that seamlessly connects related or previously explored concepts.
Proficient	Students at the proficient level independently demonstrate competence within the standards. Whether basic or sophisticated, these students have met the standards and are capable of selecting the appropriate strategy for most atypical situations or circumstances. With assistance, these students can occasionally apply their proficiency to more authentic situations or circumstances. While they haven't consistently achieved more advanced demonstrations, these students have fully met the expectations of the intended learning.
Developing	Students at the developing level are those who inconsistently demonstrate an understanding of the grade-level standards but require assistance and guidance to reach full proficiency. Connections to related or previously explored concepts are minimal or inconsistent. Developing students will occasionally reach the proficient level on some standards, but will also demonstrate learning at the novice level. These students have some transferable skills and a limited conceptual understanding that goes beyond right/wrong.
Novice	Students at the novice level are those who can only demonstrate a very basic understanding of the grade-level standards and concepts. These students are at the beginning stages of learning; explanations and demonstrations are task specific, inconsistent, linear, and isolated in that they show little connection to any related or previously explored concepts. These students operate at the recall and replication level.
Insufficient	Students at the insufficient level have not submitted the requisite amount of evidence to justify a passing level. Either whole pieces of evidence are missing or the submitted evidence is incomplete or incorrect.

Figure 8.2: Five-point scale with descriptions example.

The North East School Division (NESD) in Melfort, Saskatchewan, uses a four-point scale. As one can see in figure 8.3 (pages 112–113), the descriptions for each level are thorough, which goes far in ensuring consistent application among teachers and consistent understanding by students and parents. Visit NESD's website at http://curriculum.nesd.ca /assessment/assessment-tools for a more comprehensive look at NESD's assessment process and systems.

Why Avoid the Term *Exceeding*?

Some educators use the term *exceeding* to reference the top level of proficiency (for example, *exceeding standards*). Unfortunately, this leads to confusion. To *exceed* is to go beyond the standard, which in theory sounds the same as *advanced*; however, in execution it often morphs into *the next grade level*. In other words, to reach the highest level, students would need to meet standards at the next grade level, which is both inaccurate and unfair. This inadvertently makes the highest level next to impossible to reach. The traditional system never asked, for example, for seventh-grade students to work at an eighth-grade level to earn an A, so our levels of proficiency shouldn't either.

In addition, if they are not careful, teachers can also raise the level of performance too much on the lower levels. There is a difference between setting high standards and making the levels unreachable for most students, which is why teachers need to work together to understand how to apply the various levels.

How to Determine Levels of Proficiency

Determining student proficiency requires clear performance criteria, continual practice among colleagues teaching the same subjects, and an investment from students in understanding the difference between levels and percentages. The shift to levels is not difficult to understand but does require some purposeful action to implement with high fidelity, especially in the early stages where the entrenched paradigm of points and percentages as well as the uncertainty of the unknown may influence the habits of teachers, students, and even parents.

Establish Clear Performance Criteria

The accuracy of our judgments regarding student proficiency hinges on the quality of the assessments we conduct as well as our competence in matching performance to the established success criteria (Moss, 2013). The first step toward greater accuracy is to establish clear criteria with levels of performance that teachers can distinguish from one another.

Assessment items closely tied to both curricular standards and classroom instruction increase both the validity and reliability of the results, which allows teachers to draw more accurate conclusions about student proficiency (Parkes & Giron, 2006). Teachers can enhance the validity and reliability of performance assessment, in which they must infer that student performance matches a particular level of proficiency, when they specifically define performance criteria (Baron, 1991).

Level	Phrases and Descriptors Often Associated With These Levels
Fully meeting grade-level expectations with enriched understanding (EU)	• Consistently applies concepts to new situations (for example, uses examples [different than those used in class] to clarify concepts on assessments) • Extends ideas and draws connections to real-world situations • Thoroughly explains concepts and consistently demonstrates a deep understanding of the concept or skill • Demonstrates understanding of interconnected details by drawing complex connections to other concepts and models, to oneself, and to the world • Can teach the concept to other students (often through a variety of methods) • Works independently or works confidently and collaboratively in groups • Consistently uses established skill set for problem solving, selects the most appropriate tools and strategies for the situation, and can justify (explain) the chosen method • Solves problems in multiple ways and can verbalize strategies and solutions • Describes and analyzes topics with detailed and insightful supporting evidence • Poses new questions of strong personal significance • Takes risks and analyzes results • Insightfully analyzes relevant information and conveys own thoughts and connections regarding the outcome and concept in a personally meaningful and engaging way • Not only clearly understands the outcome but begins to assess the impacts and challenges on self, the class, society, and the environment • Exceeds level as shown by assessment evidence (visible in reflections, portfolio, discussions, exams, and other assessments) • Consistently reflective and solution oriented • Engages in a variety of contexts and accurately uses new vocabulary • Includes problem solving as an integral part of work along with reflection on the work in discussions with the teacher

Fully meeting grade-level expectations (FM)	• Applies the concept to new situations with increasing confidence (for example, uses examples [often the ones discussed in class] to clarify concepts on assessments) • Explains (examines, describes, identifies) concepts with detail and consistently demonstrates an understanding of the concept or skill • Demonstrates an understanding of interconnected details by drawing connections • Includes and demonstrates key elements of the outcome per the assessment criteria and rubrics • Shows evidence of learning in reflections, portfolios, discussions, and assessments • Needs few refinements • Works independently or collaboratively when required • Has an established skill set • Analyzes relevant information and conveys thoughts and connections to the outcome or concept • Asks strong questions and supports analysis with relevant details and examples • When problem solving with a teacher (getting feedback or an assessment), comes prepared with questions and possible solutions to think through the assessment • Submits original and well-thought-out work after feedback
Mostly meeting grade-level expectations (MM)	• Demonstrates a basic understanding of the concept but needs more practice to apply it • Leaves out key elements or aspects of the concept that require elaboration • Begins to examine, describe, and explain the concept or skill but more attention to detail is required to fully demonstrate understanding of the topic • Shows a developing skill set • Needs to explore connections to texts, self, and others • Needs to continue to explore the topic to learn more • Starts to ask questions and support analysis with details and examples • Needs assistance to meet goals (for example, attending tutorial sessions) • When problem solving with a teacher (getting feedback on an assessment), looks for answers to general questions • Submits work after feedback that required teacher's ideas
Not yet meeting grade-level expectations (NY)	• Identifies key elements of the concept • Demonstrates an understanding of the topic • Goes beyond an emerging skill set • Interprets the context or meaning of the problem • Needs to revisit the topic to develop more understanding and attention to detail

Source: Adapted with permission from the North East School Division, Melfort, Saskatchewan. To view the original version, visit http://curriculum.nesd.ca/assessment/assessment-tools and select "Understanding NESD Rubrics (K–8)." Original document created by Stephanie Pipke-Painchaud.

Figure 8.3: North East School Division four-point scale.

In her book *Formative Assessment: Making It Happen in the Classroom*, Margaret Heritage (2010) highlights the importance of establishing both learning goals and success criteria, and while her book focuses primarily on formative assessment, the same fundamental holds true for summative assessment, since learning goals specifically identify what the students will learn during the course of the lesson or lessons and summative assessment is about verifying the achievement status of students.

Teachers can word learning goals and success criteria almost identically when dealing with fundamental knowledge or skills, though *learning goals* tend to highlight conceptual understanding while *success criteria* focus on what it looks like to achieve the learning goal. The link between goals and criteria is murkier when dealing with deeper, more complex learning goals; these demonstrations require the teacher to infer whether students have successfully learned what's expected. As such, it is essential that both teacher and student have an aligned understanding of how they may represent specific levels of proficiency. Without such alignment, it will be challenging for students to accurately monitor their work for discrepancies between what they produced and the desired outcome. As well, it will be exponentially more challenging for teachers to accurately infer student proficiency related to the intended learning goals and standards.

April Davenport (@davenport78), Thomas Metcalf Laboratory School, Normal, Illinois

When I first started standards-based grading in 2006, I did it on my own within my language arts classroom. I was already grading everything on a rubric, which made the change to standards-based grading a little easier. It also made sense to use a five-point scale (1–5) since it correlated nicely with the letter grades I was expected to use for report cards.

Two years later, the Common Core State Standards were introduced. My superintendent asked me to try the standards in my classroom to see what I thought of them, which led me to change the way I set up my rubrics. Instead of just the raw numbers (1–5) representing different levels of criteria for each assignment, I decided to define what the numbers would now represent: 5 = Fully explains; 4 = Meets the standard; 3 = Getting part of the standard; 2 = Beginning to get it; 1 = Little work done; 0 = Nothing done. After the switch, I immediately felt as though I was more effectively communicating the students' progress as it related to the learning standards. However, I didn't think that my descriptors were very well defined.

Within a few months, I had the opportunity to attend two workshops that were exactly what I needed to improve my grading practices in a more meaningful way. The first was specific to grading practices while the second focused more on formative and summative assessment. It was after the second workshop that we (myself along with my colleagues who were exploring the possibility of changing as well) realized that our descriptors should be more about proficiency. We knew we had to make a change, but we knew it wasn't going to be easy. As a team we met, read, and discussed. We met with our administrators and they immediately were on board; they knew what I had been doing over the last several years and were excited that my teammates were now willing to move in the same direction.

Our initial decision was to adopt a four-point grading scale. We knew we wanted *mastery* and *proficiency* as two of our descriptors, but we didn't feel we had a need for three additional levels. We also discussed the possibility of a three-point scale, but already convinced *mastery* and *proficiency* had to be a part of it, we realized we needed more than one category to represent the different levels of understanding. Four seemed to be the perfect fit for how we wanted to represent the levels of understanding.

During the summer, our middle-school team met. One takeaway from the workshops that stuck with us had been the big idea that the scores we assigned had to mean something. If we were going to assign a 3, students needed to know what that meant. Coming up with the descriptors proved to be a challenging task. We met for eight hours, reading, researching, and discussing what we wanted to do. Each of us defined what we thought each number or level should mean and then we compared. Sometimes our definitions were close, and sometimes they weren't. There were times the discussions became a little heated, but after eight hours we had found common ground.

We worked hard discussing each individual word in each definition to describe each main focus—mastery, proficiency, emergent learning, significant gaps, and too little work. We finally arrived at the following descriptors; we added back a fifth level, which was essentially a not-enough-evidence category:

- 4—Demonstrates complete and masterful work by effectively communicating and flexibly applying understanding of the assessed standard

- 3—Demonstrates proficient work by communicating a meaningful understanding of the assessed standard

- 2—Demonstrates an ability to communicate an emergent understanding of the assessed standard. Some gaps in understanding exist.

- 1—Demonstrates significant gaps in understanding the assessed standard. Guidance and practice are necessary in order to progress.

- 0—Too little or no work submitted to show evidence of the assessed standard

We decided that there was a difference between proficiency and mastery, and our goal was to make sure all of our students reached at least the proficiency level, but we were also going to push for mastery. According to our shared philosophy, 0s and 1s were unacceptable, and it would be through a retake process that we would work with our students to get them to a proficient level of understanding.

Our middle-school team adapted standards-based grading on a number-based scale for one year, before the rest of our preK-8 teachers got on board. In the second year, our entire school used the scale; within two years, our school no longer correlates any grades with letter grades. Going through this meaningful process together as a team was extremely beneficial and necessary to ensure we were on the same page. I feel that it's an essential first step for any school moving to standards-based grading.

Calibrate With Colleagues

Accurate inferencing by individual teachers is half the battle; the other half is consistency among colleagues teaching the same subjects. In a standards-based instructional paradigm, there is no such thing as high standards or low standards, only *the* standards. A student who reaches the advanced level in a subject should earn that level regardless of who the teacher is.

Granted, teachers may not judge students identically when they're on the very edges of two neighboring levels because of the slight margin of error involved, but this is the exception, not the rule. To pass the accuracy test, grading mechanisms must produce accurate results, which means it is non-negotiable that teachers actively calibrate their determinations in collaboration with their colleagues. There is no formula or quick fix that replaces the process of teachers purposefully sharing student work samples and discussing the consistent inferencing of proficiency based on the established success criteria. For teachers with limited experience or those teaching new subjects, this collaborative process is invaluable since they have no point of reference to draw on. There is no trick; this is quite simply the work of accurate assessment that takes an intentional commitment of time, energy, and practice.

Personal Reflection: Honing Assessment Skills

During my two years working at central office, one of my responsibilities was coordinating the administration and scoring of the Foundation Skills Assessment (FSA). In British Columbia, students in grades 4 and 7 take the FSA, which consists of three content areas—reading, writing, and numeracy—divided into two sections per area (a total of six tests). The purpose of the FSA is to measure learning skills linked to the provincial curriculum and performance standards, and while there has been some political tension as to how the FSA data are used both within and outside the school system, the exercise in scoring the assessments is some of the best professional learning I have ever participated in.

To score the exam, a district team consisting of teachers and administrators was organized. Within that team were three team leaders whose additional responsibilities included leading the scoring session for each content area. These were teachers who had a specialization within the content area as well as experience in scoring the FSA; I was not one of the team leaders but was a full participant in the scoring of the assessments.

With approximately four to six people on each team, the calibration of assessment scoring was a priority. The scoring had to be consistent for the results to be both fair and useful. Each team leader began with a set of what were called *anchor papers*, which were sample answers prepared by the team leaders ahead of the scoring session. These were not responses from the current assessments we were about to score, but answers from years past or practice questions completed by the team leaders' own students; the assessments were scored on a four-point scale.

The process with the anchor papers was simple. Each individual would go through the answer and determine a score based on the holistic rubric that was to be used. After each team member had individually scored the answer, a discussion ensued to see how consistent each team member was in applying the performance criteria to the answer provided. As we discussed discrepancies between individuals, we used the rubric to justify the inference between the criteria and the anchor paper. Some slight discrepancy on the edges of performance was to be expected, but overall the consistency grew with each subsequent example.

For those inexperienced in scoring, the conversation was invaluable. I discovered that my assessment of fourth-grade math was much too rigorous; I was examining the work through my middle and high school teacher lens as opposed to the performance criteria. Without the exercise of calibrating, I would have misclassified the performance of the students whose papers I was scoring artificially low. Predictably, the beginning of the calibration brought forth initial variation in assessing performance, but as we went through the exercise, we became more aligned in our scoring. The calibration was done until the team felt as though everyone was ready to independently apply the criteria to the set of papers each was responsible for scoring.

Not only did the calibration occur at the beginning of the scoring session, the team leaders would periodically stop the individual scoring and provide yet another anchor paper for the team to discuss. Returning to more anchor papers ensured the performance criteria were consistently being applied, and while this exercise did extend the time spent scoring individual assessments, team members were unanimous in their support of recalibrating at regular increments. The members of the scoring teams believed that the professional learning that occurred during the scoring sessions was invaluable and would have a residual impact on their daily work within their classrooms.

The FSA was a standardized test that, despite not contributing anything to report-card grades, created a healthy debate about the role of large-scale assessment. The exercise of scoring the assessments was unrivaled as a professional exercise of applying clear performance criteria to a variety of student samples. After that experience, it became clear to me that individual schools, departments, grade levels, or teaching partners would all benefit from a similar exercise in honing their assessment skills.

Get Student Investment

In her book *Design in Five: Essential Phases to Create Engaging Assessment Practice*, Nicole Dimich Vagle (2015) identifies student investment as an essential component of high-quality assessment experiences. Teachers can create student investment by intentionally bringing students in as partners in their own learning so that they can more readily connect the learning, assignments, results, and improvement. Vagle (2015) points out that investment goes beyond involvement by establishing "a reciprocal relationship between student and teacher . . . that leads to the student taking the reins and beginning to own and value his or her own learning" (p. 11).

To be invested, students must actively participate in the process of self-regulating their learning, including reflecting on the grades they've earned. Students are the definitive source of assessment information since they have continual, immediate access and control over what they think, what they do, and how efficacious they are (Andrade, 2010; Brookhart, 2013a). The connection between student investment and standards-based grading is that for students to use report card grades to self-reflect, grades must only show achievement. We must teach students to reflect on and use their grades for self-regulation and improvement.

The responsibility of determining proficiency is the teacher's alone. Given the potential consequences of final grade determination (grade advancement, transcripts, college acceptance, and so on), students should not be involved in final decisions; they don't have the training or expertise to make these important determinations without the teacher judging their accuracy. That doesn't mean students can't contribute during the process. There is no harm in soliciting student input about where they believe they are in relation to the standards.

Courtney Bebluk (@CBebs), Teacher, Richmond, British Columbia

Rubrics are an essential assessment tool in my grades 6 and 7 classroom. At the beginning of each school year, the students complete an assignment designed to assist them in understanding the assessment process and the application of different levels of proficiency. Originally this assignment was called "Go for 5" based on a five-point scale, where five was the top level. However, I began to notice that numbered levels were disadvantageous. Students became less focused on the feedback and more concerned with the number on their assignment; the scores and feedback I was giving were unhelpful. My students' obsession with numbers made it clear that I needed to take a different approach when it came to using levels.

I decided to make the activity more effective in order to refocus my students on learning. I changed the name of the activity to "Go for Exemplary." The purpose remained the same: to unpack the levels of proficiency on the rubrics, but now instead of using the numbers (1–5) for the levels, I used descriptive language headings. The five levels were now described (from lowest to highest) as *not there, developing, acceptable, accomplished,* and *exemplary.*

First, as a whole class, we created a clear exemplar of "how to bake the perfect cake" so students could more clearly understand the differences between the levels. In this whole-class example, a *not there, developing, acceptable, accomplished,* and *exemplary* cake example was developed with both pictures and description. Following the whole-class example, each student then had to create his or her own example that began with "How to make the perfect _____." The students explained their own rubric through leveled visuals and descriptions.

Since the shift to using descriptive language, I have noticed that students are more engaged in the process of learning. The descriptive language has fostered more conversation about assignment criteria—specifically what is working for the students and where they can make improvements in future assignments. The students are also using descriptive language; therefore, the feedback becomes more useful.

Student reflections about the purpose of the activity made me realize that this was a worthwhile activity. Here's what a few of them said:

> Greg—"I understand how to do my best work and go for exemplary in my assignments."

> Bradley—"[I understand] how we will assess our work, but also how we can improve."

> Michelle—"We get the big picture of our assignments, how to succeed, and clear examples of work."

> Rylan—"[This assignment] shows expectations for the year. . . . I now know how to go for exemplary all year long!"

These reflections emphasize the process of learning and how the different levels represent progress toward the highest level. The process of teaching students how to use levels is time well spent and is essential for student success and investment. When students have a clear idea of assignment criteria and how levels are utilized, they understand how their own learning is assessed. I found students to be more invested in the assessment process and more motivated to learn. Ultimately students can own their learning, which creates a classroom environment where high standards for learning are clearly achievable.

How to Use Levels of Proficiency

Teachers vary in how they use levels in standards-based grading. There is no one right way; it only requires that the final grade determination accurately reflects students' true level of understanding as it relates to the standards. Teachers make decisions about how to use levels locally and must consider context. The ideal standards-based grading routines may not be possible if existing policies demand procedures that are less than desirable (such as the use of percentage grades, which I explore later in this section). Teachers, schools, and districts must make the best decisions they can within the limitations of their existing conditions, which are often outside their control.

When to Use Levels

The most immediate decision is whether to use the levels of proficiency on every summative assessment, only for performance assessments, or exclusively to determine the overall grade. Each possibility has advantages and limitations, and what is right for one school or district may not be right for another. Grade level (elementary, middle, or high school) is also an influential factor.

The advantage to using levels (0–4) on every assignment is that both teachers and students become comfortable with the practice of *holistic assessment*—making an overall judgment rather than evaluating specifics at a more granular level. Students (and parents) quickly learn that advanced doesn't mean perfect; students can make mistakes and still be advanced. The consistency of using one scale will undoubtedly make the formal report cards more consumable.

The disadvantage of exclusively using levels comes in the interpretation. While performance assessments and the corresponding rubrics align perfectly with the use of levels for specific assignments, ratio-based assessments (in which the score is the number correct versus the number asked) will require some interpretation. How many incorrect answers can a student have and still be at a 4? Are some questions more important than others? Does the fact that two students scored fifteen out of twenty mean they earn the same level even though each answered a different set of five questions incorrectly? By exclusively using levels, educators must develop and establish a set of rules that they can share with students and parents.

Assessment results must be transparent and relatively easy to interpret, so it must be obvious how students can achieve each level with any given assignment. To achieve accuracy with interpreting results, teachers can intentionally reorganize their assessments by standard so that each section relates to the standards rather than question type. Rather than each section focusing on a singular question type (such as multiple choice, long-answer, and so on), each section would anchor on the standards that are most closely connected and contain an appropriate sampling of all question types necessary to elicit accurate evidence of learning. In addition, within each section, teachers can intentionally sequence questions from novice to advanced so the proficiency levels are obvious within the assessment. Their progress determines their level. A limitation, of course, is that some questions may feel redundant since correctly answering advanced questions inherently requires proficiency in the previous levels; teachers would need to be mindful of this potential overlap.

The advantage to only using levels on performance assessments (and thereby using traditional ratio-based scores when counting correct and incorrect answers) is that teachers enhance alignment with the established success criteria articulated in the rubric, especially when they use a holistic rubric to make their overall judgments. *Analytical rubrics*—rubrics that separate each aspect of quality along the established levels—while invaluable for formative assessment, can lead to inconsistent application when used for grading. *Holistic rubrics,* on the other hand, are more useful for summative assessment because they increase consistency by reducing the number of classification combinations (Brookhart, 2013c). Rather than containing individual descriptions for each aspect of quality, the *holistic* rubric contains a holistic description of each level of proficiency; figure 8.2 (page 110) is an example of a holistic rubric for overall grading.

The disadvantage to using levels only on performance assessments is that students must navigate both levels and percentages. In the early stages of implementation, it may confuse students and parents to mentally bounce back and forth. For example, if one assignment earns a 3 while another assignment earns an 81 percent, it could be difficult for students and parents to know whether a subsequent assignment represents a drop or an increase in proficiency, or whether nothing has changed at all. As well, teachers may compromise student investment by making the process of clearly identifying overall proficiency awkward. That could lead to the teacher having to determine it for the student, which defeats the purpose of actively involving students in the first place.

Regardless of the local decision, the consistent application and use of the levels are critical. While the arguments on both sides of the each-and-every-assignment versus only-the-overall-grade discussion are valid, both sides would agree that clarity of process and consistency in application are non-negotiable.

When to Use Percentage Equivalents

A common dilemma many teachers face is fitting levels of proficiency in a system that only uses percentage grades. This could mean that the computerized grading program only accepts percentage grades or the summarizing and reporting system is driven by a policy based on percentage scores, or both. In any case, it may be necessary for teachers to determine a percentage equivalent from the levels of proficiency students demonstrate. This is more often related to overall judgments; however, teachers can use percentage equivalents on individual performance assessments and then convert them into a percentage score. Figure 8.4 illustrates how teachers can convert levels to percentage grades to determine the overall proficiency should a single grade be required.

Level	50 Percent = Pass	60 Percent = Pass	70 Percent = Pass
4.00	99	99	99
3.75	95	95	97
3.50	91	92	95
3.25	87	89	92
3.00	83	86	90
2.75	79	83	87
2.50	75	80	85
2.25	71	77	82
2.00	67	74	80
1.75	63	71	77
1.50	59	68	75
1.25	55	64	72
1.00	50	60	70

Figure 8.4: Percentage equivalents to levels.

Figure 8.4 only relates to converting levels into an overall percentage when it's absolutely necessary; I do *not* mean that there are thirteen levels of proficiency in the far-left column.

As well, notice that level 1 equates to the minimum passing level; anything below pass would be a level 0. This scale would only be used if a teacher was required to convert a 0–4 level to a percentage grade for entry into the electronic gradebook. Figure 8.5 provides an example of how this could be done.

How to Calculate With an Ounce of Tradition

Unless the grading and reporting system is purely standards based, some mathematical calculation may be necessary. There is theory, and then there is practice; sometimes when we put theory to practice, we must make compromises. In some cases, we can use an ounce of tradition—in this case, mean averaging—in the process of determining an overall score.

Consider the following scenario. In the example in figure 8.5, a teacher made an overall determination of a student's proficiency at the end of each unit.

Unit 1	Unit 2	Unit 3	Unit 4	Unit 5	Unit 6	Unit 7	Unit 8	Unit 9	Unit 10
2	3	4	3	3	2	4	3	3	2

4 = Advanced, 3 = Proficient, 2 = Developing, 1 = Novice, 0 = Insufficient

Figure 8.5: A student's proficiency in levels.

Given the ten units of study, and the levels for each unit, what percentage might this student earn in a system where 60 percent is the minimum passing level? A teacher may simply average the units of study together, assuming each unit is of equal importance, and then determine an equivalent along a traditional grading scale. In figure 8.5, the student's mean average level is 2.90, which the teacher decides equates to an 85 percent. How? Well, 2.90 is between 2.75 and 3.00 (see figure 8.4, page 121), which equate to an 81 percent and 86 percent, respectively. As 2.90 is slightly closer to 3.00 than 2.75, the teacher chose 85 percent instead of 84 percent. As readers will recall from the discussion in chapter 5, mean averaging is a viable mathematical calculation that, when used along a relatively small range, eliminates the impact of outlier scores and produces a fairly accurate picture. The limitation within figure 8.5 is that the teacher has organized the evidence by units, rather than standards. Nonetheless, levels within standards can work in an identical fashion.

Now imagine that within unit 2, a student fails to submit the requisite amount of evidence to justify a passing level (figure 8.6); this results in the teacher scoring unit 2 as an overall zero.

Unit 1	Unit 2	Unit 3	Unit 4	Unit 5	Unit 6	Unit 7	Unit 8	Unit 9	Unit 10
2	0	4	3	3	2	4	3	3	2

Figure 8.6: A student's proficiency in levels with a zero included.

The mean average of all ten units drops from 2.90 to 2.60, which on the percentage equivalent scale (figure 8.4) would likely result in an overall grade of 81 percent. The zero clearly results in a drop—as it should—but since the teacher determines the mean along a five-point scale, the zero does not act as an outlier that annihilates the student's score.

Keep in mind the examples in figures 8.5 and 8.6 do not represent ideal scenarios. The reality is that many schools still operate on the percentage system, so teachers must find acceptable alternatives that allow a standards-based approach within what appears to be a traditional system. Organizing instruction and evidence by units does not account for the fact that some standards will overlap into more than one unit. Organizing instruction and evidence by standards is preferable and prevents this overlap on standards that longitudinally run through an entire curriculum. This is critical if students are to earn full credit for meeting standards regardless of how low or slow the start; once mastery is reached, it's irrelevant how long it took to get there.

How to Bring Parents on Board

Moving to levels of proficiency represents a monumental shift in mindset for parents, especially if the new system uses levels on report cards. Schools that use levels to determine percentage increments will have a little less to explain, but no matter what, they must ensure that grade determination is transparent. Even with a hybrid system in place (and parents don't see any tangible evidence of a move to levels), parents must know that the grades they see accurately reflect their children's true level of understanding in the moment.

One way to help parents is to use simple examples from outside the school context. As I mentioned in chapter 1, the example of swimming programs is a great way to explain the levels of learning; swimmers achieve each level regardless of how slow they started. It's not that the concept of levels is beyond parents' comprehension; however, parents' own experiences as students, along with those of their children, affect their perceptions. At first, many parents may attempt to equate a level with a traditional grade (for example, they may ask if developing is the same as a C), which, again, makes communicating the differences between levels and traditional grades—and the process for determining them—all the more critical.

Bringing clarity to the shift from traditional percentage increments to levels of proficiency is mostly an issue of time. First, take the time to ensure that parents have ample opportunity to understand the intimacies of this shift through multiple points of communication. Open houses, newsletters, blog posts, and emails (to name a few) can all contribute to parents' eventual understanding of the new language of learning. Second, allow parents time to digest the change. In this case, the saying "slowing down to speed up" holds true. The most effective communication plan is one where the teachers or school leaders strategically spread out the multiple points of communication. This gives parents time to consume the information and ask questions; it also provides teachers, schools, and districts time to tailor the communication to the needs parents identify in their questions. Being thorough and purposeful will go a long way in eliminating the many potential hiccups along this important transition.

Conclusion

Moving to levels of proficiency will represent a fundamental change to the way teachers view the quality of student work. On the surface, A–F grading is no different than 0–4 grading since both are nothing more than symbols used to summarize learning; what separates the two are the mechanics behind their determination. In the traditional system, A–F is assigned via predetermined percentage increments based typically on mean averages, while levels of quality are a full reflection of student proficiency regardless of how low or slow the start.

The number of levels is not as critical as being able to clearly distinguish between the levels, though two to seven levels seems to be most common. Once the number of levels is agreed upon, schools or districts must then define the levels by establishing a sequential learning progression that shows a logical path to proficiency. The distinctions between levels need to be relatively obvious to make clear the necessary steps that will move a student from one level to the next. With fewer levels, the progression through the levels may not be immediate as it would be with an increase in the accumulation of points that mathematically impact the percentage of points attained. Progression through levels is likely to be more methodical, yet more permanent as specific performance criteria are detailed and overt.

The move to levels is most desirable; however, some schools and districts are dealing with grading policies and processes beyond their control. It may seem futile to even consider levels if, for example, a state or province demands percentage-based grades. Even so, using levels up to the point of reporting is still possible with equivalent scales that allow the reporting of percentage-based grades based on levels of proficiency. Here is where the standards-based mindset comes to life; the mechanics behind the achievement are level-based while the optics of reporting are percentage-based. These workarounds are the reality of systems in transition and, at the very least, represent meaningful steps forward toward a more aligned system.

QUESTIONS FOR LEARNING TEAMS

1. What quote or passage represents your biggest takeaway from chapter 8? What immediate action will you take as a result of this takeaway? Explain both to your team.

2. Choose one of the subjects you teach. How would you explain the overall differences between an advanced, proficient, developing, and novice student in that class?

3. What aspects of your instructional routines would make it easier for students to understand the concept of grading on levels? Are there any aspects that could potentially be inhibitors?

4. Do you favor using levels on every assignment or just for an overall determination of proficiency? Explain.

Visit **go.solution-tree.com/assessment** *for free reproducible versions of the questions for learning teams.*

CHAPTER 9

How to Teach and Assess Student Attributes and Competencies

If our objective is to improve student behavior, then our first obligation as teachers and leaders is to describe with clarity and specificity the behavior that we wish to achieve.

—Douglas Reeves

A prevailing fear among those who resist moving from traditional to standards-based grading is that eliminating important attributes from proficiency grades—characteristics and habits such as respect, punctuality, responsibility, and so on—will cause teachers to marginalize them, if not ignore them altogether. If educators are serious about their importance, then being proactive and purposeful in developing these traits, rather than simply punishing students for not having them, must become a priority.

While some attributes are universal (such as responsibility), much of what schools teach and assess should be contextually driven, representing the attributes the school, district, or community at large believe are important for students to develop. Schools would be wise not to simply adopt the first example of important attributes they find on the web, but rather develop a list of attributes of their own. Examples from other schools can certainly guide them, but if teachers and students are to connect with the attributes on a deeper level and understand their importance, the process of developing the attributes is as important as the final product.

Teaching attributes separately aligns with the grading true north. It passes the accuracy test because it ensures that subject grades only reflect learning and important student attributes receive the attention they deserve. It also passes the confidence test, as it helps students know what it takes to develop and sustain habits for lifelong success, which are every bit as important as subject-specific proficiency to ensure that they are prepared to take on the challenges of college or career.

How to Determine Student Attributes

We can say we want students to be ready for success in college or their chosen career, but unless we identify what that means and teach it, the proclamation is nothing more than lip service. If we're serious about this, the first step is to identify which attributes matter and what the success criteria are within those attributes. In this section, I identify several universally accepted attributes along with examples of success criteria that teachers could use for assessment purposes. I discuss the assessment of the attributes in more depth in the subsequent section.

Responsibility

More than any other attribute, teachers reference responsibility most often as they explore the possibility of moving to standards-based grading. No one would argue against students learning to be responsible, but intentionally confronting what that actually means is the only way to enable students to identify specific elements of responsibility that need attention. Following are some specific examples of what student responsibility looks like.

- The student has a strong attendance record.
- The student arrives to class on time and prepared to learn.
- The student reports planned absences in advance.
- The student reports unplanned absences the day of and provides verification upon returning to school.
- The student submits work on time.
- The student makes up missing work in a timely manner.
- The student follows through on commitments and shows integrity and reliability.
- The student resists blaming others for things within his or her control.

Admittedly, the age of the student influences how much responsibility he or she can be reasonably expected to show and may also influence how much teaching of responsibility happens at home. For very young students (K–3) the focus, for example, may be on responsibility as it relates to personal character when no one is watching since other issues (such as attendance) are likely beyond their control.

Respect

It is hard to imagine a school that doesn't expect students to be respectful of themselves, others, adults, the learning environment, and physical property. The expectation may be universal, but the process for teaching it to students is not. Some schools expect respect but fail to take any measures to help students close the gap between their demonstrated actions and the desired behavior; others, of course, take the same proactive instructional approach to respect as they would with mathematics, language arts, or any other subject. Following are some specific examples of what respectful student behavior looks like.

- Students show respect for themselves by dressing, speaking, and acting in accordance with the established norms within the school setting, as well as through honesty and integrity.

- Students show respect for themselves by attending all classes, being prepared to learn, and staying current with all schoolwork.

- Students show respect for others by keeping their hands to themselves, using appropriate language, and being courteous to the people around them.

- Students show respect for others by sharing equipment, taking turns, and following the appropriate safety guidelines both inside and outside the school.

- Students show respect for school property by cleaning up after themselves and putting trash in the appropriate containers.

- Students show respect for school property by using equipment and furniture only in the manner for which it was intended.

- Students show respect for learning through attentive listening and by following directions.

- Students show respect for learning by recognizing that others may need extra time and support, and by contributing positively to the learning of others.

Citizenship

While similar to respect, citizenship tends to focus on the bigger picture both in and out of school, such as how the student contributes to the greater good. Within the school, students follow through with their individual duties as well as contribute to a more positive experience for others. Outside school, students fulfill their responsibilities and are positive ambassadors for the school. While the specific definition of what it means to be a good citizen will undoubtedly need to be defined at the local level, there are some characteristics that most schools would agree define what being a good citizen is all about.

- Students work for the betterment of others, even in cases where the benefit to them is minimal.

- Students demonstrate ethical and moral behavior that aligns with school, community, or cultural norms.

- Students have integrity (do what they say they're going to do), and are honest and trustworthy.

- Students are willing to take on more than their fair share of the workload in order to complete a project that has a non-negotiable timeline.

- Students volunteer their time beyond the regular hours of school to assist with optional activities or opportunities.

- Students recognize that every student has a right to an education and work to enhance (not interfere with) the learning of others.

- Students are inclusive and work to make all students feel welcome and appreciated.

- Students are proactive in resolving conflicts and overcoming difficulties within groups.

Work Ethic

As the nuts and bolts of the attributes, many see work ethic as the great equalizer and the key to developing a growth mindset. Developing a strong work ethic can overcome shortcomings and allow students to push through their inevitable stumbles on the path to success. Work ethic really is nothing more than a decision to stay focused, push through, and persevere. As we discussed in chapter 2, confidence is a factor that influences how willing a student is to work; however, the initial successes that emerge from a strong work ethic could also help develop students' optimism about future learning that may appear, at first glance, to be out of reach. Work ethic could entail the following characteristics.

- The student completes all of the required assignments to the best of his or her ability.

- The student submits all assignments on or before the established deadline.

- The student is both neat and thorough when completing assignments.

- The student arrives to class on time, has all of the necessary materials, and is ready to learn.

- The student is an active participant in the activities related to the lesson.

- The student perseveres through challenging tasks and views initial failures as steps toward a resolution.

Organization

Schools may choose to be more specific about certain attributes, like organization. For elementary and middle school students, these more basic attributes may serve as a solid foundation for complex attributes. High schools often choose to embed organization within more broad-based attributes like work ethic or career readiness. Being disorganized exacerbates the challenge of reaching academic proficiency. By focusing on specific characteristics of organization, schools can guide students to a more efficient and effective school experience. Organization includes the following characteristics.

- The student uses class time wisely.

- The student is able to plan ahead to coordinate the completion of multiple tasks or projects.

- The student easily retrieves information and notes from previous lessons.

- The student communicates potential challenges to work completion ahead of the pending deadline.

- The student sets regular routines for review and study.

- The student balances both curricular and extracurricular responsibilities.

Personal Reflection: Separating Attributes From Proficiency Grades

My first attempt at separating attributes from proficiency grades was, admittedly, quite pedestrian. I possessed neither the fluency nor capacity to implement a sophisticated system; I was just learning myself. At the time, our school had no established criteria, no formal instructional process, and certainly no frequency scale to assess and report. We did, however, have something called *work habits* where students would be rated as either good (G), satisfactory (S), or unsatisfactory (U). Despite this existing structure that *could* have lent itself nicely to creating a more robust system, it didn't. I, like most of my colleagues, often attributed the work habit rating to the grade that was earned. A student who earned an A or B would likely be rated a G; a C+ or C would equate to an S; while a C– down to an F would earn a U.

As an administrator, I had the opportunity to review a good portion of the report cards during each reporting period. As I started to shift my mind to a *real* separation between grades and work habits, the inconsistencies became more obvious. For example, a student might have earned an A and been rated a G, but then have anecdotal comments that referenced poor organization, a less-than-desirable attitude, or marginal work habits. As I started to wrap my head around the idea of separating student attributes, these mixed messages became more prominent.

The big lessons for me were twofold: First, it is clearly more advantageous to have a proactive process that treats the attributes as a separate, yet equal part of the summative paradigm. Second, in the absence of a more formal process, much can be accomplished in creating a culture that has the mindset of separation. Despite the lack of established criteria, several of the schools I worked in began to talk about the reality of a student earning an A but being rated as an S or even a U in terms of work habits; that discrepancy would be addressed in the anecdotal comments. Parents and students began to see—and feel—that the work habits were now a more serious part of our overall assessment of student performance.

As we became more comfortable with the separation, the grade-level teams (in middle school) and our departments (high school) began the process of establishing some criteria related to the G-S-U rating. None of it was as sophisticated as so many of the examples now available, but it was a start, which is really the point. Establishing formal routines takes time as agreements pertaining to criteria, process, and methods have to be secured. That said, this mindset of separation is something any teacher can begin tomorrow by simply disconnecting proficiency and habits; disconnecting from the idea that achievement is a simple function of effort.

The decision about which attributes matter is a local one. Schools face some difficult decisions about what they will or won't include. Once they have made the decision, the next step is to agree on a performance scale to assess the attributes.

How to Assess Student Attributes

If teachers intentionally develop these important student attributes, they are responsible for assessing them and informing parents about the level of proficiency their children have reached. If they don't, they send the signal that the attributes don't really matter. The assessment of student attributes follows the same fundamental pattern as that of academic skills: identify the learning goal and success criteria, create a progression toward proficiency, and provide feedback to students along the way to accelerate their progress.

Clear Performance Criteria

Once teachers have decided what attributes matter, then they must establish clear performance criteria. Some schools may take a more holistic approach while others choose a detailed and specific method. Figure 9.1 shows an example of an expectations rubric from Spring Garden Middle School in St. Joseph, Missouri. Rather than identifying specific categories, Spring Garden Middle School took a holistic approach by combining the desired attributes. This is certainly efficient in that it allows teachers to make an overall determination of advanced, proficient, and so on, based on numerous attributes, rather than making discrete distinctions between specific characteristics.

Advanced **4**	• Acts as a leader or exemplary team member • Always values and encourages all members of team • Always demonstrates both respectful and helpful behaviors with peers and staff • Always engages in learning activities and strives to reach full potential to ensure tasks are well done • Always prepared with appropriate and needed materials • Always completes tasks and meets due dates
Proficient **3**	• Acts as a team member • Values and encourages team members • Demonstrates both respectful and helpful behaviors with peers and staff without prompting • Engages in learning activities and seeks assistance as necessary • Prepared with appropriate and needed materials • Completes tasks and meets due dates
Basic **2**	• Participates minimally and requires some prompting as a team member • Sometimes values and encourages team members • Sometimes demonstrates both respectful and helpful behaviors with peers and staff with limited prompting • Sometimes engages in learning activities and occasionally seeks necessary assistance • Sometimes prepared with appropriate and needed materials • Sometimes completes tasks and meets due dates
Below Basic **1**	• Rarely participates in team activities • Rarely values and encourages team members • Rarely demonstrates both respectful and helpful behaviors with peers and staff • Rarely engages in learning activities, nor seeks necessary assistance • Rarely prepared with appropriate and needed materials • Rarely completes tasks and meets due dates

Source: Reprinted with permission from Spring Garden Middle School, St. Joseph, Missouri.

Figure 9.1: Spring Garden Middle School expectations rubric.

By contrast, the Calgary Board of Education (CBE) has separated the attributes and taken a more specific approach to identifying the important attributes it expects schools to develop in their students. Figure 9.2 outlines what the Calgary Board of Education refers to as *results 3, 4, and 5*, which, along with *result 1* (the mission to enable students for success after graduation) and *result 2* (maximizing academic success), form the strategic focus for the district.

CBE Results	Specific Outcomes
Result 3: Citizenship in learning Each student will be a responsible citizen.	Students will: 3.1. Participate in developing and maintaining our Canadian civil, democratic society 3.2. Understand the rights and responsibilities of citizenship in local, national, and international contexts 3.3. Respect and embrace diversity 3.4. Be responsible stewards of the environment by contributing to its quality and sustainability
Result 4: Personal development through learning Each student will identify and actively develop individual gifts, talents, and interests.	Students will: 4.1. Demonstrate resilience and perseverance to overcome failure and adapt to change 4.2. Take initiative, set goals, self-evaluate, and strive to continuously improve 4.3. Have the confidence to embrace ambiguity and complexity 4.4. Take risks appropriately 4.5. Make lifestyle choices based upon healthy attitudes and actions, and be able to assume responsibility for personal well-being 4.6. Be able to lead and follow, as appropriate, and to develop and maintain positive relationships with other individuals and groups in order to manage conflict and to reach consensus in the pursuit of common goals
Result 5: Character in learning Each student will demonstrate good character.	Students will: 5.1. Possess the strength of character to do what is right 5.2. Act morally with wisdom 5.3. Balance individual concerns with the rights and needs of others

Source: Reproduced with permission from the Calgary Board of Education, the copyright holder.

Figure 9.2: Calgary Board of Education results 3, 4, and 5.

Students are assessed on the four-level scale of *EX* (exemplary strengths), *EV* (evident strengths), *EM* (emerging strengths), and *SR* (support required). While the results (attributes) are universal, each school establishes more specific success criteria to fit the age and maturity of their students.

The Hawaii State Department of Education has also taken a specific approach to what they refer to as *general learning outcomes* (GLOs). They expect each school to focus on six GLOs, which lead students to be (1) self-directed learners, (2) community contributors, (3) complex thinkers, (4) quality producers, (5) effective communicators, and (6) effective and ethical users of technology. Each GLO has its own corresponding rubric that specifically outlines both the success criteria and the corresponding levels. Figure 9.3 shows an example of the specific rubric developed by the Hawaii State Department of Education to assess students as self-directed learners.

Indicators	Consistently Demonstrates 4	Usually Demonstrates 3	Sometimes Demonstrates 2	Rarely Demonstrates 1
Sets priorities and establishes achievable goals and personal plans for learning*	Consistently sets challenging, achievable goals and personal plans for learning Consistently sets priorities to achieve goals Develops a thorough action plan for short- and long-range learning goals (in pursuit of career choices)	Usually sets achievable goals and personal plans for learning Usually sets priorities to achieve goals Develops an adequate action plan for short- and long-range learning goals (in pursuit of career choices)	Sets achievable goals and personal plans for learning with moderate assistance Sets priorities to achieve goals with moderate assistance Develops an incomplete action plan for short- and long-range learning goals (in pursuit of career choices)	Sets achievable goals and personal plans for learning with ongoing assistance Sets priorities to achieve goals with ongoing assistance Unable to develop short- and long-range learning goals (in pursuit of career choices)
Plans and manages time and resources to achieve goals	Consistently manages time and resources in an efficient manner to achieve goals Consistently uses a variety of credible and relevant resources	Usually manages time and resources in an efficient manner to achieve goals Usually uses a variety of credible and relevant resources	Manages time and resources with moderate assistance to achieve goals Sometimes uses a variety of credible and relevant resources	Manages time and resources with ongoing assistance to achieve goals Rarely uses a variety of credible and relevant resources
Monitors progress and evaluates learning experiences	Consistently checks on progress and learning experiences to resolve problems that may be interfering with learning	Usually checks on progress and learning experiences to resolve problems that may be interfering with learning	Checks on progress and learning experiences with moderate assistance to resolve problems that may be interfering with learning	Checks on progress and learning experiences with ongoing assistance to resolve problems that may be interfering with learning

*= Descriptors for grades 5 and 6; ** = Descriptors for grades 1–6.*

Source: Hawaii State Department of Education (2013), p. 1. Used with permission.

Figure 9.3: Rubric for GLO 1, self-directed learner.

Lara Gilpin (@DrLGilpin), Principal, St. Joseph, Missouri

In 2010, Spring Garden Middle School transitioned from traditional grading practices to a standards-based system. In 2013, we implemented our Garden Expectations rubric that allowed behavior to become part of a student's grade. Students who were well behaved and completed tasks could receive an advanced or proficient mark, even if they were unable to meet the required academic standards at that level. The separation between our academic grading scale and our nonacademic grading scale has allowed our staff to measure a separate set of skills that can be an asset or inhibit student success within the classroom or workforce.

How has incorporating a nonacademic mark influenced our students, parents, staff, and the overall culture of SGMS? Ionya Sharp, a teacher, says that "assigning students a nonacademic mark gives me an opportunity to reflect on the behaviors that are affecting student progress. This reflection aids conversations that I have with my students to help them see the relationship between their behavior and academic success." Veteran teacher Melody Townsend believes that "in using nonacademic marks, students and parents are given a true picture of the whole child and can accurately reflect on learning separate from behaviors."

Angie Klaassen, a publication teacher, uses the school expectations rubric for student reflection and teacher feedback. One student reflected, "The reason I chose a four was because I worked very hard on a topic that I wasn't interested in. I have met all of my due dates and have plenty of pictures." Angie responded, "You really stepped up and took a story assignment that you didn't sign up for; I appreciate that! You put forth 100 percent effort into all that you do. Thanks for being a great example."

Kati Reid is a teacher who believes the culture of our school has been positively impacted by our nonacademic marks. She says, "Students understand that it is not just the subject content that is important to the school; the school also focuses on helping students develop as functional members of society or any social group." Our social studies staff believe that nonacademic marks reinforce consistent expected behaviors across the building and that if teachers feel the nonacademic mark is important, then students find it important too. The ultimate goal is that students will see work ethic and life skills as just as important as an academic mark.

As we continue to evolve at Spring Garden, we believe the separation of academic and nonacademic grading allows us to assess and communicate more accurately, not only on academic performance, but also within a nonacademic skill set that is imperative for success beyond the school setting. With continued professional practice and learning, we anticipate an increase in student reflection on nonacademic marks earned, thus helping students identify their strengths as well as the areas in which they need to grow. As a staff, we must explicitly teach and provide interventions for expected nonacademic skills. We hope to continue to highlight the significance of how two important marks can impact school and future performance for our students.

Frequency Scales

If readers examine the scale used by the Hawaii State Department of Education (figure 9.3, page 132) more closely, they will notice that it uses a *frequency scale* for each level. While most academic rubrics focus on levels of quality, attribute-based rubrics often utilize frequency scales that focus on how consistent the performance is; the consistency with which a student displays the desired attribute is more important than the level of quality at one particular moment. The scale for Hawaii is *consistently, usually, sometimes,* and *rarely.* This type of frequency scale would not apply to most curricular standards since consistency is often based on counts, which is incongruent to quality with most demonstrations of proficiency. An exception to this may be a performance assessment in which behavioral frequency (such as maintaining eye contact with the audience during a presentation) is more applicable.

Figure 9.4 shows the elementary school global citizen rubric from The International School Yangon in Yangon, Myanmar. Two things stand out with this example. First is the use of the frequency scale. Second, the scale clearly defines the criteria. Not only does it list the desirable traits, but it defines each trait in student-friendly terms through "I can" statements. This tells students what they are striving for (attribute goals) and what reaching the goal would look like (success criteria). The more user friendly the rubric is, the more apt students are to use it in a meaningful way.

The use of frequency scales is more a preference than a requirement; schools can just as easily apply levels of quality to student attributes or behaviorally based performance standards. Each scale has both advantages. One potential disadvantage of a frequency scale is that it may deny students full credit for lately developed consistency. Imagine a student who begins the year with a very poor work ethic but finishes the last third of the school year at an exemplary level. Depending on the scale they use, teachers may not rate the student at the highest level. If, for example, the highest level is *always,* a teacher might decide that the student didn't *always* display an exemplary work ethic since the first part of the year was poor. This is not a reason to avoid frequency scales, but it is something to be mindful of when developing the process using the scale.

The advantage to using scales with levels of quality for student attributes is consistency. The move to standards-based grading can be challenging enough; if we employ levels as well as frequency scales, now we're asking stakeholders to navigate two scales instead of one. Another advantage to a levels scale is that it may more readily prevent the scenario I previously mentioned where the student reaches the exemplary level but doesn't receive full credit. When the highest level is advanced, teachers may be less inclined to count and more inclined to make an overall judgment based on recent displays by the student.

The disadvantage to using the same levels as with curricular standards is the potential misalignment with the assessment process. Again, it comes down to quality versus counts, which are unrelated in their applicability. Another disadvantage could be redundancy. In all likelihood, the levels of quality will reference frequency anyway; teachers will describe advanced students in terms of how consistent their displays of organization, work ethic, and responsibility are. As such, it may make more sense to simply embed a frequency scale within the levels.

Trait	Consistently	Usually	Sometimes	Rarely
Appreciation of the values, traditions, and perspectives of others I can be open minded and work with others who are different from me. I can appreciate and respect other cultures, nationalities, races, and the other gender.	• Consistently communicates, interacts, and works positively with individuals from different cultural groups • Seeks opportunities to collaborate or interact with those who have different values or perspectives from his or her own • Consistently demonstrates an awareness of and sensitivity to the dangers of stereotyping and cultural and gender bias	• Usually communicates, interacts, and works positively with individuals from different cultural groups • Usually seeks opportunities to collaborate or interact with those who have different values or perspectives from his or her own • Usually demonstrates an awareness of and sensitivity to the dangers of stereotyping and cultural and gender bias	• Sometimes communicates, interacts, and works positively with individuals from different cultural groups • Sometimes seeks opportunities to collaborate or interact with those who have different values or perspectives from his or her own • Sometimes engages in behaviors that demonstrate lack of awareness of or sensitivity to the dangers of stereotyping and cultural and gender bias	• Rarely communicates, interacts, or works effectively with individuals from different cultural groups • Rarely seeks opportunities to collaborate or interact with those who have different values or perspectives from his or her own • Engages in behaviors that demonstrate lack of awareness of or sensitivity to the dangers of stereotyping and cultural and gender bias
Honesty and integrity I can be truthful and honest.	• Consistently truthful in words and actions	• Usually truthful in words and actions	• Sometimes truthful in words and actions	• Rarely truthful in words and actions
Respect for others I can be fair and kind.	• Consistently uses words and actions that are fair and kind to others	• Usually uses words and actions that are fair and kind to others	• Sometimes uses words and actions that are fair and kind to others	• Rarely uses words and actions that are fair and kind to others
Care for the environment and welfare of the world community I can help others. I can help The International School Yangon, Yangon, or the world. I can take care of the environment.	• Consistently is willing and glad to help others • Consistently shows a commitment to taking care of or supporting the school and the local and global communities • Consistently takes care of this place	• Usually is willing and glad to help others • Usually shows a commitment to taking care of or supporting the school and the local and global communities • Usually takes care of this place	• Sometimes helps others—may require prompting or may not always be willing or glad to help • Sometimes shows a commitment to taking care of or supporting the school and the local and global communities • Sometimes takes care of this place	• Rarely helps others without complaining • Rarely shows care or support of the school and the local and global communities • Rarely takes care of this place

Source: The International School Yangon. Used with permission.

Figure 9.4: International School Yangon global citizen rubric.

Again, the decision is a local one. Our task is to be clear on which scale is most relevant given the specific context, why it's the most relevant, what each level represents, and how we can consistently apply the levels. As we discussed in chapter 5, frequency can play a role in determining student proficiency within specific curricular standards (the most frequent evidence). One school may decide, for consistency, that it will use the same four level descriptors for both proficiency and attributes; another may decide it's necessary to establish a clear distinction between the two processes. Both are correct as long as teachers align the decision to local mores.

A Look at Cross-Curricular Competencies

A set of student attributes that has emerged since the turn of the century is cross-curricular competencies. Also known as 21st century skills, these competencies represent a significant shift in emphasis for schools. While content standards remain an integral part of the instructional paradigm, these competencies have become equally important. Proficiency on 21st century skills gives students the ability to keep learning as well as adjust to an ever-changing reality (Kay, 2010). Initially, assessing these cross-curricular competencies may feel foreign, but the reality is that our assessment fundamentals are equally applicable regardless of what we assess.

What Are the 4Cs?

While each school district develops and emphasizes its own unique set of competencies, four competencies tend to be ubiquitous and serve as the core of competency-based learning. Often referred to as the *4Cs*—(1) critical thinking, (2) communication, (3) collaboration, and (4) creativity—these core competencies have almost universal acceptance as being essential for students to be successful in the modern, post-graduation world of the 21st century (Kay & Greenhill, 2013). School districts may emphasize additional competencies (such as cultural awareness or character development), but the 4Cs tend to form the foundation.

The truth is that the 4Cs are not new to teachers; we asked students in the 20th century to think critically, communicate, collaborate, and be creative. The difference is that these competencies once served as a means to acquire content. It was not necessary for teachers to develop formal performance criteria or to assess the competencies because schools did not claim to intentionally develop these skills in their students. The shift in emphasis means the competencies *are* an end; schools now use curricular content to develop skills within the competencies. The good news is that multiple curricular disciplines can develop these competencies, hence the label *cross-curricular competencies*; the mathematics teacher, the science teacher, the social studies teacher, and the English language arts teacher can all use the same performance criteria.

It is important to note that 21st century skills are most relevant within specific disciplines. The point, for example, is not to be abstractly creative, but to think with creative intent within a specific curricular discipline. This means that content proficiency is vital (as a means) for students to think critically or determine creative solutions. The reason surgeons can creatively resolve acute situations is that they have content mastery over the human body; the reason engineers can push the envelope of automobile design is because they have content mastery over how automobiles operate. The ability to assess both curricular content and cross-curricular competencies is essential in the new reality. In fact, we may need to assess them simultaneously, which requires both skill and finesse.

What Do We Assess?

The most salient point about assessing cross-curricular competencies is to be clear on what we are assessing and what success looks like, which means establishing transparent performance criteria. In doing so, teachers must ensure that they understand the differences between competencies as a means and as the end. Assigning a group project, for example, doesn't automatically translate into assessing collaboration; allowing students opportunities to creatively show what they know is not the same as intentionally assessing creativity. To be clear, there is nothing ill-advised about providing creative opportunities or group projects; it just doesn't automatically equate to developing the competencies within our students. We must do that with intent and purpose. Critical thinking and communication are relatively accessible competencies for teachers, while collaboration and creativity often present a greater challenge. Let's examine the latter two competencies in more detail.

How Do We Assess Collaboration?

Let's look at collaboration as an example. What is the difference between working in a group and developing collaborative skills? Table 9.1 shows, from an assessment perspective, the characteristics of group work versus collaboration.

Table 9.1: Assessing Group Work Versus Assessing Collaboration

Assessing Group Work	Assessing Collaboration
• Focus is on demonstrating proficiency with curricular content standards. • Contributions by individuals contribute a portion to one singular outcome or product. • An end product is the goal; the collective effort serves as a means.	• Focus is on demonstrating proficiency as an effective collaborator. • Contributions by individuals contribute to a collective goal and multiple outcomes. • The collaborative process is the goal; the end product serves as a means.

Assessing a group project and the collaboration itself can happen simultaneously. That is, a teacher can assess proficiency on content standards and assess the students' proficiency within the collaborative experience; they are mutually exclusive but can occur concurrently. When assessing collaboration, a teacher would consider the following processes embedded within effective collaborative efforts.

• Is the collaborative team able to determine roles and responsibilities?

• Does the collaborative team have an established process for holding each other accountable?

- Does the collaborative team have a self-assessment process for judging progress toward the common goal?

- Has the collaborative team established a process for managing and resolving conflict?

- Has the collaborative team established a protocol for consensus building?

- Does the collaborative team practice active listening during discussions, especially when differences of opinion arise?

The key to assessing collaboration is to establish specific, separate criteria. And the teacher must purposefully assign tasks that elicit the characteristics of effective collaborative teams.

How Do We Assess Creativity?

Creativity as a cross-curricular competency is about thinking with creative intent. In her book *Sparking Student Creativity*, Patti Drapeau (2014) writes that students who think creatively share the following characteristics. They:

- Express ideas other students don't think of
- Like to choose their own way of demonstrating understanding
- Ask questions that may seem off-topic or silly
- Enjoy open-ended assignments
- Prefer to discuss ideas rather than facts
- Prefer to try new ways of approaching a problem rather than accepted ways (p. 6)

Notice that nothing Drapeau refers to has anything to do with aesthetically appealing artwork. For teachers to establish a creative learning environment, Drapeau (2014) writes that teachers "must make teaching creativity intentional and explicit" (p. 7); to establish the habit of creative thinking, "students use creative thinking consistently and continually while engaged in authentic tasks with meaningful content in a safe environment" (p. 13).

Howard Gardner (2010) identifies creativity as one of the five important *minds* that teachers must cultivate for the future (the others being the disciplined, synthesizing, respectful, and ethical minds). Gardner (2010) emphasizes that educators should not see these minds as separate silos but as interlocking parts of a greater whole; synthesizing involves some discipline mastery as well as creativity. As he states so succinctly, "It's not possible to think outside the box unless you have a box" (p. 17). Gardner further illustrates this interconnectedness when he asserts an element of creativity is required when students synthesize, a process more often associated with critical thinking. That suggests an element of originality when one synthesizes. The point, again, is that creativity is more about mind and less about artistic demonstration. Developing our students' ability to think with creative intent requires unique criteria and purposeful assessment.

Like the collaboration–group work comparison, there is a difference between allowing creative opportunities and assessing creativity. Allowing students to show what they know through creative expression is a positive opportunity for students to use their talents and passions to demonstrate proficiency within content-specific standards, but it doesn't mean the teacher is actually assessing creativity. Table 9.2 outlines a few of the differences between providing creative opportunities and assessing creativity.

Table 9.2: Creative Opportunities Versus Assessing Creativity

Providing Creative Opportunities	Assessing Creativity
• The focus is on demonstrating proficiency with curricular content through creative expression. • Creativity is the means. • The assignment tends to focus more on atypical, aesthetically pleasing products as alternatives to traditional tests.	• The focus is on demonstrating proficiency as a creative thinker. • Creativity is the end. • The assignment tends to emphasize internal creativity over the production of creative products.

Now, despite how they appear in table 9.2, providing creative opportunities and assessing creativity are not necessarily mutually exclusive. It is quite possible for a teacher to provide creative opportunities and assess creativity simultaneously; the teacher simply has to ensure that the criteria for each are isolated and transparent. A science teacher could ask students to develop hypotheses related to climate change, which would require content mastery (that the student could present through creative means) and original thinking (creativity). A social studies teacher could have students create an advertising campaign to encourage more people to participate in the political process, which would require original thought, but would also demonstrate, through plausible alternatives, a deep understanding of the issue that students would creatively present through the specifics of the campaign message. It is possible for students to simultaneously reach content proficiency, show proficiency in a creative way, and demonstrate their creative thinking. Assignments that require students to either produce new ideas or reorganize existing ideas in a new way are more likely to foster creativity (Brookhart, 2013c).

Since our goal is to develop students into habitual creative thinkers, a frequency scale paired with clear criteria would be the most appropriate for summative purposes. For individual demonstrations, teachers may focus on a more specific scale (such as [4] uniquely creative, [3] creative, [2] generic, or [1] imitation) that identifies levels of creativity shown within the context of the individual assignment. For our purposes, reporting an overall judgment of the students' abilities to think creatively would be more beneficial if we emphasized frequency; how frequently does the student demonstrate the habits of creative thinkers? Establishing the specific characteristics along the levels of frequency (always, mostly, rarely, never) is the first step to establishing an environment that nurtures the attributes of creative thinkers as well as a process for assessing and reporting the development of these habits.

How Do We Assess the Competencies?

The assessment of cross-curricular competencies is only necessary if we collectively proclaim that we are intentionally developing these attributes in our students. We can't say, on the one hand, that we are progressive, 21st century schools that will develop the necessary skills, but establish no process for assessing (but not necessarily testing) and reporting students' progress within those skills. If we claim to develop critical thinkers, then we need to gather evidence to support that claim and illustrate how students are developing their cross-curricular competencies.

The critical step is narrowing the assessment criteria to a manageable amount and making them transparent for students. With clear criteria and purposeful execution, we can assess anything because the fundamentals of sound assessment are universally applicable.

How to Bring Parents on Board

Critical to the conversation with parents is making sure they understand why we have separated attributes and competencies from the proficiency grades. It can be helpful to relate this separation back to the grading true north of accuracy and confidence; proficiency grades are more accurate (and for them more clear) and students feel more confident about addressing growth areas in a transparent communication of current skill levels, both within curricular standards and for positive attributes and characteristics. When students understand the levels and how they can progress through them, they are more likely to respond with optimism.

Remember, what adults pay attention to is what students learn to believe is important; it's the same with the relationship between teachers and parents. Parents will quickly discover that teachers give lip service to the attributes without any meaningful action or purposeful instruction. Most parents will agree with the concept of the separation, but they will need to see action to ensure that the articulated attributes are a priority. No one would dispute the importance of the proficiency grade, but parents might argue that the attributes are more important for their children's ultimate success. Without overt evidence of attribute development, parents may be inclined to suggest that separating them makes matters worse.

The bottom line is that parents need to understand that proficiency grades don't always tell the whole story, even if the grade is satisfactory. From a traditional one-grade-per-subject paradigm, a high proficiency grade may actually mask a student's inconsistent work habits, disrespectful attitude, or limited collaborative skills. Likewise, low grades may overshadow a student's strong work ethic, respectful approach to learning and others, and his or her mastery at working collaboratively with others. Once parents see tangible evidence of purposeful action, they will feel increased comfort with the idea.

Conclusion

The claim to be teaching responsibility—or any other important attribute—without established criteria is hollow. If schools want to be taken seriously about their work in developing these lifelong attributes in students, then a more purposeful approach is required. While it is quite likely that the attributes and characteristics will be similar from school to school or district to district, there is much to be gained from the decisions about which attributes to focus on, and the subsequent success criteria being local and somewhat autonomous. Establishing some kind of focus will create the necessary alignment within (and throughout) all grade levels.

The fundamentals of sound assessment practices hold true, whether assessing proficiency, attributes, or cross-curricular competencies. Clear learning intentions and specific performance criteria (that allow for a wide variety of demonstrations), along with purposeful opportunities to develop the skills will be most productive. Knowing what competency is being assessed, what specific performance criteria are connected to proficiency within that competency, and what activity will elicit that specific performance is how we intentionally teach and assess competencies that are universally applicable across subject areas and in life after graduation.

QUESTIONS FOR LEARNING TEAMS

1. What quote or passage represents your biggest takeaway from chapter 9? What immediate action will you take as a result of this takeaway? Explain both to your team.

2. Given the age of the students you teach, which attributes are the most important? List your top three in order and then explain your reasoning. Do you already focus on any of those attributes with your students?

3. Would you prefer a different scale (frequency) or the same scale (proficiency) when assessing student attributes? If you already have a process in your school, do you think it needs any adjustment?

4. In addition to the 4Cs, are there any cross-curricular competencies that you think should be a priority for your school? Explain.

5. Do you think your parent community is ready to see student attributes separated from the proficiency grades? If not, what needs to happen in order to get them ready?

6. Do you think your parent community is ready to see cross-curricular competencies as a separate category on the report card? If not, what needs to happen in order to get them ready?

*Visit **go.solution-tree.com/assessment** for free reproducible versions of the questions for learning teams.*

CHAPTER 10

How to Use Standards-Based Reporting

On the basis of our belief that grades should show what a student knows and is able to do, we developed a policy for consistently and objectively reporting student academic achievement.

—Jeffrey Erickson

The more embedded the standards-based mindset is, the easier the transition to standards-based reporting becomes—not easy, but *easier*. The standards-based report card is ideally the last thing to change and ends the process of creating a fully standards-based instructional paradigm. Therefore, discussing standards-based reporting is premature without examining the purpose of reporting itself and the organization of evidence, which includes reorganizing the traditional gradebook. After we explore standards-based reporting, I conclude this chapter with a look at the importance of reporting progress, which is more about growth than achievement.

There is no one template for reporting by standards. Schools, districts, and even states and provinces have the opportunity to decide what it is they want to communicate and the format that communication takes on. I do not intend the examples within this chapter to be definitive; they are simply samples of what other schools or districts have done. What is right for one school may not be right for another, so the readers' goal should not be to find a template that they can quickly adopt; rather, they should aim to develop their own template, using those of other schools as guidelines for function and form.

Set the Stage for Standards-Based Reporting

With the endless possibilities available for how standards-based reporting might look, it is important to remain grounded in some non-negotiable fundamentals to ensure that the process remains on point—that the stage is set for maximum success of any standards-based reporting routine. These non-negotiable fundamentals include (1) defining one's purpose for grading and reporting, (2) organizing the evidence of learning by curricular standards, and (3) ensuring that whatever teachers send home to parents is user-friendly.

Define One's Purpose

When teachers do not explicitly state the purpose of the report card and what grades represent, the reader must interpret the meaning of grades. Not only do very few report cards explicitly state the purpose (Friedman & Frisbie, 1995), it is not uncommon for schools or districts to be vague or silent about grades, other than the fact that they will be given (McElligott & Brookhart, 2009). Vague or nonexistent statements about the grading and reporting process make it vulnerable to multiple interpretations from various stakeholders.

In *Developing Standards-Based Report Cards*, Thomas Guskey and Jane Bailey (2010) share six broad categories researchers have found educators often cite in response to the question, What is the purpose of grading and reporting? Those six categories are:

1. To communicate information about students' achievement to parents and others.

2. To provide information to students for self-evaluation.

3. To select, identify, or group students for certain educational paths or programs.

4. To provide incentives for students to learn.

5. To evaluate the effectiveness of instructional programs.

6. To provide evidence of students' lack of effort or inappropriate responsibility. (Guskey & Bailey, 2010, p. 27)

Debating the legitimacy of each of the categories is likely a healthy exercise for any group of educators, and while that isn't the purpose here, the six categories may help explore tension that could exist if all six were at play within one school. Even if, for argument's sake, teachers deem all six legitimate, the notion that any school or district could accomplish every category with one letter of the alphabet and a couple of comments is absurd. When teachers agree on the purpose of grading and reporting, they narrow their focus on what they want to accomplish.

Guskey and Bailey (2010) go on to suggest three important questions that, when answered, will clarify the purpose of grading and reporting for any school or district:

1. What information will be communicated in the report card?

2. Who is the primary audience for the information?

3. What is the intended goal of that communication? or How should that information be used? (p. 31)

Grading Dilemma: Balancing Interests

Sometimes what is most effective for students and parents is inversely proportional to what is most efficient for teachers. This is especially true with developing standards-based report cards. Reporting to parents is one of the most important aspects of the teaching profession, however, few aspects create more stress for teachers than report-card time. There is no question that traditional report cards are more efficient than standards-based report cards, however, efficiency gains are neutralized by a loss in effectiveness.

The dilemma is how to balance both. How do we develop a report card that provides more meaningful information about student learning without making the reporting process an impossible chore for teachers? Creating an efficient and effective report card is ideal, one where parents are thoroughly informed about their child's achievement and teachers experience a manageable workload. These decisions, as is often the case, will be considered in relation to the specific context.

- *What specific, unique aspects of your school or district must remain front and center while you develop your standards-based report card?*

- *How will you ensure that the balance between effectiveness and efficiency is achieved?*

Once teachers answer these questions with some specificity, the necessary structure of the actual report card becomes clearer. While it is certainly advantageous—even recommended—to state the purpose of grading and reporting explicitly on the report card, the real value lies in making sure all stakeholders are sure about what teachers intend to communicate with the report card.

If teachers do not state the purpose of the report card on the report card itself, it may be wise to develop (and make public) a policy that clearly defines the purpose of grading. Figure 10.1 (page 146) is an excerpt from the Grades 6–12 Grading and Assessment Procedures and Guidelines from the Denton Independent School District (ISD) in Denton, Texas. The policy is "intended to define the philosophy, purpose, and procedures behind the changes in secondary grading practices adopted by Denton ISD for the core content areas" (Denton Independent School District, 2014, p. 1). Specifically, I excerpt sections of that policy that explicitly state the district's beliefs about grading (section 2) and what grades are supposed to represent (section 3). Take note of how sections 2 and 3 pass both the accuracy and the confidence tests in terms of intention and how they both outline a set of guiding principles to fall back on.

Having a policy does not mean the process of aligning practices is quick or easy. But a policy that outlines the parameters of the grading procedures can decrease the chances of inconsistent application as long as teachers introduce it at the right time. The advantage of policies is forced compliance; everyone follows the same procedure. The downside is also forced compliance; now everyone has to do it instead of feeling compelled. Premature policy without a standards-based mindset can easily backfire. After teachers have firmly established the standards-based mindset, policies at their best make their grading and reporting routines definitive in the school or district.

Section 2: Beliefs and Practices Statements
"As secondary educators in Denton ISD, we are committed to grading practices that support the learning process, encourage student success, and accurately reflect student progress toward mastery of state standards, the Texas Essential Knowledge and Skills (TEKS)." (p. 1)
Section 3: Standards-Referenced Grades and Assessments
"Because we believe assessment is a process for providing feedback that influences learning and that grades should reflect mastery of standards, Denton ISD will support accuracy in grading through standards-referenced assignments and assessments." (p. 2)
"Denton ISD will enact a grading procedure that requires secondary classroom teachers to assign grades that reflect mastery of the TEKS or AP/IB course standards. This procedure is designed to communicate accurate information to parents and students regarding progress towards mastery." (p. 2)

Source: Reprinted with permission from the Denton Independent School District. Visit www.dentonisd.org/cms/lib /TX21000245/Centricity/Domain/7857/secondarygrading.pdf for a full version of the Denton ISD policy.

Figure 10.1: Denton ISD grading and assessment procedures and guidelines (2014–2015).

Nowhere in education do we try to say so much with so little than through traditional reporting methods. At the same time, we can, if we're not careful, attempt to say and accomplish too much with an overzealous, all-encompassing approach to standards-based grading. The report card can't be everything to everyone; a focus on purpose creates a more meaningful and manageable summative assessment experience for all involved.

Organize Evidence of Learning

In chapter 8, we discussed the idea of teachers reorganizing their assessments by standard (instead of question type) in order to create a more coherent and targeted reassessment experience. A further step—and one that truly sets the stage for standards-based reporting—is to reorganize the gradebook by standard. Without doing so, teachers run the risk of double dipping by combining old evidence and new evidence within the same standard. Clearly, the electronic gradebook each school or district uses dictates what is and isn't possible. This section is intentionally conceptual in nature, and I do not intend to endorse one grading program over another. Once the purpose of grading and reporting is clear, districts should seek electronic gradebooks that serve that purpose in the most effective and efficient manner.

Reorganizing the gradebook represents a fundamental shift in how it functions. Figure 10.2 (page 148) shows an example of a traditional gradebook organized by task types for an English language arts class. As a traditional gradebook, it includes a category for homework, which as we discussed in chapter 6 is a potential contributor to the inaccuracy of what teachers ultimately report about student achievement.

Personal Reflection: Electronic Gradebooks

The electronic gradebook has been, simultaneously, the best and worst invention in education. On the positive side, we have never been more clinically efficient with organizing our data. On the negative side, we've become collectively obsessed with numbers.

When I first started teaching in 1991, we didn't have an electronic gradebook. When students approached me at a moment's notice to ask, "Mr. Schimmer, what's my overall grade?" I would have no idea. I would have to flip to the back of my day planner to the pages where my class rosters and assessment results were stored and try to figure out, by hand, what the student's overall grade was. There was no instant access, no email at a push of a button (actually there was no email at all where I worked), and no real-time calculation.

Now, don't get me wrong, I was as excited about the advent of the electronic gradebook as anyone else. I *thought* it was only going to enhance my opportunity to track, organize, and manipulate assessment information, and while that was, true, I didn't anticipate losing the art of assessment (something we discussed in chapter 2), nor did I anticipate becoming so driven by percentages, which I did for a short period of time.

As advantageous as instant access can potentially be, I reflect now on whether it's necessary. How did students and parents survive all those years without having immediate online access to the overall grade? This is not about eliminating the electronic gradebooks as I know they are here to stay; this is a reflection based on the notion of *just because you can, doesn't mean you should.* New technology can enhance our experience, but it can also become a hindrance.

Is it necessary that parents have 24/7 access to our gradebooks when learning is so fluid and developmental? Do students *have to* know their overall grades whenever they demand it? To be clear, I'm not advocating that we keep secrets from parents, but I wonder if we are almost providing them too much information that can easily be misinterpreted. If we are going to use levels via the most recent or most frequent evidence then the calculations may be the definitive decision point. Instant access to gradebooks has made it more challenging for teachers to eliminate old evidence, as parents will undoubtedly ask, "Why did you remove those scores?"

Just as no one would advocate the elimination of cell phones, the Internet, or any other technological advancement, I'm not advocating the elimination of electronic gradebooks, but I am reflecting on whether we could use them more effectively and whether or not having parents log in to check grades almost daily is really positive, or does it exacerbate the mindset that grades equal learning?

The real challenge to accuracy here is the potential for overlapping evidence. The teacher could assign homework designed to introduce the students to the concept of irony, create an assignment focused on developing his or her students' understanding of irony, conduct a quiz on irony, give a test with a section (or multiple sections) about irony, and assign a major writing assignment that asks students to demonstrate how much they know about irony.

Major Writing and Projects	Tests	Quizzes	Assignments	Homework
35 percent	25 percent	15 percent	15 percent	10 percent

Figure 10.2: Traditional gradebook organization.

As a result, evidence of proficiency as it relates to irony is present in all five tasks. Through weighting and averaging, the teacher will combine the old evidence (homework) with the more recent evidence (major writing) to produce a grade most likely somewhere in the middle, assuming a positive growth trajectory.

That process will never produce an accurate grade because students will never earn full credit for what they come to know. With traditional gradebooks, teachers add a column for each corresponding assignment. With standards-based gradebooks, teachers consider the evidence more holistically and decide whether the current level needs adjusting. Teachers can set up a standards-based gradebook at the beginning of the year or term since they need add nothing later. That said, some teachers may insert levels or scores for individual assignments rather than storing them in a portfolio. This is not about sloppy record keeping. It does allow information about student proficiency to be readily available should anyone inquire how they determined a grade.

Figure 10.3 represents an example of how a teacher could organize a standards-based gradebook. It uses the grade 7 mathematics domains as outlined in the Common Core State Standards for mathematics (NGA & CCSSO, 2010b); however, this reorganization works with virtually any curriculum guide organized by standard or outcome.

Bin 1	Bin 2	Bin 3	Bin 4	Bin 5
Ratios and Proportional Relationships	The Number System	Expressions and Equations	Geometry	Statistics and Probability
3 (Proficient)	2 (Developing)	3 (Proficient)	4 (Advanced)	2 (Emerging)

The levels represent the student's most recent or most frequent level of understanding, depending on the teacher's determination of what is most accurate. (See chapter 5.) The term bin *refers to the top layer of organization in the electronic gradebook. Bins here represent the standards.*

Source for domains: NGA & CCSSO, 2010b.

Figure 10.3: Standards-based gradebook example.

Each bin should contain specific evidence as it relates to the domain. The teacher determines the amount of evidence necessary for each domain; it could be all summative assignments, or the teacher could decide to limit the number based on, for example, the number of variations possible within each domain and the specific standards. Regardless of what the teacher decides, a final determination is necessary. The teacher could come to a conclusion holistically or, if he or she assessed each specific piece of evidence along the same scale, through a calculation (which I discuss later). Even if the choice is a calculation, the teacher (not the computer) still has the final say on the overall level that he or she reports.

The standards-based report card could have these five domains as headings, which would make it simple for the teacher to transfer the information from the gradebook to a report card. While that may not be specific enough, something we'll address later in this section, it does prevent the combination of unrelated evidence. Yes, it's all mathematics, but geometry and statistics and probability, for example, are separate concepts and require some differences in operation.

What if the report card requires a single-level grade? In this case, the teacher has a couple of options. First, he or she could look at the results and use the median result (which is 3) to determine the overall level; the teacher would then report that, overall, this student is proficient in mathematics. The teacher could also average the five levels. (Remember, the issue with averaging is that teachers calculate the mean along a wide range of results, which can create outliers; on a four- to seven-point scale there are no true outliers.) The average of the five is 2.8, meaning the teacher, assuming a slight margin of error, would likely round up and report proficient.

What if the report card requires a single letter grade? The conversion to a letter grade is quite simple if the school has redefined letter grades along proficiency levels. If *A* means advanced, *B* means proficient, *C* means developing, and *D* means novice, then the teacher would likely assign the student a B.

What if the report card requires a single percentage grade? In this case, the teacher could use an equivalency scale like the one I outline in figure 10.4. The average of the five domains is 2.8. On the equivalency scale where 60 percent is equal to a pass, a 2.8 equates to roughly an 84 percent. I cannot stress enough that teachers should only employ this conversion to percentages if their school or district requires it. Standards-based levels and percentages are not congruent and best avoided.

Level	Percentage Equivalent
4.00	99
3.75	95
3.50	92
3.25	89
3.00	86
2.75	83
2.50	80
2.25	77
2.00	74
1.75	71
1.50	68
1.25	64
1.00	60

Source: Adapted from Brookhart, 2013c.

Figure 10.4: Percentage equivalent scale.

For some, a gradebook or report card organized by domain heading may not be specific enough. Figure 10.5 illustrates how a teacher *could* organize a standards-based gradebook at one more layer of depth, which distinguishes among the specific topics underneath each domain. Instead of the five bins representing the five domains, this gradebook has the major topic headings within each domain, which provides a little more detail.

Mathematics Standards by Domain	Level
Ratios and Proportional Relationships	
(A) Analyze proportional relationships and use them to solve real-world and mathematical problems.	4—Advanced
The Number System	
(A) Apply and extend previous understandings of operations with fractions.	3—Proficient
Expressions and Equations	
(A) Use properties of operations to generate equivalent expressions.	3—Proficient
(B) Solve real-life and mathematical problems using numerical and algebraic expressions and equations.	2—Developing
Geometry	
(A) Draw, construct, and describe geometrical figures and describe the relationships between them.	3—Proficient
(B) Solve real-life and mathematical problems involving angle measure, area, surface area, and volume.	2—Developing
Statistics and Probability	
(A) Use random sampling to draw inferences about a population.	3—Proficient
(B) Draw informal comparative inferences about two populations.	2—Developing
(C) Investigate chance processes and develop, use, and evaluate probability models.	2—Developing
1. **Single-level determination:** Average of all nine levels is 2.67; teacher could determine that student is proficient or a 3. The teacher could also determine the student is developing or a 2 since the specific topics and skills that are at a greater level of sophistication are at the developing or 2 level. 2. **Letter grade:** With a 2.67, the equivalent letter grade could be a B or a C, depending on the way the evidence has emerged for this particular student. 3. **Percentage equivalent:** A 2.67 equates to an 81 percent (using the equivalency scale in figure 10.4, page 149).	

Source for standards: NGA & CCSSO, 2010b.

Figure 10.5: Standard-specific, standards-based gradebook.

Again, it's up to the teacher to determine how granular the evidence is within each of the major topics. Every task ensures that teachers consider all evidence, but limiting the sample size may be more conducive to using the most recent or most frequent performance. Remember, tasks overlap standards, so a standards-based approach is typically more aligned with standards-based evidence and organization.

For reporting purposes, the major topics ideally stand alone to provide a more specific level of proficiency without being lost in mathematical calculations or single-grade determinations. Teachers can use the numbers to guide decisions, but they must audit the accuracy of the numbers based on the student's actual evidence of learning and his or her trajectory of growth.

Still, some may feel that the major topics don't provide enough detail and may choose (staying with the grade 7 mathematics example) to list the twenty-four standards separately. Figure 10.6 shows levels with the twenty-four specific Common Core Mathematics Standards included. Included in figure 10.6 are the single level per standard using the process outlined earlier. Again, it would be ideal if the reporting by standards could mirror the gradebook in figure 10.5, but if combinations are required, then the single level may help with that process.

Mathematics Standards by Domain	Level
Ratios and Proportional Relationships	
7.RP.A.1: Compute unit rates associated with ratios of fractions, including ratios of lengths, areas, and other quantities measured in like or different units.	3—Proficient
7.RP.A.2: Recognize and represent proportional relationships between quantities.	3—Proficient
7.RP.A.3: Use proportional relationships to solve multistep ratio and percent problems.	2—Developing
The Number System	
7.NS.A.1: Apply and extend previous understandings of addition and subtraction to add and subtract rational numbers; represent addition and subtraction on a horizontal or vertical number line diagram.	3—Proficient
7.NS.A.2: Apply and extend previous understandings of multiplication and division and of fractions to multiply and divide rational numbers.	3—Proficient
7.NS.A.3: Solve real-world and mathematical problems involving the four operations with rational numbers.	3—Proficient
Expressions and Equations	
7.EE.A.1: Apply properties of operations as strategies to add, subtract, factor, and expand linear expressions with rational coefficients.	3—Proficient
7.EE.A.2: Understand that rewriting an expression in different forms in a problem context can shed light on the problem and how the quantities in it are related.	3—Proficient
7.EE.B.3: Solve multistep real-life and mathematical problems posed with positive and negative rational numbers in any form (whole numbers, fractions, and decimals), using tools strategically.	2—Developing
7.EE.B.4: Use variables to represent quantities in a real-world or mathematical problem, and construct simple equations and inequalities to solve problems by reasoning about the quantities.	2—Developing
Geometry	
7.G.A.1: Solve problems involving scale drawings of geometric figures, including computing actual lengths and areas from a scale drawing and reproducing a scale drawing at a different scale.	4—Advanced
7.G.A.2: Draw (freehand, with ruler and protractor, and with technology) geometric shapes with given conditions.	4—Advanced
7.G.A.3: Describe the two-dimensional figures that result from slicing three-dimensional figures, as in plane sections of right rectangular prisms and right rectangular pyramids.	3—Proficient

Figure 10.6: More detailed, standard-specific, standards-based gradebook.

Continued →

Mathematics Standards by Domain	Level
7.G.B.4: Know the formulas for the area and circumference of a circle and use them to solve problems; give an informal derivation of the relationship between the circumference and area of a circle.	2—Developing
7.G.B.5: Use facts about supplementary, complementary, vertical, and adjacent angles in a multistep problem to write and solve simple equations for an unknown angle in a figure.	3—Proficient
7.G.B.6: Solve real-world and mathematical problems involving area, volume, and surface area of two- and three-dimensional objects composed of triangles, quadrilaterals, polygons, cubes, and right prisms.	3—Proficient
Statistics and Probability	
7.SP.A.1: Understand that statistics can be used to gain information about a population by examining a sample of the population; generalizations about a population from a sample are valid only if the sample is representative of that population. Understand that random sampling tends to produce representative samples and support valid inferences.	3—Proficient
7.SP.A.2: Use data from a random sample to draw inferences about a population with an unknown characteristic of interest. Generate multiple samples (or simulated samples) of the same size to gauge the variation in estimates or predictions.	2—Developing
7.SP.B.3: Informally assess the degree of visual overlap of two numerical data distributions with similar variabilities, measuring the difference between the centers by expressing it as a multiple of a measure of variability.	2—Developing
7.SP.B.4: Use measures of center and measures of variability for numerical data from random samples to draw informal comparative inferences about two populations.	3—Proficient
7.SP.C.5: Understand that the probability of a chance event is a number between 0 and 1 that expresses the likelihood of the event occurring. Larger numbers indicate greater likelihood.	2—Developing
7.SP.C.6: Approximate the probability of a chance event by collecting data on the chance process that produces it and observing its long-run relative frequency, and predict the approximate relative frequency given the probability.	3—Proficient
7.SP.C.7: Develop a probability model and use it to find probabilities of events. Compare probabilities from a model to observed frequencies; if the agreement is not good, explain possible sources of the discrepancy.	3—Proficient
7.SP.C.8: Find probabilities of compound events using organized lists, tables, tree diagrams, and simulation.	2—Developing
1. **Single-level determination:** Average of all twenty-four levels is 3.0; teacher determines that student is proficient or a 3. 2. **Letter grade:** With a 3.0, the equivalent letter grade would be a B. 3. **Percentage equivalent:** A 3.0 equates to an 86 percent (using the equivalency scale in figure 10.4, page 149).	

Source for standards: NGA & CCSSO, 2010b.

As we discussed earlier, within each layer of the gradebook (figures 10.5 and 10.6), the teacher would likely add another layer of data collection to store and track individual scores on individual assignments. Teachers should accumulate information about student learning, but they must be cautious about linking the individual data to the layer above with a distinct algorithm. Grade determination and grade calculation are not the same thing; the numbers can help with decision making, but they should not be the final decision maker should an overall grade or level still be required by state or district policy.

Figure 10.7 illustrates a possible way to organize each layer of the gradebook. In this example, the specific standard 7.G.B.6 from figure 10.6 represents one bin within the gradebook.

7.G.B.6: Solve real-world and mathematical problems involving area, volume, and surface area of two- and three-dimensional objects composed of triangles, quadrilaterals, polygons, cubes, and right prisms.								3*
Area (3)**			Volume (3)**			Surface Area (2)**		
SA1	SA2	SA3	SA1	SA2	SA3	SA1	SA2	SA3
2***	3***	4***	3***	3***	3***	2***	2***	2***

SA = Summative assessment

*Represents the overall level within the entire standard (should that be necessary)
**Results represent a more specific level for each specific topic.
***Results on specific summative assessments. These could be entirely separate events or simply separate demonstrations within the same event (when organized by standards).

Source for standard: NGA & CCSSO, 2010b.

Figure 10.7: Gradebook example.

Figure 10.7 represents some implicit decisions. First, the teacher decided to limit the amount of evidence that would contribute to the overall summative grade to three items. This does not necessarily mean there would only be three summative moments, but only three would contribute to the grade. This allows the teacher to reflect on the most recent versus most frequent evidence in order to use only the most accurate. Second, the teacher uses the four-point scale (with numbers) on each demonstration. Third, the teacher did not go more specific and distinguish between two- or three-dimensional objects; nor did he or she identify the specific objects. Within the formative assessment paradigm, the teacher would likely need that very specific separation to pinpoint specific hurdles and challenges the student faces. But recording evidence at that grain size for summative purposes surpasses the necessary level for accurate decision making. On the summative assessments, the teacher would simply ensure that he or she represented two- and three-dimensional objects in the assignment, and that each specific object (triangle, quadrilaterals, and so on) appeared.

What if a number isn't necessary? Figure 10.8 (page 154) shows the same gradebook organization with level descriptors rather than numbers. Using descriptors may prevent over-reliance on mathematical calculations, but it may make the process of overall determination more cumbersome.

7.G.B.6: Solve real-world and mathematical problems involving area, volume, and surface area of two- and three-dimensional objects composed of triangles, quadrilaterals, polygons, cubes, and right prisms.								P
Area (P)			Volume (P)			Surface Area (D)		
SA1	SA2	SA3	SA1	SA2	SA3	SA1	SA2	SA3
D	P	A	P	P	P	D	D	D

A = Advanced; P = Proficient; D = Developing; N = Novice

Source for standard: NGA & CCSSO, 2010b.

Figure 10.8: Gradebook example with descriptors.

Erin Wilson (@ewilson_10), Teacher, Prince George, British Columbia

My first experience as a new teacher included a class of grade 9 students who had previously failed math in grade 8. Being a new teacher, I had little idea of how to assess students. My more experienced colleagues told me how to set up my gradebook; it was the usual tests, quizzes, assignments, and so on. Now with this group of students, many of them could pass the tests, but for a variety of reasons, could not (or would not) finish and submit the assignments. As the end of the year approached, I continued to pressure them, call home, hold them in at lunch, and do whatever I could to get them to finish the missing assignments; slowly, their overall grade would inch up to a pass. Meanwhile, I kept thinking, Why am I doing this? I know they understand the material because they passed the test, so what is the point of having them complete the missing assignments?

During my next teaching assignment, I met Cathy, a teacher who was also new to the school. At the beginning of the year, our department was discussing how to arrange our gradebooks; it was the typical assignments, tests, and quizzes set up. However, after some discussion, Cathy spoke up. She told us she had a different way of assessing and would not change back. We all listened intently, as we had never heard of another way of assessing students and organizing the gradebook. She explained how she assesses students based on their understanding of concepts, rather than on how many assignments they complete or how they perform on a quiz. This seemed to fit me perfectly. Why would I enter a low quiz mark for a student who may have missed the initial lesson? Usually by the test, the quiz mark was insignificant since students had since shown me their understanding.

One of the most difficult changes I had to make was how to set up my gradebook to work with my new approach to assessment. First, I looked closely at the curricular outcomes and decided how to combine them into some bigger ideas since it would have been overwhelming trying to give a mark for each one. I categorized the curricula into four or five big ideas as indicated in the curriculum. These would include things like number sense, patterns and relations, and trigonometry. Next, in my gradebook, I used these as the categories instead of the traditional categories I had used in the past. I used the curriculum guide's suggested time allotments to determine the weighting of each category. I then changed my gradebook so that I was entering marks for understanding of concepts such as "shows understanding of solving one-step equations" rather than labels like "chapter 2 test."

Next, I decided on a five-point scale for assessment of a student's understanding. A four means the student understands all concepts, while three means they understand most. A two means the student understands some of the concepts, while one and zero mean the student needs more practice. I also decided that some outcomes were more important than others, so I adjusted the weighting on each of the concepts. I did still enter marks for assignments and quizzes, however, that category was zero weighted because I considered them formative.

The next stage in my assessment transformation was to change the layout of my tests so that each concept was in a specific section of the test. That way, I could quickly know if a student understood each concept (and to what degree). I am still working on this, as the division isn't always clear, though I don't think it will ever be perfect. Instead of entering one test mark in my gradebook, I now enter as many marks as the number of concepts that particular test covers. Then I compare them with the formative work to check for anomalies. I might find, for example, a student performed well on a quiz but not on that same concept on the test. In this case, I would talk to the student to determine why this has happened and come up with a course of action so that the student can show understanding.

Admittedly, this is still a work in progress, but so far, this has worked well for me (and my students). I'm now more accurate in assessing my students' true understanding, and my reported grades are no longer a reflection of student work habits.

Make Report Cards User-Friendly for Parents

Throughout the book, I have discussed topics related to parents at the end of each chapter, and while that is still the case within this chapter, it's worth mentioning here that teachers should ensure that parents can easily consume any new reporting processes. Educators understand curricular standards and the processes for grading and reporting at an intimate level; parents won't. Most parents perceive the traditional report card as easy to understand and interpret. One may convince educators that a B calculated via a mean average doesn't say much at all about student proficiency, but many parents believe they know what it means. An important priority, then, must be to ensure that whatever replaces the traditional report card is as easily interpreted by parents.

When moving to a standards-based system, it is easy for educators to remain insular in focus and hypothesize about the rubrics, work samples, and the descriptive feedback that they can provide to parents. However, too much information leaves parents frustrated with their inability to interpret the report card. While the transition to standards-based reporting is in progress, it is wise to have a cross-section of parents involved with the early drafts of report card templates so that they might temper any overzealous attempts that turn the report card into an arduous document.

Examples of Standards-Based Reporting

The following report card examples illustrate how a school and a district decided to structure their standards-based report cards. They are not meant to be the definitive examples; they are simply samples that illustrate some of the key principles of standards-based reporting. Again, these should guide discussions; I don't recommend blindly adopting without first vetting them for alignment with one's individual context.

The first example (figures 10.9 and 10.10, pages 157–166) is an elementary school report card from The International School Yangon (ISY) in Yangon, Myanmar. The sample includes several positive attributes.

- The report card articulates its primary purpose immediately.

- Separate, stand-alone boxes contain both behaviors that support learning and the schoolwide learner results of being a global citizen, a successful communicator, a complex thinker, creative, and a lifelong learner.

- The scale for achievement is a 1–4 proficiency scale; the scale for behaviors is a frequency scale (the CUSR scale [consistently evident, usually evident, sometimes evident, and rarely evident]).

- The report card thoroughly explains the CUSR scale on the third page.

- The frequency scale uses U for usually; initially the school used an O for often, but parents were misreading it as a zero and mistakenly thinking their children were doing poorly.

- Teachers added an asterisk symbol (*) to indicate when grades carried over from the previous trimester and no assessments occurred in between.

- The school added separate proficiency levels to the world languages program because it assesses students on the standards that correlate with their language level (based on the American Council on the Teaching of Foreign Languages [ACTFL] proficiency levels).

While the ISY example (figure 10.10) and the Calgary Board of Education (CBE) example (figure 10.11, page 167) have much in common (such as standards-based, separate scales for proficiency and attributes), there is a slight difference to note. The ISY example is a school-based example whereas the CBE example is a districtwide report. As such, the CBE is more general in scope as it requires maximum applicability and consistency between schools. The broader the scope, the more generic a template will need to be since alignment and consistency will be paramount. Schools permitted to develop their own report card templates will likely be afforded the freedom to tailor the report to the specific needs of both the students

The International School Yangon
Elementary Report Card (Grades 2–5)

Student: _____   Grade: _____   School Year: _____
Teacher: _____   Principal: _____

The primary purpose for reporting is to communicate student achievement and behaviors that support learning. This report documents student performance within a period of time and provides information regarding strengths and areas to improve. The intent of this report is to provide a common understanding of your child's progress and to facilitate growth.

Behaviors That Support Learning	Trimester		
	I	II	III
Stays focused and uses time effectively			
Completes work and tasks			
Demonstrates organizational skills			
Resolves conflicts in appropriate ways			
Follows directions			
Works independently			
Seeks help when needed			
Actively participates in classroom activities			
Exhibits qualities of a growth mindset			
Trimester 1: Strengths and Areas to Improve—			
Trimester 2: Strengths and Areas to Improve—			
Trimester 3: Strengths and Areas to Improve—			

Figure 10.9: Report card from The International School Yangon.

Continued →

Expected Schoolwide Learner Results (ESLRs)	Trimester		
	I	II	III
Exhibits qualities of a global citizen			
Exhibits qualities of a successful communicator			
Demonstrates complex thinking and creativity			
Demonstrates qualities of a lifelong learner			

Mathematics	Trimester		
	I	II	III
Operations and algebraic thinking			
Numbers and operations			
Measurement and data			
Geometry			
Mathematical practices			

Trimester 1: Strengths and Areas to Improve—

Trimester 2: Strengths and Areas to Improve—

Trimester 3: Strengths and Areas to Improve—

Marking for Achievement, Behaviors That Support Learning, and ESLRs		
4	Exemplary	C	Consistently evident
3	Proficient	U	Usually evident
2	Partially proficient	S	Sometimes evident
1	Novice	R	Rarely evident
N/A	Not assessed	yes	Absences and tardiness
U/A	Unable to assess	no	Absences and tardiness
*	Grade is carried over from previous trimester. This area of learning was not addressed at this time.		

Absences and Tardiness

There are approximately sixty school days per reporting period.

	Trimester			
	I	II	III	Total
Days absent				
Absences affected learning.				
Days tardy				
Tardiness affected learning.				

Language Arts

	Trimester		
	I	II	III
Reading foundational skills			
Phonics, word recognition, and fluency			
Reading			
Literature			
Informational texts			
Writing			
Opinion and argument			
Narrative			
Informative			
Research			
Listening and speaking			
Comprehension and collaboration			
Presentation of knowledge and ideas			
Language			
Conventions of standard English			
Vocabulary acquisition and use			

Continued →

Trimester 1: Strengths and Areas to Improve—

Trimester 2: Strengths and Areas to Improve—

Trimester 3: Strengths and Areas to Improve—

Social Studies	Trimester		
	I	II	III
Change and conflict			
Culture and geography			
Government and economics			

Trimester 1: Strengths and Areas to Improve—

Trimester 2: Strengths and Areas to Improve—

Trimester 3: Strengths and Areas to Improve—

Science	Trimester		
	I	II	III
Physical science			
Earth and space sciences			
Life science			
Scientific inquiry and process			

Trimester 1: Strengths and Areas to Improve—

Trimester 2: Strengths and Areas to Improve—

Trimester 3: Strengths and Areas to Improve—

Physical Fitness and Health	Trimester		
	I	II	III
Behaviors that support learning (nonlearning attributes)			
Attainment of physical fitness			
Knowledge of physical fitness concepts			
Motor skills and movement			
Trimester 1: Physical Fitness Comments—			
Trimester 2: Physical Fitness Comments—			
Trimester 3: Physical Fitness Comments—			

World Languages B (French or Mandarin)	Trimester		
	I	II	III
Behaviors that support learning			
Language proficiency level			
Reading and writing			
Listening and speaking			
Trimester 1: World Languages B Comments—			
Trimester 2: World Languages B Comments—			
Trimester 3: World Languages B Comments—			

Continued →

Computer Technology	Trimester		
	I	II	III
Behaviors that support learning			
Digital citizenship			
Technology operations and concepts			
Trimester 1: Computer Technology Comments—			
Trimester 2: Computer Technology Comments—			
Trimester 3: Computer Technology Comments—			

Visual Arts	Trimester		
	I	II	III
Behaviors that support learning			
Creating art			
Perceiving and evaluating art			
Making visual art connections			
Trimester 1: Visual Arts Comments—			
Trimester 2: Visual Arts Comments—			
Trimester 3: Visual Arts Comments—			

Music	Trimester		
	I	II	III
Behaviors that support learning			
Creating music			
Producing and performing music			
Responding to and reflecting on music			
Trimester 1: Music Comments—			
Trimester 2: Music Comments—			
Trimester 3: Music Comments—			

Promoted to grade _____ for the _____ school year.

Teacher signature: _____ Principal signature: _____

Source: The International School Yangon, Yangon, Myanmar. Used with permission.

The International School Yangon Elementary Report Card Guide

Achievement Grade Descriptors

4	Exemplary	A 4 indicates the student demonstrates mastery, with excellence, of the grade-level standards with relative ease and consistency, and often exceeds the cognitive level of the standards. The student applies and extends the key concepts, processes, and skills of the grade level.
3	Proficient	A 3 indicates the student demonstrates mastery of grade-level standards at the cognitive level the standard is written. The student consistently grasps and applies key concepts, processes, and skills with limited errors.
2	Partially proficient	A 2 indicates the student demonstrates mastery of some grade-level standards. The student inconsistently grasps and applies some of the key concepts, processes, and skills with significant errors.
1	Novice	A 1 indicates the student has minimal understanding and does not meet grade-level standards. Performance is inconsistent even with guidance and support.
N/A	Not assessed	These standards or areas of learning have not been addressed at this time.
U/A	Unable to assess	Insufficient assessment data exist to make a fair evaluation of student performance of expectations.

Specialist Classes: Behaviors That Support Learning Grade Descriptors

C = Consistently evident U = Usually evident S = Sometimes evident R = Rarely evident	• On task, engaged with, and focused on learning without teacher influence • Exhibits a positive and respectful attitude toward class guidelines, class expectations, and classmates • Comes to class prepared in every way needed • On time for class and ready to begin learning

Expected Schoolwide Learner Results Descriptors

C = Consistently evident U = Usually evident S = Sometimes evident R = Rarely evident	Exhibits qualities of a successful communicator who … • Demonstrates the skills of effective collaboration (communicators) • Uses appropriate technology as a tool to convey ideas (communicators) • Writes, speaks, reads, and listens with purpose (communicators) • Is multilingual (communicators)	Exhibits qualities of a global citizen who … • Is environmentally aware and active (caring) • Contributes to the welfare of the world community (caring) • Respects the dignity and worth of others (principled, open minded) • Manifests the virtues of honesty and integrity (principled) • Understands and appreciates the values, traditions, and perspectives of others (open minded)
	Demonstrates complex thinking and creativity by … • Gathering, analyzing, and processing information from a variety of sources (thinkers) • Being an effective and creative problem solver (thinkers) • Being an effective decision maker (thinkers) • Pursuing inquiry and curiosity within learning (inquirers) • Building a foundation of knowledge and applying understandings to new situations (knowledgeable)	
	Demonstrates qualities of a lifelong learner who … • Takes responsibility for his or her learning (reflective) • Values all types of learning: academic, social, athletic, aesthetic, and emotional (balanced) • Has the confidence to take on new challenges (risk takers) • Gives thoughtful consideration to his or her own learning (reflective)	

World Languages B Proficiency Levels (French or Mandarin)

		Novice range of proficiency:
NL	Novice low	• Expresses self in conversations on very familiar topics using a variety of words, phrases, simple sentences, and questions
NM	Novice mid	• Understands simple words, phrases, and formulaic language; understands the meaning of the main idea from simple, highly predictable oral or written texts, with strong visual support
NH	Novice high	• Communicates information on very familiar topics using a variety of words, phrases, and sentences

Figure 10.10: Report card guide from The International School Yangon.

Continued →

IL	Intermediate low	Intermediate range of proficiency:
IM	Intermediate mid	• Expresses self and participates in conversations on familiar topics using sentences and series of sentences. Handles short social interactions in everyday situations by asking and answering a variety of questions. Can communicate about self, others, and everyday life
IH	Intermediate high	• Understands main ideas and some supporting details on familiar topics from a variety of texts • Communicates information and expresses own thoughts about familiar topics using sentences and series of sentences

Note: By the end of grade 5, students who have been enrolled in the French or Mandarin program since grade 1 with two 45-minute class sessions per week could potentially reach the novice-mid to novice-high levels of proficiency in all skills of communication (listening, speaking, reading, and writing) depending on a student's age, cognitive ability, level of literacy, and language performance in the student's mother tongue, and how similar the student's mother tongue language is to the new language.

Source: The International School Yangon, Yangon, Myanmar. Used with permission.

Calgary Board of Education Report Card

Last Name, First Name: _____   Grade: _____

Homeroom: _____   Alberta Education ID: _____

Indicator Legend

	Achievement of Alberta Program of Studies		Citizenship, Personal Development, Character Summative Indicators of Success	
4	Excellent	The student has demonstrated excellent achievement of grade-level expectations.	EX	Exemplary strengths
3	Good	The student has demonstrated good achievement of grade-level expectations.	EV	Evident strengths
2	Basic	The student has demonstrated basic achievement of grade-level expectations.	EM	Emerging strengths
1	Not meeting	The student is not meeting grade-level expectations.	SR	Network of support required
NER	No evaluation recorded	Insufficient evidence is available to be able to determine an accurate grade at this time.		
ELL	English language learning	The student's language proficiency level impacts the evaluation of achievement.		
IPP	Individual program plan (IPP)	Achievement of this report card outcome is reported through the student's Individual Program Plan (IPP).		
*4 *3 *2 *1	Modified	A numerical indicator with an asterisk (*1, *2, *3, or *4) is used when a student is formally identified with an Alberta Education Special Education code and is accessing modified programming. Modified means programming in which the learning outcomes are significantly different from the provincial curriculum and are specifically selected to meet students' special education needs. Student achievement has been evaluated against these modified learning outcomes.		

The use and processes of technology outcomes, as defined by Alberta Education Information and Communication Technology (ICT), are infused into core subjects and some other subjects and are included in the calculation of these marks. Citizenship, personal development, and character are integral parts of all programs and not separate courses.

*R3: Citizenship in Learning

Teachers:

Exercises democratic rights and responsibilities within the learning community	
Demonstrates respect and appreciation for diversity	
Works and collaborates effectively with others	

Continued →

Figure 10.11: Calgary Board of Education grade 9 report card.

	Report 1	Report 2
*R4: Personal Development Through Learning		
Teachers:		
Sets and works toward learning goals		
Engages in learning with confidence and persistence		
*R5: Character in Learning		
Teachers:		
Treats others with respect and compassion		
Makes responsible decisions		
English Language Arts 9		
Teachers:		
Reads to explore, construct and extend understanding		
Writes to develop, organize and express information and ideas		
Manages and evaluates information and ideas		
Constructs meaning and makes connections through speaking		
Constructs meaning and makes connections through listening		
Represents ideas and creates understanding through a variety of media		
Mathematics 9		
Teachers:		
Understands mathematical concepts and relationships		
Uses mathematical reasoning to analyze and solve problems		
Explores and develops strategies for mental mathematics and estimation		
Develops and applies appropriate and efficient strategies for computation		
Models, represents and communicates mathematical ideas		

Physical Education 9	Report 1	Report 2
Teachers:		
Performs and refines movement skills		
Cooperates to demonstrate fair play and teamwork		
Explores and applies strategies for leading a healthy, active life		

Science 9	Report 1	Report 2
Teachers:		
Understands and makes connections between concepts		
Analyzes and solves problems through scientific reasoning		
Develops skills for inquiry and communication		

Social Studies 9	Report 1	Report 2
Teachers:		
Demonstrates knowledge and understanding of citizenship and identity		
Explores events and issues from different points of view		
Demonstrates skills and processes for inquiry and research		
Communicates ideas in an informed and persuasive manner		

Drama 9	Report 1	Report 2
Teachers:		
Demonstrates individual and collaborative decision making that leads to creative expression		
Performs dramatic works with clarity and precision		
Analyzes, evaluates, and responds critically to dramatic works		

Continued →

Health and Life Skills 9	Report 1	Report 2
Teachers:		
Makes safe and healthy choices based on experiences and information		
Develops skills to form and maintain healthy relationships		
Explores roles and responsibilities to work toward life and learning goals		

Music 9	Report 1	Report 2
Teachers:		
Demonstrates technical ability with clarity and precision		
Analyzes, evaluates and responds critically to music		
Understands and expresses musical ideas		

Power Up Your Learning 9	Report 1	Report 2
Teachers:		
Explores and refines understandings of oneself as a learner		
Develops, adjusts and applies learning strategies, tools, and techniques		
Gathers, reflects on and responds to evidence of learning		

Career and Technology Foundations (CTF) Recreation Leadership 9	Report 1	Report 2
Teachers:		
Explores interests and skills in the design of approaches to challenges		
Creates a product, performance or service in response to challenges		
Appraises process, product and personal contribution in response to challenges		
Communicates and demonstrates knowledge and skills in response to challenges		

Attendance	Report 1	Report 2	Total
Number of days enrolled	90	91	181
Number of days late			
Number of days absent			
Attendance is calculated to the day report cards are printed. For a more accurate report, please call the school.			

Source: Reproduced with permission from Calgary Board of Education, the copyright holder.

and parents within their context. Elementary-level templates tend to be more granular and specific as they pertain to standards, attributes, and other competencies; secondary templates tend to be more generic since the diversity of course offerings and the variety of standards is considerable.

The Importance of Reporting Progress

Student progress (also referred to as *growth* or *improvement*) is another essential aspect of reporting that teachers can inadvertently overlook. Articulating the story of progress is arguably more important in a standards-based system, since improving from one level to the next entails much more than simply answering a greater percentage of questions correctly. Articulating the progress students make along their learning continuum can neutralize feelings of frustration, especially when the grade or level hasn't changed. Our grading true north insists that we maintain student confidence throughout the grading experience; intentionally reporting progress clearly passes the confidence test and allows students to know that they're getting closer to proficiency, even when they're not there yet.

Progress Versus Achievement

While certainly complementary, achievement and progress are not the same thing. *Achievement* refers to student proficiency as it relates to the curricular standards, while *progress* means how much the student has grown. The emphasis on reaching proficiency would have educators highlight achievement since there would be a consistent standard from which student achievement is measured, but the story of progress matters. No one wants highly proficient students to settle or struggling learners to become discouraged. Tracking individual progress and setting an expectation of growth allow teachers to personalize reporting within the standards-based instructional experience. Growth is relevant and somewhat tricky to report since less proficient students have the most room to grow, but making the most progress doesn't always equate to reaching the highest level of proficiency. As well, a highly proficient student may have little opportunity to show much growth since his or her achievement, from the start, was already close to the advanced level.

It's important that standards-based grades reference achievement because for them to be valid, teachers must derive grades from similar (if not the same) processes across the same subjects; however, they must also tell the story of progress so that students and parents can know that their trajectories are positive and proficiency is closer.

The Story of Progress

We need to tell the story of progress; how schools choose to tell that story is a local decision. Some may choose a formal, stand-alone section on the report card dedicated to showing the growth each student has made. Others may address progress more informally and separately from the formal report card. Some may do a little of both. The intent of this section is to provide a few salient points to consider when reflecting on how to report students' progress.

When Achievement Shows Progress

Certainly at the macrolevel, students indicate growth when they move to the next level of proficiency within a standard; a student who was at the developing level in the first reporting period but is now at the proficient level in the second reporting period clearly indicates both progress and achievement. While this does show growth, the downside is twofold. First, using achievement levels to show growth, especially within a standards-based system, is not specific enough. The change in levels does indicate improvement, but this omits the specifics of what improved, how it improved, and which aspects improved the most. Second, using achievement levels to show progress is not reliable for the majority of students. As we discussed earlier, with four overarching levels, much of the improvement occurs within the levels; again, moving up a level is not as simple as, say, moving from a 71 percent to a 74 percent. Waiting for a level change before indicating any progress fails to recognize the improvement students make along the way.

When Achievement Doesn't Show Progress

Even if the students' achievement levels do indicate growth, our process of reporting progress can't rely on that possibility. Progress is more granular than achievement because students take many progress steps on their journey to achieve. Purposefully reporting those smaller steps is a way to neutralize the cracks that may form in a student's optimism. Remember, for real confidence to develop, students must experience some—even small—success. While there are several ways teachers can report this progress, the comment boxes on formal report cards are a particularly useful one. With the standards already listed on the standards-based report card, the comment boxes can convey the more specific improvements the teacher noticed. Replacing comments like "worked on argumentative writing" with explanations like "has improved her ability to support her arguments with more relevant details" will allow both students and parents to see that, despite achievement levels remaining the same, the student is making progress.

When Achievement Is Low

We have students at the novice level who may, based on the evidence submitted so far, remain there for some time. For these students, the story of progress is even more critical, as frustration and hopelessness can quickly set in. Despite their lack of proficiency, these students must know that their trajectory is positive and inching closer to the threshold of the next level. To pass the accuracy test, our routines must stop short of giving students a false indication of their proficiency just to maintain confidence; it won't be real confidence if feedback isn't based on any real achievement indicators. On the other hand, to pass the confidence test, we must avoid exclusively reporting novice levels without any indication of how much closer the student might be to the next level. For low-achieving students, the story of progress must be an even higher priority.

A More Frequent, Less Formal Process for Reporting Growth

While the report card is certainly a place to tell the story of progress, it might be more effective (and more productive) to establish a more frequent, less formal process for communicating growth. While there is a place for formal pre- and postassessment information that shows growth on the achievement scale, the progress that really matters are the incremental steps students take toward proficiency. The story of progress may get lost on a report card, as most parents and students have a laser-like focus on proficiency grades. Developing a separate, more frequent, less formal process for reporting progress may allow student improvement to receive the attention it deserves.

Increasing the frequency prevents progress reporting from becoming an epic event since it reduces the scope of each increment. As well, using an informal process allows the story of progress to be more personal. However, informal should not be mistaken for arbitrary or random. If the story of progress becomes a predictable routine, both parents and students will see that the teacher is serious about the importance of progress. If the teacher pays no attention to progress, then students may dismiss it as, at best, a tangential part of their learning experience.

Teachers can report on progress using email, Google Docs, texting, student webpages, or even digital portfolios. Obviously they must account for privacy issues, but when they do, the options are endless. Texting, for example, allows the teacher and parents to send and read messages at their convenience. Parents may appreciate these smaller, more in-the-moment messages more because they know teachers are not required to send them. Teachers need not always communicate the story of progress through written correspondence, since many of our students' nonlinguistic demonstrations of learning can literally show the progress they're making. In our digital age, we can store much in the cloud and draw on it at a moment's notice to illustrate to parents their child's progress toward a final result (such as draft versions of writing or partially completed projects) or the final product or result itself.

Student Self-Reflection

Self-assessment has, as part of the broader formative assessment movement, emerged as an integral part of students' learning experiences (Brown & Harris, 2013). There is widespread agreement that self-assessment has a direct benefit to students, especially in terms of raising achievement, as the process of self-assessment teaches them the important self-regulatory skills that allow them to measure their work against the standards (Andrade, 2010; Black & Wiliam, 1998; Hattie & Timperley, 2007; Ramdass & Zimmerman, 2008). *How* attention to self-assessment improves learning is not yet clear (Wiliam, 2011).

Through self-assessment, students take more ownership and become the source of their own feedback by identifying for themselves the discrepancy between where they are now and where they're going. There is, however, a caveat. While self-assessment has much to offer in terms of improving student learning, it is not free of potential limitations and problems (Brown & Harris, 2013). Potential inaccuracies and a lack of content mastery (just to name a few possible problems) could compromise the integrity of the self-assessment process.

Teachers must remain active in the process to ensure that it has a maximum positive impact on the overall learning experience.

It is through the self-assessment process that students can identify the specific areas in which they have improved. If we design the instructional experience well and are consistently clear about establishing the learning goals, the targets that support those goals, and the success criteria for reaching proficiency (or higher), then students can have the opportunity to track their own story. This does not release the teacher of all responsibilities, but it does bring students in as partners. Crafting the story of progress is not complicated, and students can follow a simple formula by answering the following five questions.

1. Am I improving?

2. If so, what specific aspects have improved?

3. How will I ensure that I keep improving in those areas?

4. What am I still struggling with?

5. What are my next steps to improve within those areas of struggle?

Students' age and sophistication dictate whether teachers need to simplify the five questions; we want to avoid creating an additional hurdle. The point is that teachers can craft a regular, predictable routine of having students reflect on their improvements and then communicate their findings to others.

One place where students could tell their own story of progress is through a personal blog. Imagine students documenting their progress toward proficiency through blog posts. Now imagine the students' parents subscribing to that blog so that each new entry generates an email notification. Now imagine the parents reading the posts and following up with conversations at home about what's improved, what's being worked on, and what the next steps are. The teacher's responsibility now shifts to validating and verifying what the students have written to ensure its accuracy instead of drafting all the stories of progress for his or her entire class. Others can read these blog posts, including students in other classes, other schools, other cities—even other countries. In fact, students could eventually find a learning partner—perhaps someone halfway around the world—who can help them continue their progress toward proficiency. The possibilities are endless if we have the will to make room for the story of progress within our often aggressive pursuit of proficiency.

How to Bring Parents on Board

As we previously discussed, whatever changes educators make in reporting evidence of learning and progress, the end result must be a process or product that parents can understand. Having parents involved early and often in the development of the new report card is an effective barometer to ensure the changes are efficient and effective in practice.

If teachers involve parents, they must be sure to be clear on the parents' roles and responsibilities—that they are advisors, not necessarily decision makers. Parents are there to ensure that educators' interpretations of promising practices remain as promising in practice as they are in theory. Parents are usually not educators, so we can't expect them to know or understand a lot about assessment. They are, however, critical partners whose voices we need to hear proactively to avoid developing a flawed process.

At some point, there may be tension between what parents want and what the system is prepared to do (for example, some parents might want to keep percentage grades). Educators must, with finesse, let parents know that they are not willing to consider some directions. Critical to that process is providing explanation. Nothing is more dismissive than asking for input and then offering no explanation for not considering some ideas. In any consultation, but especially with parents, people deserve an explanation. Parents must know, in advance, that teachers will not do everything they want; however, their criticism is justified if teachers don't provide a sound explanation why their ideas won't work. If the lack of explanation becomes habitual, parents will most likely lose interest in participating in any meaningful way.

Conclusion

The formal move to a more standards-based reporting system should be a final step in establishing a new summative assessment paradigm. The reporting on standards is simplified when grades are standards based and the evidence of learning that produces the grades is also standards based; standards-based evidence is more possible from standards-based assessments born from standards-based instruction. Establishing a culture of learning focused on the achievement of standards is a prerequisite of a full standards-based reporting system. This natural progression simplifies the process from instruction to reporting. To teach by activities and task types while attempting to navigate a standards-based report card is daunting; change the report cards last, not first.

Now, whatever changes do occur must be user-friendly and consumable to parents. It is easy to be overzealous with work samples, rubrics, portfolios, and detailed descriptions; however, nothing schools or districts move to is better if the parents can't consume and interpret the information. Traditional reporting systems tend to provide too little information; schools and districts must be cautious of providing too much. Having a few parents involved can ensure that the end result of any change effort is going to be a welcome enhancement.

While accuracy is the priority of the proficiency grade, confidence is the priority when reporting the story of progress. Some students need longer to learn, so in the meantime, students and parents must also gain insight as to how much progress is being made. Whether through a separate "grade" or a narrative, this essential story honors the fact that, while the student may not yet be proficient, their work toward proficiency is admirable and their trajectory toward closing their own learning gap is recognized.

QUESTIONS FOR LEARNING TEAMS

1. What quote or passage represents your biggest takeaway from chapter 10? What immediate action will you take as a result of this takeaway? Explain both to your team.

2. Does your entire staff agree on the purpose of grading and reporting? If yes, then articulate how you came to that consensus. If no, then what do you believe is the source of that disagreement?

Continued →

3. Are there any school, district, state, or provincial policies that currently prevent grading and reporting from fulfilling their primary purpose? If so, which specific policies are you thinking of? What would it take to change those policies?

4. Is your gradebook organized by standard? If so, how specific and detailed is it? If not, is that something you would now consider, and how specific do you think you would get?

5. How do you tell the story of progress? What do you think would make that a more meaningful experience for both parents and students? If you don't, discuss how you might begin including progress as part of your regular communication with parents.

6. How involved are your students in tracking both their achievement and progress? Are there any nontraditional ways (such as blog posts) that you allow students to own and communicate their own learning?

*Visit **go.solution-tree.com/assessment** for free reproducible versions of the questions for learning teams.*

AFTERWORD

How to Navigate the Road Ahead

Most people won't go on the long march unless they see compelling evidence in 12 to 24 months that the journey is producing expected results. Without short-term wins, too many people give up or actively join the ranks of those people who have been resisting change.

—John Kotter

Now the tough part begins. Reading this book was easy; the heavy lifting is taking action. While readers may not agree with every idea I put forth in these pages, my overall hope is that teachers feel reinvigorated or newly inspired to examine their grading practices. Grading is an emotional topic that can create tension and divide colleagues, so they must conduct any close examination with purpose and finesse. A haphazard approach to exploring more sound grading practices will undoubtedly be counterproductive and leave many wondering why they bothered to change any grading practices in the first place.

Establish Clarity

Effective changes to grading practices happen when educators and schools or districts contextualize the proposed changes, initiate a non-negotiable focus, and establish clarity about what the proposed changes are (and are not). The modern assessment paradigm demands a rethinking of our traditional grading practices, and it is within this context that I have seen the most effective grading conversations begin. Our collective work in building our assessment fluency and capacity is now decades long, and while there is still much to learn, it is time our grading practices realigned with how we now teach within a standards-based instructional paradigm.

Once colleagues are open to the possibility, initiating a non-negotiable focus brings a necessary predictability to conversations that can otherwise go sideways. Using the grading true north as a collective lens through which all teachers can focus on their current (and future) grading practices brings much-needed alignment that philosophical debates often don't produce. There are many local—even personal—decisions necessary when one shifts to a more standards-based approach, which makes our metaphorical compass all the more important. While the specific practices for each teacher may vary slightly in implementation and execution, accuracy and confidence can serve as two guiding principles that keep everyone on the same page.

Since grading is such an emotionally charged topic, establishing clarity as a first step is important. It may help to discuss and debunk the myths about grading in advance of any move forward to clear up misunderstandings about the potential changes before anyone is too far along in the process. They also serve as a reminder of what not to do when it comes to modernizing grading practices. Once everyone is aware of myths, possible misunderstandings, and likely misinterpretations, staying on track becomes much easier. Trying to debunk myths after the fact is more challenging since new (and misguided) habits may have already become entrenched.

Change Thinking to Change Grading

From there, changes begin from the inside with the development of the standards-based mindset. Rather than using policy to force change, educators can give others the flexibility to develop a standards-based mindset on a more personal level. One teacher may begin by repurposing homework, while another revamps his or her reassessment procedures. Simultaneously, the entire school may begin discussions about redefining accountability, especially for the didn't-do–infrequent students. From my experience, the three fundamental practices of the standards-based mindset (giving students full credit, repurposing homework, and redefining accountability) will eventually (and undoubtedly) overlap. Giving homework a more formative purpose increases the likelihood that students will earn full credit for what they know; redefining accountability will impact reassessment practices, especially in instances of academic dishonesty.

Educators accomplish two things by developing a collective standards-based mindset. First, they create the necessary space for teachers to begin reforming their grading practices without being forced to go through premature policy changes. Teachers can immerse themselves in the unavoidable messiness of change without worrying that missteps become policy violations. Second, the built-in delay of working on the mindset first allows teachers, schools, and districts time to experience the groundswell of change and feel out which direction some of the local decisions are going. From my experience, the most effective changes to the grading paradigm within any context are more bottom-up than top-down. That doesn't mean leadership doesn't matter—it does—but the leadership is about guiding principles, a common purpose, and the ends; the means rest with those responsible for implementing the new practices.

Some immediate policy changes may be necessary; some traditional practices may be so egregious that they need immediate attention. Even so, collectively rethinking our grading practices provides the catalyst for dynamic discussions about how to modernize grading practices within our own context. There are countless what-if scenarios, and while it's not possible to address every one of them in advance, the standards-based mindset provides a fresh lens through which we can examine all of the possible problematic scenarios. Working from the inside out is the most efficient and effective way to shift the culture of grading within any school or district.

Once We Think It, We Will Do It

Rethinking grading first gives everyone a fresh perspective from which to form new policies, procedures, and practices. Teachers must find a balance between being methodical without being slow and being thoughtful without overthinking. Plan how to establish consensus about levels, attributes, gradebooks, and report cards; a collective standards-based mindset creates some efficiency in doing that. However, these changes will not be free of challenges, so as the saying goes, be prepared to slow down in order to speed up. With policy and procedural changes, it's better to get them right than change them quickly.

Achieving consensus about levels of proficiency and what they mean creates a framework for everything else. While the other necessary changes or enhancements to performance criteria, to the teaching of attributes, or to report cards will not happen without purpose, moving from a percentage-based system to a level-based system will effectively set up all future discussions about new grading policies and procedures.

The treatment of student attributes is an important test for any shift in grading and reporting practices. Separating them from proficiency grades cannot make them seem less important. While the accuracy of what we report about student proficiency demands that we protect the integrity of the proficiency grade, it doesn't mean we demote those desirable characteristics to afterthoughts. Many teachers believe the traditional grading paradigm keeps these attributes in the forefront, despite knowing that punishing the absence of an important attribute doesn't teach students how to develop that attribute. Those who hesitate to modernize their grading practices would be right to criticize the implementation effort if the result is that responsibility, work ethic, respect, and the other attributes do not have at least equal status to proficiency grades. It is the proficiency grades that get students into college; it's their attributes that keep them there and allow them to graduate. Even for those students not going to college, proficiency may secure them a job, but it's the attributes that will allow them to keep it.

In a perfect world, the report card is the last change teachers make. Standards-based grading and reporting are most effective within the context of standards-based instruction and standards-based assessments, which result in standards-based evidence. Teachers do need to thoughtfully consider the purpose, structure, and interpretation of the report card. By establishing the foundation of both the standards-based mindset and a standards-based approach, teachers can simplify decisions about any potential changes to the reporting structures. There are countless examples of standards-based reporting, but while it's tempting to adopt a template from another school, meaningful, long-lasting changes will happen only when teachers first make decisions about the purpose, structure, and meaning of the report card; finding existing exemplars should happen only once they have decided what exactly they're looking for.

A Transformation in Grading Practices

In his article "Leading Change: Why Transformation Efforts Fail," John Kotter (2007) identifies the eight steps to transforming any organization.

1. Establish a sense of urgency

2. Form a powerful guiding coalition

3. Create a vision

4. Communicate the vision

5. Empower others to act within the vision

6. Plan for and create short-term wins

7. Consider improvements and produce still more change

8. Institutionalize new approaches

While the article addresses the business context, these eight steps transfer easily to the education paradigm and, specifically, the prospect of moving to a standards-based approach to grading and reporting. What follows is a brief consideration of each of the eight steps and their applicability to the transformation of grading practices.

Establish a Sense of Urgency

It's worth repeating here that establishing an internal sense of urgency while maintaining an external sense of patience is the optimal balance. The time for teachers and their schools to act is now (urgency), but the time it will take to fully implement any changes across a grade level or school could vary (patience). Comparing oneself to others is not helpful. It might take one school a little longer to change than some others, but as long as the delay is not the result of heel dragging, then it doesn't matter that one school was slower or that another school is progressing faster.

Form a Powerful Guiding Coalition

One of the first agreements teachers establish may simply be an agreement to examine the grading norms within their context. Kotter's (2007) advice is to assemble a guiding coalition with enough power to lead the change effort. In schools, a microcosm of the staff is most beneficial. A blend of new and veteran teachers brings both experience and a fresh perspective; multiple grade levels and departments can work together to contextualize ideas that often begin in the abstract. While many people will likely volunteer to participate on a grading committee, it would be wise for leaders to recruit a few influential staff members—those who can move people simply with their own personal sponsorship of the proposed ideas.

Create a Vision

Vision is about the ends, while mission is about the means. When it comes to creating a vision, establishing the grading true north we discussed throughout this book is the most helpful thing an educator can do. While there may be multiple paths to follow, the universal end result is a grading system that increases the accuracy of what teachers ultimately report and leaves students feeling optimistic about their potential success. The specific practices that lead to this end can vary from classroom to classroom, as long as they pass both the accuracy and confidence tests. My experience has taught me that leading outcomes as opposed to methods is the most effective way for leaders and teams to set direction without telling teachers specifically what to do at each step along the way. The vision will create the alignment necessary to keep everyone moving in the same direction without expecting uniformity in execution.

Communicate the Vision

Communication of the vision is critical within the school context and with all stakeholders—especially parents. Within the school context, members of the guiding coalition have to be responsible for communicating their vision as well as the tone and flavor of what they discuss and propose. Though a small group does most of the initial work, everyone within the school has to be involved on some level; no one should be surprised by the direction the school is heading with grading and reporting practices. For those stakeholders outside the school context (such as parents, businesses, colleges, and so on), being proactive about the direction grading practices are headed is advantageous. Certainly, the communication will not be as frequent, and it's not about seeking approval, but it is good practice to keep stakeholders informed, especially with a hot-button issue like grading.

Empower Others to Act Within the Vision

Kotter (2007) writes that we must encourage risk taking and consider nontraditional ideas; nothing is more nontraditional than standards-based grading. We know the move to standards-based grading and reporting is messy. Educators must give everyone the necessary space to try new approaches, learn from errors in execution, and make adjustments without fear of judgment or reprimand. Keeping the vision of accuracy and confidence in mind, teachers should feel free to explore new practices and approaches to grading. The guiding coalition, along with administration and individual colleagues, should collectively work to remove any potential obstacles or unnecessary hurdles so free exploration is possible. Rarely is any new idea executed to perfection; we learn as much from doing as we do from preparing.

Plan for and Create Short-Term Wins

Making significant changes to grading and reporting routines will take time, and, as Kotter (2007) writes, transformation efforts risk losing momentum if there are no short-term wins to celebrate. This is where the standards-based mindset really proves its worth. An individual teacher can, in very short order, transform his or her classroom with a shift toward homework as a more formative exercise; another teacher can do the same by using an incomplete instead of a zero. Planning for rapid results deepens the investment everyone has in seeing the important changes through. There is a protocol to changing district (even school) policies and procedures, but teachers can very quickly get a glimpse of what is possible through the small changes made to specific practices. Developing the overall mindset first also allows teachers to begin where they are most comfortable, which increases the likelihood that they'll stick with the potential change. The long-term win is a change to grading policies and procedures; the short-term wins happen quickly for individual teachers and students who develop a new way of thinking about grading and reporting.

Consider Improvements and Produce Still More Change

We are not one rubric or reassessment policy away from long-lasting transformations. To consider improvements is to think about ways of establishing greater alignment with teachers' initial implementation efforts. Initially, the freedom to explore is beneficial, but from my experience, the most effective long-lasting changes occur when teachers establish collective alignment within the natural context. There will, of course, be subtle differences in how teachers reassess or manage late work, but they must stay subtle, since we are all familiar with how important consistency is for children. Consistency is not uniformity, but eventually considering new practices under a more universal banner will take the guesswork out of how grading works in individual classrooms. Producing more change is about the long-term goals of gradebooks, report cards, and attribute rubrics. Trying to do everything at once is not possible, which means educators will need to delay some changes. Strategically delaying (and communicating that delay ahead of time) will keep the implementation effort fresh and let everyone see the progression toward the long-term goals.

Institutionalize New Approaches

Once teachers have considered individual practices to create the necessary alignment, then policy changes are more palatable. Notice that institutionalizing new approaches comes last, not first. As we discussed earlier, introducing policy changes before the context is ready forces changes that some may not be comfortable with; this leads to reluctant implementation and half-hearted attempts. Remember, change policies when there is a collective sense that policies should be changed. Institutionalizing new practices, at its best, is simply a formal adoption of what is already happening within the school. Once practices take hold, they mitigate potential hiccups from staff turnover; new staff members can quickly pick up how grading works in the school. As well, the institutionalization of practices prevents a change in principal or teacher leadership from derailing the grading transformations that may, at that point, have taken a few years to achieve.

From establishing a sense of urgency to institutionalizing new grading approaches, sustainable grading reform is more likely to succeed when it is planned, thoughtful, and intentionally sequenced. The prospect of grading reform can bring about the kind of visceral responses unrivaled by most change initiatives in schools. That's not to say we should be fearful of moving ahead; far from it. But it is important to be mindful that a strategic approach will likely produce the best results.

Change Can Start With You

Not everyone who reads this book will have the good fortune of working with a team to guide the collective change efforts; some of you will initially go it alone. While it is certainly advantageous to have others alongside you, there is much you can accomplish as an individual. Why can't you be the one to bring the perils of punitive grading to the attention of your colleagues? Why can't you be the one to forge ahead with a different approach to late work? Why can't you be the one who challenges the established norms and decides that your school needs a different grading experience? Maybe you cannot alter board policies and procedures, but you can monumentally shift how your students experience the grading paradigm.

Others *will* eventually follow. They may doubt you at first; they may challenge your new-age approach to grading or even accuse you of intentionally leaving students ill prepared for the real world. Stay on course and block out the noise. Despite the accusations, doubt, and potentially hostile reactions, you know that changes to the grading and reporting paradigm are necessary and right for students, and that is, after all, why we all went into this profession. Once your short-term wins become obvious, the challenges will turn into questions, and statements like "That will never work" become "How did you make that work?" I know this because I've experienced it firsthand.

For those who remain skeptical, I ask only that you maintain an open mind as you move forward and implement the one specific aspect of a standards-based approach that you most agree with. While this book has been about the progression toward standards-based grading and reporting, it's not necessary to go that far. If all you did was rethink your approach to grading in one specific area (such as reassessment), your students will experience a more learning-centered classroom. One change doesn't represent a monumental shift, but for some, shifting a long-standing practice *is* monumental.

While this book may, at times, have felt prescriptive, I really didn't write it for that purpose. My hope is that, no matter where you are with standards-based grading, this book has helped you move closer to at least considering some potential changes to your grading practices. While change is often filled with unanticipated challenges, staying grounded in the grading true north and developing a standards-based mindset will ensure that whatever grading decisions you make will contribute to the accuracy of what you report about student learning and the optimism your students feel about their potential success going forward.

REFERENCES AND RESOURCES

Andrade, H. L. (2010). Students as the definitive source of formative assessment: Academic self-assessment and the self-regulation of learning. In H. L. Andrade & G. J. Cizek (Eds.), *Handbook of formative assessment* (pp. 90–105). New York: Routledge.

Arter, J., & McTighe, J. (2001). *Scoring rubrics in the classroom: Using performance criteria for assessing and improving student performance.* Thousand Oaks, CA: Corwin Press.

Baron, J. B. (1991). Strategies for the development of effective performance exercises. *Applied Measurement in Education, 4*(4), 305–318.

Bennett, S., & Kalish, N. (2006). *The case against homework: How homework is hurting our children and what we can do about it.* New York: Crown.

Black, P. (2013). Formative and summative aspects of assessment: Theoretical and research foundations in the context of pedagogy. In J. H. McMillan (Ed.), *SAGE handbook of research on classroom assessment* (pp. 167–178). Thousand Oaks, CA: SAGE.

Black, P., Harrison, C., Lee, C., Marshall, B., & Wiliam, D. (2004). Working inside the black box: Assessment for learning in the classroom. *Phi Delta Kappan, 86*(1), 8–21.

Black, P., & Wiliam, D. (1998). Assessment and classroom learning. *Assessment in Education: Principles, Policy and Practice, 5*(1), 7–74.

Black, P., & Wiliam, D. (2010). Inside the black box: Raising standards through classroom assessment. *Phi Delta Kappan, 92*(1), 81–90.

Bloom, B. S. (1969). Some theoretical issues relating to educational evaluation. In R. W. Tyler (Ed.), *Educational evaluation: New roles, new means, part II* (Vol. 68, pp. 26–50). Chicago: University of Chicago Press.

Bonner, S. M. (2013). Validity in classroom assessment: Purposes, properties, and principles. In J. H. McMillan (Ed.), *SAGE handbook of research on classroom assessment* (pp. 87–106). Thousand Oaks, CA: SAGE.

Brookhart, S. M. (2011). Starting the conversation about grading. *Educational Leadership, 69*(3), 10–14.

Brookhart, S. M. (2013a). Classroom assessment in the context of motivation theory and research. In J. H. McMillan (Ed.), *SAGE handbook of research on classroom assessment* (pp. 35–54). Thousand Oaks, CA: SAGE.

Brookhart, S. M. (2013b). Grading. In J. H. McMillan (Ed.), *SAGE handbook of research on classroom assessment* (pp. 257–271). Thousand Oaks, CA: SAGE.

Brookhart, S. M. (2013c). *How to create and use rubrics for formative assessment and grading*. Alexandria, VA: Association for Supervision and Curriculum Development.

Brookhart, S. M., & Peretin, J. (2002, April). *Patterns of relationship among motivational and effort variables for different classroom assessments*. Paper presented at the annual meeting of the American Educational Research Association, New Orleans, LA.

Brown, B. (2009). *Standards-based education reform in the United States since "A Nation at Risk."* Honolulu, HI: Curriculum Research and Development Group.

Brown, G. T. L., & Harris, L. R. (2013). Student self-assessment. In J. H. McMillan (Ed.), *SAGE handbook of research on classroom assessment* (pp. 367–393). Thousand Oaks, CA: SAGE.

Buckingham, M. (2005). What great managers do. *Harvard Business Review*. Accessed at https://hbr.org /2005/03/what-great-managers-do on May 29, 2015.

Butler, R. (1988). Enhancing and undermining intrinsic motivation: The effects of task-involving and ego-involving evaluation on interest and performance. *British Journal of Educational Psychology*, *58*(1), 1–14.

Chan, E. (2001). Improving student performance by reducing anxiety. *Positive Pedagogy: Successful and Innovative Strategies in Higher Education*, *1*(3). Accessed at www.stlhe.ca/wp-content /uploads/2011/06/Improving-Student-Performance-by-Reducing-Anxiety1.pdf on May 29, 2015.

Chappuis, J. (2005, March). *"You be George" activity*. Presented during CASL training by Assessment Training Institute in Portland, OR.

Chappuis, J. (2012). "How am I doing?" *Educational Leadership*, *70*(1), 36–41.

Chappuis, J. (2015). *Seven strategies of assessment for learning* (2nd ed.). Boston: Pearson.

Chappuis, J., Stiggins, R., Chappuis, S., & Arter, J. (2012). *Classroom assessment* for *student learning: Doing it right—using it well* (2nd ed.). Boston: Pearson.

Cooper, H. (1989). Synthesis of research on homework. *Educational Leadership*, *47*(3), 85–91.

Cooper, H., Robinson, J. C., & Patall, E. A. (2006). Does homework improve academic achievement?: A synthesis of research, 1987–2003. *Review of Educational Research*, *76*(1), 1–62.

Covey, S. R. (1989). *The seven habits of highly effective people: Powerful lessons in personal change*. New York: Simon & Schuster.

Crooks, T. J. (1988). The impact of classroom evaluation practices on students. *Review of Educational Research*, *58*(4), 438–481.

Cross, L. H., & Frary, R. B. (1999). Hodgepodge grading: Endorsed by students and teachers alike. *Applied Measurement in Education*, *12*(1), 53–72.

Darling-Hammond, L. (1995). Equity issues in performance-based assessment. In M. T. Nettles & A. L. Nettles (Eds.), *Equity and excellence in educational testing and assessment* (pp. 89–114). Boston: Kluwer Academic.

Davis, M. H. (2003). Outcome-based education. *Journal of Veterinary Medical Education*, *30*(3), 258–263.

Dean, C. B., Hubbell, E. R., Pitler, H., & Stone, B. (2012). *Classroom instruction that works: Research-based strategies for increasing student achievement* (2nd ed.). Alexandria, VA: Association for Supervision and Curriculum Development.

Denton Independent School District. (2014). *Grading and assessment procedures and guidelines, grades 6–12, 2014–2015*. Accessed at www.dentonisd.org/cms/lib/TX21000245/Centricity/Domain /2137//Grading%20Policy/secondarygrading.pdf on May 29, 2015.

Dobbs, D. (2011). Beautiful brains. *National Geographic*, *220*(4), 36–59.

Drapeau, P. (2014). *Sparking student creativity: Practical ways to promote innovative thinking and problem solving.* Alexandria, VA: Association for Supervision and Curriculum Development.

DuFour, R. (2005). What is a professional learning community? In R. DuFour, R. Eaker, & R. DuFour (Eds.), *On common ground: The power of professional learning communities* (pp. 31–43). Bloomington, IN: Solution Tree Press.

Dweck, C. S. (2006). *Mindset: The new psychology of success.* New York: Ballantine Books.

Elawar, M. C., & Corno, L. (1985). A factorial experiment in teachers' written feedback on student homework: Changing teacher behavior a little rather than a lot. *Journal of Educational Psychology, 77*(2), 162–173.

Epstein, J. L., & Van Voorhis, F. L. (2001). More than minutes: Teachers' roles in designing homework. *Educational Psychologist, 36*(3), 181–193.

Erickson, J. A. (2011). How grading reform changed our school. *Educational Leadership, 69*(3), 66–70.

Erkens, C. (2009). Developing our assessment literacy. In T. R. Guskey (Ed.), *The teacher as assessment leader* (pp. 11–30). Bloomington, IN: Solution Tree Press.

Erkens, C. (2014, May 30). *The power of homework as a formative tool.* Accessed at http://anamcaraconsulting.com/wordpress/2014/05/30/the-power-of-homework-as-a-formative-tool on May 29, 2015.

Fakier, M., & Waghid, Y. (2004). On outcomes-based education and creativity in South Africa. *International Journal of Special Education, 19*(2), 53–63.

Feldman, A., Kropf, A., & Alibrandi, M. (1998). Grading with points: The determination of report card grades by high school science teachers. *School Science and Mathematics, 98*(3), 140–148.

Friedman, S. J., & Frisbie, D. A. (1995). The influence of report cards on the validity of grades reported to parents. *Educational and Psychological Measurement, 55*(1), 5–26.

Gardner, H. (2010). Five minds for the future. In J. A. Bellanca & R. Brandt (Eds.), *21st century skills: Rethinking how students learn* (pp. 9–31). Bloomington, IN: Solution Tree Press.

Gill, B. P., & Schlossman, S. L. (2004). Villain or savior?: The American discourse on homework, 1850–2003. *Theory Into Practice, 43*(3), 174–181.

Gittman, E., & Koster, J. (1999, October). *Analysis of ability and achievement scores for students recommended by classroom teachers to a gifted and talented program.* Paper presented at the annual meeting of the Northeastern Educational Research Association, Ellenville, NY.

Gladwell, M. (2000). *The tipping point: How little things can make a big difference.* New York: Little, Brown.

Gladwell, M. (2009). *Outliers: The story of success.* New York: Little, Brown.

Greene, R. W. (2008). *Lost at school: Why our kids with behavioral challenges are falling through the cracks and how we can help them.* New York: Scribner.

Guskey, T. R. (2004). 0 alternatives. *Principal Leadership, 5*(2), 49–53.

Guskey, T. R. (2015). *On your mark: Challenging the conventions of grading and reporting.* Bloomington, IN: Solution Tree Press.

Guskey, T. R., & Bailey, J. M. (2010). *Developing standards-based report cards.* Thousand Oaks, CA: Corwin Press.

Hamilton, L. (2003). Chapter 2: Assessment as a policy tool. *Review of Research in Education, 27*(1), 25–68.

Harden, R. M., Crosby, J. R., Davis, M. H., & Friedman, M. (1999). AMEE guide no. 14: Outcome-based education—Part 1—An introduction to outcome-based education. *Medical Teacher, 21*(1), 7–14.

Hattie, J. (2009). *Visible learning: A synthesis of over 800 meta-analyses relating to achievement.* New York: Routledge.

Hattie, J. (2012). Know thy impact. *Educational Leadership, 70*(1), 18–23.

Hattie, J., & Timperley, H. (2007). The power of feedback. *Review of Educational Research, 77*(1), 81–112.

Hawaii State Department of Education. (2013). *General learner outcomes for grades 1–6.* Accessed at www .hawaiipublicschools.org/DOE%20Forms/GLO/GLO_elem.pdf on May 29, 2015.

Heflebower, T. (2009). Proficiency: More than a grade. In T. R. Guskey (Ed.), *The teacher as assessment leader* (pp. 111–133). Bloomington, IN: Solution Tree Press.

Heritage, M. (2010). *Formative assessment: Making it happen in the classroom.* Thousand Oaks, CA: Corwin Press.

Heritage, M., Kim, J., Vendlinski, T. P., & Herman, J. L. (2008, August). *From evidence to action: A seamless process in formative assessment?* (CRESST Report No. 741). Los Angeles: Graduate School of Education and Information Studies, University of California.

Herman, J. L., & Choi, K. (2008, August). *Formative assessment and the improvement of middle school science learning: The role of teacher accuracy* (CRESST Report No. 740). Los Angeles: Graduate School of Education and Information Studies, University of California.

Holme, J. J., Richards, M. P., Jimerson, J. B., & Cohen, R. W. (2010). Assessing the effects of high school exit examinations. *Review of Educational Research, 80*(4), 476–526.

Holmes, C. T. (1989). Grade level retention effects: A meta-analysis of research studies. In L. A. Shepard & M. L. Smith (Eds.), *Flunking grades: Research and policies on retention* (pp. 16–33). Philadelphia: Taylor & Francis.

Holmes, C. T., & Matthews, K. M. (1984). The effects of nonpromotion on elementary and junior high school pupils: A meta-analysis. *Review of Educational Research, 54*(2), 225–236.

Jackson, G. B. (1975). The research evidence on the effects of grade retention. *Review of Educational Research, 45*(4), 613–635.

Jacob, B., & Lefgren, L. (2007, October). *The effect of grade retention on high school completion* (Working Paper No. 13514). Cambridge, MA: National Bureau of Economic Research. Accessed at www .nber.org/papers/w13514 on May 29, 2015.

Jimerson, S. R. (2001). Meta-analysis of grade retention research: Implications for practice in the 21st century. *School Psychology Review, 30*(3), 420–437.

Kanter, R. M. (2004). *Confidence: How winning streaks and losing streaks begin and end.* New York: Crown Business.

Karson, M. (2014, January 14). Punishment doesn't work. *Psychology Today.* Accessed at www .psychologytoday.com/blog/feeling-our-way/201401/punishment-doesnt-work on May 29, 2015.

Kay, K. (2010). 21st century skills: Why they matter, what they are, and how we get there. In J. A. Bellanca & R. Brandt (Eds.), *21st century skills: Rethinking how students learn* (pp. xiii–xxxi). Bloomington, IN: Solution Tree Press.

Kay, K., & Greenhill, V. (2013). *The leader's guide to 21st century education.* Upper Saddle River, NJ: Pearson Education.

Kluger, A. N., & DeNisi, A. (1996). The effects of feedback interventions on performance: A historical review, a meta-analysis, and a preliminary feedback intervention theory. *Psychological Bulletin, 119*(2), 254–284.

Kohn, A. (2005). Unconditional teaching. *Educational Leadership, 63*(1), 20–24.

Kohn, A. (2007). *The homework myth: Why our kids get too much of a bad thing*. Philadelphia: Da Capo Press.

Kotter, J. P. (2007, January). Leading change: Why transformation efforts fail. *Harvard Business Review*. Accessed at https://hbr.org/2007/01/leading-change-why-transformation-efforts-fail on May 29, 2015.

Kotter, J. P., & Whitehead, L. A. (2010). *Buy-in: Saving your good idea from getting shot down*. Boston: Harvard Business Review Press.

Kuhn, T. S. (1962). The structure of scientific revolutions. In *International Encyclopedia of Unified Science* (Vol. 2, no. 2). Chicago: University of Chicago Press.

Lee, S. (2013). The problem with punishment. *Reclaiming Children and Youth, 21*(4), 51–54.

Marzano, R. J. (2010). *Formative assessment and standards-based grading*. Bloomington, IN: Marzano Research.

Marzano, R. J., Pickering, D. J., & Pollock, J. E. (2001). *Classroom instruction that works: Research-based strategies for increasing student achievement*. Alexandria, VA: Association for Supervision and Curriculum Development.

Massachusetts Institute of Technology. (2014, September). Course catalog, '14–'15. *MIT Bulletin, 150*(1). Accessed at http://web.mit.edu/catalog/archive/2014-2015/catalog1415.pdf on May 29, 2015.

McElligott, J., & Brookhart, S. M. (2009). Legal issues of grading in the era of high-stakes accountability. In T. R. Guskey (Ed.), *Practical solutions for serious problems in standards-based grading* (pp. 57–74). Thousand Oaks, CA: Corwin Press.

McMillan, J. H. (2001). Secondary teachers' classroom assessment and grading practices. *Educational Measurement: Issues and Practice, 20*(1), 20–32.

McMunn, N., Schenck, P., & McColskey, W. (2003, April). *Standards-based assessment, grading, and reporting in classrooms: Can district training and support change teacher practice?* (ERIC Document Reproduction Service No. ED475763). Paper presented at the annual meeting of the American Educational Research Association, Chicago.

Meisels, S. J., Bickel, D. D., Nicholson, J., Xue, Y., & Atkins-Burnett, S. (2001). Trusting teachers' judgments: A validity study of a curriculum-embedded performance assessment in kindergarten to grade 3. *American Educational Research Journal, 38*(1), 73–95.

Messick, S. (1989). Validity. In R. L. Linn (Ed.), *Educational measurement* (3rd ed., pp. 13–103). Phoenix, AZ: Oryx Press.

Moss, C. M. (2013). Research on classroom summative assessment. In J. H. McMillan (Ed.), *SAGE handbook of research on classroom assessment* (pp. 235–255). Thousand Oaks, CA: SAGE.

National Commission on Excellence in Education. (1983). *A nation at risk: The imperative for educational reform*. Washington, DC: Author.

National Governors Association Center for Best Practices & Council of Chief State School Officers. (2010a). *Common Core State Standards Initiative*. Washington, DC: Authors.

National Governors Association Center for Best Practices & Council of Chief State School Officers. (2010b). *Common Core State Standards for mathematics*. Washington, DC: Authors. Accessed at www.corestandards.org/assets/CCSSI_Math%20Standards.pdf on August 1, 2015.

Natriello, G. (1987). The impact of evaluation processes on students. *Educational Psychologist, 22*(2), 155–175.

No Child Left Behind (NCLB) Act of 2001, Pub. L. No. 107-110, § 115, Stat. 1425 (2002).

O'Connor, K. (2009). *How to grade for learning, K–12* (3rd ed.). Thousand Oaks, CA: Corwin Press.

O'Connor, K. (2011). *A repair kit for grading: Fifteen fixes for broken grades* (2nd ed.). Boston: Pearson.

O'Connor, K. (2013). *The school leader's guide to grading*. Bloomington, IN: Solution Tree Press.

Parkes, J., & Giron, T. (2006). *Making reliability arguments in classrooms*. Paper presented at the annual meeting of the National Council on Measurement in Education, San Francisco.

Pink, D. H. (2009). *Drive: The surprising truth about what motivates us*. New York: Riverhead Books.

Popham, W. J. (2008). *Transformative assessment*. Alexandria, VA: Association for Supervision and Curriculum Development.

Ramdass, D., & Zimmerman, B. J. (2008). Effects of self-correction strategy training on middle school students' self-efficacy, self-evaluation, and mathematics division learning. *Journal of Advanced Academics, 20*(1), 18–41.

Reeves, D. (Ed.). (2007). *Ahead of the curve: The power of assessment to transform teaching and learning*. Bloomington, IN: Solution Tree Press.

Reeves, D. (2011). *Elements of grading: A guide to effective practice*. Bloomington, IN: Solution Tree Press.

Robins, R. W., & Pals, J. L. (2002). Implicit self theories in the academic domain: Implications for goal orientation, attributions, affect, and self-esteem change. *Self and Identity, 1*(4), 313–336.

Roderick, M., & Nagaoka, J. (2005). Retention under Chicago's high-stakes testing program: Helpful, harmful, or harmless? *Educational Evaluation and Policy Analysis, 27*(4), 309–340.

Rodriguez, M. C. (2004). The role of classroom assessment in student performance on TIMSS. *Applied Measurement in Education, 17*(1), 1–24.

Sadler, D. R. (1989). Formative assessment and the design of instructional systems. *Instructional Science, 18*(2), 119–144.

Scriven, M. (1967). The methodology of evaluation. In R. W. Tyler, R. M. Gagne, & M. Scriven (Eds.), *Perspectives of curriculum evaluation* (Vol. 1, pp. 39–83). Chicago: Rand McNally.

Selby, D., & Murphy, S. (1992). Graded or degraded: Perceptions of letter-grading for mainstreamed learning-disabled students. *British Columbia Journal of Special Education, 16*(1), 92–104.

Shepard, L., Hammerness, K., Darling-Hammond, L., & Rust, L. (2005). Assessment. In L. Darling-Hammond & J. Bransford (Eds.), *Preparing teachers for a changing world: What teachers should learn and be able to do* (pp. 275–326). San Francisco: Jossey-Bass.

Sinek, S. (2009, September). *Simon Sinek: How great leaders inspire action* [Video file]. Accessed at www.ted.com/talks/simon_sinek_how_great_leaders_inspire_action?language=en#t-120567 on May 29, 2015.

Spady, W. G. (1994). *Outcome-based education: Critical issues and answers*. Arlington, VA: American Association of School Administrators.

Stiggins, R. (2007). Assessment *for* learning: An essential foundation of productive instruction. In D. Reeves (Ed.), *Ahead of the curve: The power of assessment to transform teaching and learning* (pp. 59–76). Bloomington, IN: Solution Tree Press.

Stiggins, R. (2008, April). *Assessment manifesto: A call for the development of balanced assessment systems*. Portland, OR: ETS Assessment Training Institute.

Thomas, S., & Oldfather, P. (1997). Intrinsic motivations, literacy, and assessment practices: "That's my grade. That's me." *Educational Psychologist, 32*(2), 107–123.

Tiedemann, J. (2002). Teachers' gender stereotypes as determinants of teacher perceptions in elementary school mathematics. *Educational Studies in Mathematics, 50*(1), 49–62.

Tomlinson, C. A., & Moon, T. R. (2013). *Assessment and student success in a differentiated classroom*. Alexandria, VA: Association for Supervision and Curriculum Development.

Trautwein, U. (2007). The homework-achievement relation reconsidered: Differentiating homework time, homework frequency, and homework effort. *Learning and Instruction, 17*(3), 372–388.

Trautwein, U., Köller, O., Schmitz, B., & Baumert, J. (2002). Do homework assignments enhance achievement?: A multilevel analysis in 7th-grade mathematics. *Contemporary Educational Psychology, 27*(1), 26–50.

Vagle, N. D. (2015). *Design in five: Essential phases to create engaging assessment practice.* Bloomington, IN: Solution Tree Press.

Vatterott, C. (2009). *Rethinking homework: Best practices that support diverse needs.* Alexandria, VA: Association for Supervision and Curriculum Development.

Walker, C. A. (2002, April). Saving your rookie managers from themselves. *Harvard Business Review.* Accessed at https://hbr.org/2002/04/saving-your-rookie-managers-from-themselves/ar/1 on May 29, 2015.

Waltman, K. K., & Frisbie, D. A. (1994). Parents' understanding of their children's report card grades. *Applied Measurement in Education, 7*(3), 223–240.

Westbury, M. (1994). The effect of elementary grade retention on subsequent school achievement and ability. *Canadian Journal of Education, 19*(3), 241–250.

Wiggins, G. (1998). *Educative assessment: Designing assessments to inform and improve student performance.* San Francisco: Jossey-Bass.

Wiggins, G., & McTighe, J. (2005). *Understanding by design* (Expanded 2nd ed.). Alexandria, VA: Association for Supervision and Curriculum Development.

Wiliam, D. (2011). *Embedded formative assessment.* Bloomington, IN: Solution Tree Press.

Wormeli, R. (2006). *Fair isn't always equal: Assessing and grading in the differentiated classroom.* Portland, ME: Stenhouse.

INDEX

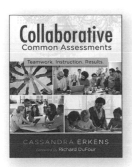

Collaborative Common Assessments
Cassandra Erkens
Reignite the passion and energy assessment practices bring as tools to guide teaching and learning. Strengthen instruction with collaborative common assessments that collect vital information. Explore the practical steps teams must take to establish assessment systems, and discover how to continually improve results.
BKF605

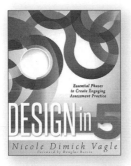

Design in Five
Nicole Dimich Vagle
Discover how to work with your school team to create innovative, effective, engaging assessments using a five-phase design protocol. Explore various types of assessment, learn the traits of quality assessment, and evaluate whether your current assessments meet the design criteria.
BKF604

On Your Mark
Thomas R. Guskey
Create and sustain a learning environment where students thrive and stakeholders are accurately informed of student progress. Clarify the purpose of grades, craft a vision statement aligned with this purpose, and discover research-based strategies to implement effective grading and reporting practices.
BKF606

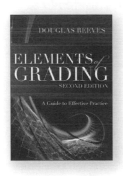

Elements of Grading
Douglas Reeves
The author provides educators with practical suggestions for making the grading process more fair, accurate, specific, and timely. In addition to examples and case studies, new content addresses how the Common Core State Standards and new technologies impact grading practices.
2nd edition **BKF648**

Solution Tree | Press
a division of
Solution Tree

Visit solution-tree.com or call 800.733.6786 to order.

"Excellent engagement
in what truly matters
in **assessment**.

Great examples!"

—Carol Johnson, superintendent,
Central Dauphin School District, Pennsylvania

 PD Services

Our experts draw from decades of research and their own experiences to bring you
practical strategies for designing and implementing quality assessments. You can choose
from a range of customizable services, from a one-day overview to a multiyear process.

Book your assessment PD today!
888.763.9045

Solution Tree